MW00620090

BRIDGING TROUBLED WATERS

Mennonite Brethren
at Mid-Twentieth Century

Perspectives on Mennonite Life and Thought is a series jointly published between Kindred Productions, the Historical Commission of the General Conference of Mennonite Brethren Churches and the Center for Mennonite Brethren Studies of Winnipeg, Manitoba, Fresno, California and Hillsboro, Kansas. *

1. Paul Toews, ed., *Pilgrims and Strangers: Essays in Mennonite Brethren History* (1977)

2. Abraham Friesen, ed., *P.M. Friesen and His History: Understanding Mennonite Brethren Beginnings* (1979)

3. David Ewert, ed., *Called to Teach* (1979)

4. Heinrich Wölk and Gerhard Wölk, *Die Mennoniten Bruedergemeinde in Russland, 1925 - 1980; Ein Beitrag zur Geschichte* (1981)

5. John B. Toews, *Perilous Journey: The Mennonite Brethren in Russia 1860 - 1910* (1988)

6. Aron A. Toews, *Mennonite Martyrs: People Who Suffered for Their Faith 1920 - 1940,* translated by John B. Toews (1990)

7. Paul Toews, ed., *Mennonite and Baptists: A Continuing Conversation* (1993)

8. J.B. Toews, *A Pilgrimage of Faith: The Mennonite Brethren Church in Russia and North America 1860 - 1990* (1993)

9. Paul Toews, ed., *Bridging Troubled Waters: Mennonite Brethren at Mid-Century* (1995)

---

* Volumes 1-4 were published by the Center for Mennonite Brethren Studies (Fresno)

Bridging Troubled Waters

Mennonite Brethren at Mid-Century

Essays and Autobiographies

PAUL TOEWS, EDITOR

WINNIPEG, MB CANADA   KINDRED   HILLSBORO, KS USA
PRODUCTIONS

BRIDGING TROUBLED WATERS
Mennonite Brethren at Mid-Century

Copyright © 1995 by the Centers for Mennonite Brethren Studies, Fresno, CA; Winnipeg, MB and Hillsboro, KS.

All rights reserved. With the exception of brief excerpts for reviews, no part of this book may be reproduced without written permission of the publisher.

Canadian Cataloguing in Publication Data
   (Perspectives on Mennonite life and thought ; 9)
   Includes bibliographical references.
   ISBN 0-921788-23-1

   1. Mennonite Brethren Church - History - 20th century.
   2. Mennonite Brethren Church - Biography.
   3. Mennonites - Canada - History - 20th century.
   4. Mennonites - United States - History - 20th century.
   5. Mennonites - Canada - Biography
   6. Mennonites - United States - Biography.
   I. Toews, Paul. II. Series

   BX8129.M373B7 1995   289.7 0971   C95-920110-6

Published simultaneously by Kindred Productions, Winnipeg, MB, R2L 2E5 and Kindred Productions, Hillsboro, KS, 67063

Cover design by Gerry Unrau, Saskatoon, SK

Book design by Derksen Printers, Steinbach, MB

Printed in Canada by Derksen Printers, Steinbach, MB

International Standard Book Number: 0-921788-23-1

Table of Contents

Acknowledgements

Most of the essays published in this book were first presented at a symposium entitled "North American Mennonite Brethren at Mid-Century (1940-1960)," which took place at the Mennonite Brethren Biblical Seminary in Fresno, California during February 1993. The symposium was sponsored by the Historical Commission of the Mennonite Brethren Church, which also recommended that the papers be published in the present form.

Kevin Enns-Rempel, Archivist of the Center for Mennonite Brethren Studies in Fresno, verified many of the details and citations in all of the essays. He also provided valuable judgement on many editorial issues. Kelly McClure and Brian Froese, both assistants in the Center for MB Studies, did additional work verifying endnotes. Marilyn Hudson at Kindred Productions oversaw the publication process. All carried out their tasks with the good humor and friendly cooperation that is required in bringing such projects to completion.

Paul Toews
Editor

Introduction

Paul Toews

In July 1951 the General Conference of Mennonite Brethren Churches met in Winkler, Manitoba for its forty-fifth convention in North America. In many ways it was like the previous conferences. The setting was a small, rural and mostly Mennonite village. The Mennonite Brethren (MB), ever since their first convention in Henderson Nebraska in 1887, had met in small hamlets. Places like Hillsboro, Kansas; Corn, Oklahoma; Mountain Lake, Minnesota; Harvey, North Dakota; Reedley, California; Coaldale, Alberta; and Hepburn, Saskatchewan were important places only in the Mennonite firmament. They were hardly convention centers for other assemblies. But Winkler was an appropriate place, for the delegates were also mostly from rural locales. The roster of delegates was almost entirely from small villages and rural towns. Other than the forty-five delegates from Winnipeg, Manitoba, there were only thirteen other delegates from cities of any significant size. Nine of those came from California: San Jose, Bakersfield, Fresno and Los Angeles. Two represented Wichita, Kansas, and one came from Enid, Oklahoma. In addition to the large Winnipeg contingent, there were four other urban Canadian delegates: one from Vancouver, British Columbia, one from St. Catharines, Ontario, and two representing Kitchener, Ontario.

The convention in many ways was like those that preceded it. All of the delegates were male. Guests stayed in the homes of the host congregation and neighboring churches and could easily share a bed with a delegate previously unknown. All meals were either in homes or at the church. The business, preaching and singing of the convention were done in English and German. The order and rhythm of the convention and the style of doing business were familiar to those who had attended a previous conference.

If the convention setting and hospitality suggested continuity with the past, elements of the program pointed to an emerging world that was different. The Board of Reference and Counsel (BORAC) offered one of the most remarkable documents submitted to a twentieth-century North American MB Conference. "A Statement to the Conference," while prosaically titled, was a trenchant analysis of issues that signaled the differing world.

"The impact of the revolutionizing changes of the political, social and economic life" of the recent past, the document, declared, had left "their imprints upon our churches" affecting both the "organizational and instructional principles" of individual congregations. The changes were the consequences of unprecedented "educational opportunities and economic advantages."[1]

It was not the educational and economic attainments that troubled the Board of Reference and Counsel, but rather "organizational and instructional" concerns. The two were distinct, but related issues. The organizational innovations, at least in this reading, could more easily accommodate instructional deviancy.

There were organizational changes underway at both the congregational and conference levels. The selection of local church leadership was increasingly borrowing the methods of "democratic policies" and giving rise to "weak, unstable and divisive" leaders. Furthermore the "unity in church polity and practice" throughout the conference was "seriously weakened" by the selective adoption of these new procedures. Leadership formerly selected from within the congregation and nurtured in the traditions of the local community was being replaced by professionals who came from divergent educational institutions. The "one man pastorate" was replacing the practice of multiple lay ministers and elders.[2]

The new congregational leadership was more prone to accept the "cry of the world for the exercise of self-will in an overemphasis of the independence of the individual." Allowing such insidious individualism to remain unchecked had caused "many evangelical denominations" to depart from the "divine principle of the Scriptural relationship of a body where Christ is the head, the members in the interdependence one upon the other, constituting the body." The historic Mennonite Brethren concept of "brotherhood"—the interrelationship of members to one another and congregations to conferences where the "independence of the individual remains subordinate to the larger body"—was in danger of giving way to an "association principle."[3]

The constitution operative in 1951 required all "churches that belong to this Conference . . . 'to keep the unity of the Spirit in the bond of peace' (Eph. 4:3) and to walk 'by the same rule' (Phil. 3:16)."[4] Yet the associational form introduced a new kind of freedom and pluralism that seemingly endangered that unity. While local churches historically were independent in the management of internal affairs the decisions of the conference had been binding. It was expected and even required that congregations carry out resolutions passed by the conference. The Board of Reference and Counsel reminded the delegates that the official name in 1951 was the "Conference of the Mennonite Brethren Church of North America," not the "Conference of Mennonite Brethren Churches of North America," and that distinction clearly implied "brotherhood" rather than "association."[5]

The fading unity in church polity and practice also "seriously weakened" doctrinal unity. While the conference declared itself free of "rank modernism" the ministry no longer maintained an "undivided camp." The differences were described as increasing "indefiniteness and difference[s] of interpretation" on some elements of the Confession of Faith and a "hesitancy in accepting defined statements of Ethical, Social and Spiritual Standards" necessary for maintaining a people "separated" from the world.[6]

These theological differences were better contextualized in the report of the Seminary Commission to the same conference. That commission, established at the 1948 conference to investigate the advisability of operating a separate denominational seminary, reported in 1951 that to "stand fast in one spirit" an MB seminary was necessary. Enumerating to the conference the list of denominations and schools from which MB church workers had received seminary training was an ample indication of emerging theological fractures: Alliance, Lutheran, Baptist (Southern and Swedish), Presbyterian, Interdenominational, Grace, Moody, Conservative Baptist, California Baptist, Pasadena College (Pentecostal), Phillips University, Princeton Theological Seminary, United Seminary.[7] The listing, if complete, would also have included Winona Lake, Southwestern Baptist, Central Baptist, Northwestern Evangelical University of Western Ontario, Hartford Seminary, United College (Winnipeg), Western Baptist, Northern Baptist and perhaps additional ones. Mennonite Brethren were indeed imbibing differing theological spirits. This was not the first conference to address virtually these same concerns. The Board of Reference and Counsel brought to the 1948 conference in Mountain Lake, Minnesota a foretaste of what would be elaborated in 1951. There they already suggested that "we do not call teachers of the Word from churches outside of our conference" because they frequently subscribed to theological positions unacceptable to the conference. In 1948 the "spirit of individualism" was also identified as destructive to the interdependence and unity of the church. Furthermore, the prevailing "political concepts" (i.e., democracy), when brought into the church, "invariably result in destructive results."[8] What distinguished the 1951 conference, however, was the readiness of the Board of Reference and Counsel to offer strong proposals for dealing with the crumbling "brotherhood" polity and ascending theological diversity. The board placed four important recommendations before the delegates: 1) the creation of a Board of Elders; 2) a requirement that all ministers be in conformity with the Confession of Faith and those who, after appropriate instruction and counsel from the Board, could not make such a profession "shall be asked to withdraw" from the ministry; 3) the preparation of a ministers manual that would carefully define the protocol for congregations to follow in calling a minister and in establishing the appropriate relationship between the minister and other church leaders and the congregation; 4) the commissioning of three separate books on the history, doctrine and polity of the MB church.

The strategy for dealing with the troubling currents was clearly an appeal to an earlier authoritative tradition. Reconstituting a Board of Elders with the charge to "guide our Brotherhood in all matters pertaining to Scriptural doctrines and church polity" gave enormous power to the nine individuals selected. Not only were they to be powerful but they were to be drawn from the established ranks of proven clergy. Only individuals who had already been ordained for not less than ten years would be eligible for membership in the Elder board. Those recent seminary graduates with new theologies and technologies would not be able to affect quick changes either in the structure or thought of the conference. Rulings of the Board of Elders were to be "final" unless reversed by the Conference itself.

The other three recommendations, while less authoritative, also had ample ability to realign the denomination more closely with some of its historic moorings. The 1943 conference, no doubt feeling some of the same concerns, advised the preparation of a ministers manual. The 1951 convention elaborated and emphasized the need for the manual to establish the guidelines that would insure more uniformity in ministerial selection and the exercise of ministerial gifts. The codification of doctrine and polity offered possibilities for greater coherence, and the search for a useable past was also an appropriate means for bounding the fraying impulses.

ORGANIZATIONAL CHANGES

The year 1951 was a good time to assess change. At mid-century, and at the mid-point in the two decades that the essays in this book examine, there was ample reason for concern about how much of the past could be carried into the future. While change is endemic to all groups in the modern world, and particularly to a recent immigrant group like the Mennonite Brethren, the pace of change in the immediate post-war period seemed to overwhelm in ways that previous decades, at least in North America, had not.

Many Mennonite Brethren into the mid-twentieth century had been able to shelter themselves from much of the cultural changes of the twentieth century. Into the 1940s most Mennonite Brethren were immigrants from the Russian empire or were children of such immigrants. Those that came between 1874 and the beginning of World War I in 1914 settled mostly in small rural communities, among other immigrants where they could recreate something of the village life of the old world. Distinctive cultural and religious practices and the maintenance of the German language created a protective barrier that separated them from many of their North-American neighbors. Furthermore, they often settled in areas adjacent to other German-speaking immigrants with whom they shared not only a language but also cultural aspirations. The immigrants into Canada during the 1920s settled both in rural villages and in emerging urban centers in Canada. Their arrival marks the beginning of Mennonite Brethren urbanization in North America. During the fifty years after the 1870s migrants left, many Mennonites remaining in Russia entered vocations more suited for urban environments—teachers, physicians, nurses, bankers, and business pursuits. The immigrants that came following World War II had not been able to continue these entrepreneurial activities in the Soviet Union during the 1930s and 1940s but they also gravitated to the cities where employment was easier to find. While many of these latter groups became urban residents, sociologists have long noted the capacity of urban Mennonite dwellers, particularly the immigrant generation, to carve out distinctive ethnic neighborhoods and rebuild at least remnants of the village cultural surroundings.[9]

The consequence of these settlement patterns was that, while most Mennonite Brethren or their ancestry had undergone the wrenching experience of being uprooted from the old world and transplanted to the new, they had been able to retain a remarkable continuity with the past. There was a unity of culture and life into the 1940s. That is not to suggest that the Mennonite Brethren were static. Life for immigrants, even if one or two generations removed from that experience, is hardly static. But for all of the disorder with which it was attended, there remained a reasonably stable family, vocational, moral and religious framework that was almost entirely so. The authority of the traditional church leadership, the economics of the family farm, and the preference for German language and culture, while buffeted, were not seriously challenged. For Mennonite Brethren who remained living within the confines of Mennonite village society—and in 1940 that was the majority—there remained an inner stability.[10]

The maintenance of any form of this cultural and religious solidity is intriguing given the centrifugal forces operative in Mennonite Brethren history since its inception in 1860. The beginning of the Mennonite Brethren movement engaged the plurality of forces seeking change within the constricted opportunity for reform within the Russian Mennonite world. Thus, divergent forces became linked with each other. Cultural progressives seeking greater liberation from a closed community and cultural conservatives seeking a tighter morality worked together. Some early Mennonite Brethren reached back to Menno Simons and Anabaptism; others reached out to British Evangelicalism and European Pietism.[11]

This incipient theological pluralism was soon matched by a geographical scattering. Given the difficulty of carving out a new religious community within the context of the Russian environment, the Mennonite Brethren experienced differing kinds of hostility and rejection from the parent body. To avoid further unpleasantness, as well as to seek new opportunities, some of the Mennonite Brethren moved from the larger colonies in the Ukraine—Molotschna and Chortitza—to the new Kuban region to the southeast. The process continued when, in 1874, the initial migration of Russian Mennonites to North America began. Among the eighteen thousand Mennonite migrants of the 1870s were some two hundred MB families who settled in Kansas, Nebraska, South Dakota and Minnesota.[12] From these fledgling settlements they soon moved out to North Dakota and Montana, westward to Colorado, Oregon, Washington and California and southward into Oklahoma and Texas. In the early twentieth century others moved into Manitoba and Saskatchewan. The history of Mennonite Brethren wandering in the North American West searching for cheap and good land and seeking to establish new communities is yet to be fully written. Calvin Redekop's essay notes the opening and closing of seventy-three congregations between 1876 and 1954. Most of those stories are part of this geographical dispersion rather than the attempt at starting new mission outposts.

By 1909 these far-flung congregations had difficulty gathering for an annual conference and so changed the General Conference schedule to a triennial meeting. They created four regional conferences that began to meet yearly: the Southern (Kansas, Oklahoma Colorado); the Central (North and South Dakota, Minnesota and Nebraska); the Pacific (Oregon and California) and the Northern (later renamed the Canadian Conference), which included all of the Canadian provinces with MB churches.

The depression of the 1930s and the demographic shifts accompanying and following World War II only accelerated this geographical movement. Sociologist E. K. Francis, in his study of Manitoba Mennonites, calculated that as many as half of the *Rusländer* (those who entered Canada during the 1920s) settlers lost their farms and relocated during the terrible 1930s.[13] While towns and urban centers across Canada received those transplanted, many, during the 1930s and in subsequent decades, found their way westward. John Schmidt of Columbia Bible College has tallied the growth of MB membership in British Columbia: 292 members in 1931, 1174 members in 1940, and 3525 members in 1950.[14] The Pacific District Conference also grew dramatically during the same two decades. While not tenfold as in British Columbia, the increase was significant: 1779 members in 1930, 2850 members in 1940 and 4359 members in 1950.[15] The numbers do not distinguish between transfers and children of members joining versus new converts, but any reading of congregational records for the 1930s and 1940s will show that the growth was preponderantly through transfer and population growth.

The full impact of these diverse theological moorings and geographical wanderings was not felt, however, before the mid-century decades. Earlier they could not dislodge the fundamental ethnic, linguistic, and familial ties that produced cohesion and solidarity. Similar musical styles and forms of piety reinforced a sense of oneness. There were differences between those who came in the 1870s and those who came in the 1920s. A dominant theme of Canadian Mennonite history is the difference between the *Kanadier* (1870s) and the *Russländer* (1920s). There were differences between those touched by pentecostalism and those who remained aloof from such movements of the spirit, between those who strongly identified with American fundamentalism and those who did not. To be sure, there were also differences between regional communities. Those differences, however, were pale compared to the things that tended to insulate them from their Anglo-Saxon neighbors.[16]

Overlaying these cultural boundaries was a high doctrine of separation from the world that into the 1940s also remained reasonably intact. Ever since the sixteenth century, Mennonites have worked at defining a theology for understanding the appropriate relationship between the people of God's kingdom and Caesar's kingdom. The theology that emerged over the centuries sharply distinguished the obligations of citizenship from those of membership in the Kingdom. This ethical dualism, while forged out of a hermeneutical tradition, was also nourished by a cultural dualism. Mennonites marginalized in Polish/Prussian lands and living on the margins of the Russian empire could easily think of the requirements of faith as inimical to participation in the dominant social system.

Into the 1940s this cultural and theological separatism remained visible. But that same decade also revealed the degree to which they were eroding. The year 1951 was indeed an appropriate time for angst among leaders wishing to preserve the traditions of an earlier day. The essays and autobiographies in this volume address the changes and transitions that marked the mid-century period. With the exception of the contribution by Doreen Klassen, they were prepared for a symposium on "North American Mennonite Brethren at Mid-Century" that convened at the Mennonite Brethren Biblical Seminary in Fresno, California in February 1993. Organized by the Historical Commission of the MB Church, the purpose of the symposium was to examine the period 1940 to 1960. While the essays do not rigidly adhere to those boundaries they do focus on the two decades. Without exception they underline changes that were troubling and required bridging to insure continuity. For a people sociologically shaped by their rural enclaves, these decades were indeed a time of troubles. Bridging the troubles and transitions, while necessary, was not always easy.

Mennonites like others were caught up in a post-war economic boom that provided unprecedented opportunities in both Canada and the United States. Calvin Redekop's study of economic development among United States Mennonite Brethren reveals the number of Mennonite Brethren owned businesses in one community — Hillsboro, Kansas — jumped from twenty-six in 1945 to forty-five in 1960. While the documentation is lacking for other small towns with a significant Mennonite population, there is every reason to assume a similar rise in enterprising activity. Both the essays by Redekop and Ted Regehr show the degree to which Mennonite businesspeople and agriculturalists were drawn into new economic markets. Farmers increasingly became business-people with economic relationships far beyond the boundaries of their rural Mennonite villages. Mennonite growers and producers joined agricultural cooperatives. The forces of increasingly integrated national economic systems, which were the consequence of depression reforms and World War II national planning, moved Mennonites toward business integration rather than separatism.

The affections of business wealth were increasingly visible— spacious and well-appointed homes, vacation houses, and luxurious automobiles. Many a photo album reveals the difference. Driving well and dressing well replaced the rural, depression and immigrant look of a decade earlier.

The new economic opportunities also increasingly pulled people into the orbit of cities. Kevin Enns-Rempel's essay notes that the percentage of Mennonite Brethren living within the cultural shadow of cities of fifty thousand or more residents more than doubled between 1941 and 1960. The percentage jump from 10 percent to slightly more than 23 percent is significant, but even more so is that in California, Manitoba and Ontario, all regions with large Mennonite populations, the urban population approached 40 percent of the total.

Increasing urbanization also accelerated the transition from German to English. Among the United States congregations, that transition was virtually completed during World War II and the years immediately following. In several U.S. churches the change came immediately following the American entry into the war in December 1941. Remembering the crises of citizenship that enveloped German-speaking communities in World War I, these congregations were unwilling to again be dubbed German sympathizers because of persistent German usage in corporate worship. In Canada the infusion of new German-speaking immigrants in the 1920s and the 1940s stayed off the language transition into the 1950s and 1960s. But even the most persistent efforts to maintain the *muttersprache* could not prevent, already in the 1940s, the emergence of an English subculture within predominantly German speaking congregations. Gerald Ediger's essay notes that by 1958 the transition in Sunday schools and youth groups was virtually complete, though it remained for the 1965 Canadian conference to formally make English the language of the Conference.

The devotion to German, Ediger makes clear, was much more than stubborn insistence on an old language. Language shifts presage cultural shifts and alterations in the forms of piety. Germaneness was a way of perpetuating the past in the new North American environment. Those conservatives wishing to preserve the language may have been shortsighted in thinking they could retain its usage. They were, however, entirely correct in sensing that the loss of language would also bring with it the loss of cultural forms.

The economic, linguistic and residential transitions only mirrored other alterations. Mennonite Brethren became increasingly comfortable with their Canadian and American citizenship, and as they did, the traditional conceptions of church-state relationships underwent alteration. Both Abe Dueck and John Redekop's papers detail the ways in which the state and political institutions became less alien entities. Redekop's essay amasses significant data that point to these decades as critical for Mennonite political acculturation. Mennonites in the United States and increasingly so in Canada were integrating into the political polity. Earlier bans on political participation vanished. Now Mennonites not only voted, but in significant numbers ran for political office. In the U.S. they tended to do so in local elections— school boards, city councils, county supervisors, town mayors; in Canada it more frequently extended beyond those local positions into provincial and national offices. The Board of Reference and Counsel had reason to worry about Mennonite Brethren bringing "political democracy" into congregational and conference life. As they became active participants in the political system of both countries, it was easy to import those forms of decision making and governance into their religious institutions.

INSTRUCTIONAL CHANGES

These "organizational" changes clearly also had their impact on the "instruction" of the Mennonite Brethren church. While Mennonite Brethren, since 1860, have been open to varying and even contradictory theological currents, the more open association with the larger cultures in the United States and Canada also eased the entrance of variant theologies. Ever since the 1920s, Mennonite Brethren—particularly in the United States— were drawn slowly but surely toward American fundamentalism. In a protestant world divided into two sharply defined camps— fundamentalists and modernists—most Mennonites instinctively leaned toward the fundamentalist party. Although its theology contained elements foreign to Anabaptist-Mennonite reflection, there was no question as to which side would gain Mennonite Brethren allegiance. While Mennonite Brethren felt sympathetic toward the fundamentalist movement they did not develop the institutional linkages that came after fundamentalism metamorphosed, during the 1940s, into Evangelicalism.

Both Richard Kyle's and Doreen Klassen's essays document the influence of these theologies. Kyle looks at the influence on formal theologizing and in institutional contexts. Klassen analyzes its impact on music and styles of worship. Both help us to understand why the members of the 1951 Board of Reference and Counsel worried about the infiltration of these theological changes.

The instructional function in the church also changed with the coming of the professional and paid pastorate. Part of the attraction of fundamentalism was that it appealed to the newly trained ministerial class with their greater concern for theological precision and more systematic formulation. Kyle notes that by the early 1950s nearly all of the MB churches in the United States had made the transition from the multiple lay leadership to the professional pastoral system. Whereas this transition was virtually complete in the U.S. by 1960 it would take most of that decade to complete the same in Canada.

The Board of Reference and Counsel's 1951 proposals for

reigning in both the organizational and instructional changes of the mid-century failed. The intellectual capital and concentration required to produce the volumes on ministerial practice, history, doctrine and polity were difficult to achieve in a tradition where leaders emerged through churchly activism rather than through scholarship. Of their four book proposals, only two were published and neither had the significance that the 1951 planners hoped they would have. In 1969 *The Minister's Manual* was finally published. By then the pressing issue of how to call ministers, in the switch from the collective leadership drawn out of the congregation to the calling of a pastorate from the professional ranks, was virtually complete. The volume on history—Abraham H. Unruh's Die Geschichte der Mennoniten-Bruedergemeinde: 1860-1954—was published in 1954. Unfortunately, its impact was limited since it was published in German and relied almost exclusively on earlier Mennonite Brethren histories by Peter M. Friesen and John F. Harms. Unruh's history was utilized in the Bible schools of Canada, where German was still the language of choice, but it did not tell the story in a way that provided the necessary connectors to arrest the fraying identity of the denomination. That task was left undone until John A. Toews's *A History of the Mennonite Brethren Church* was published in 1975.[17] The books on Mennonite Brethren doctrine and polity, to this day, remain unpublished.

The fate of the proposal for the creation of a Board of Elders was worse than either the benign neglect or limited significance of the book projects. Because of its far-reaching implications, the proposal was sent out to the district and provincial conferences for discussion and adjudication. At the 1954 conference the Board of Reference and Counsel indicated that "in view of the reactions of all the district conferences" the duties envisaged for the newly created Board of Elders would be carried out by the Board of Reference and Counsel.[18] The tradition of congregational polity, even radical congregationalism, was too deeply established and the remembrances of the role of Elders too mixed to return to more authoritarian practices.

FROM BOUNDARY MAINTENANCE TO MISSIONAL ACTIVISM

Historians and sociologists have long suggested that definable communities in North America have both boundaries and a nucleus or center. The boundaries mark the differences with other peoples. The nucleus consists of those cherished values, understandings, and traditions that give vitality and purpose. The 1951 resolutions were a combination of both boundary maintenance and nucleus revitalization. Boundary maintenance, long a strategy of Mennonite communities, was ill-suited as a carrier of Mennonite identity in the more pluralistic and cosmopolitan world of twentieth-century North America. What did catch the eye of Mennonite Brethren people, like other Mennonites during the 1940 to 1960 period, was a missional and service activism. As the cultural boundaries of the past became more permeable, Mennonite Brethren identity increasingly was carried by a greatly enlarged missional, educational and service activism. Precisely as an identity rooted in sociological factors gave way, an identity hinged to missions and service took its place. Of the many facets of this activism these essays address only one. The three essays on the women's missionary organizations capture one segment of the church expanding their service to peoples around the world in need and unreached by the gospel. The essays by Rempel, Redekop and Wiebe open up new understandings about the degree to which these women's organizations became the vehicle for carrying forward much of this post-World War II activism. Mission administrative personnel soon realized that at the congregational level the motivation for missions giving and involvement could more easily be nurtured through these organizations than through any other means. Women sewed and baked goods for sales with the proceeds going to missions; they gathered relief supplies for shipment abroad either with Mennonite Central Committee or through the mission board; they funded specific overseas projects and they unlocked the family resources for greater missions giving.

In other ways Mennonite Brethren were also able to bridge the troubled waters introduced by the changes of these mid-century decades. Increasing ease of citizenship did not undermine the doctrine of nonresistance. More democratic polities transformed but did not abridge the continuing tradition of peoplehood that bound Mennonite Brethren congregations and communities together. National conferences did become more important, particularly after 1954 when all educational institutions came under their jurisdiction, but the General Conference Board of Reference and Counsel continued as the most visible articulator and guardian of theology. From the vantage point of 1960 it would be plausible to suggest that American fundamentalism and Evangelicalism were about to overwhelm Anabaptist Evangelicalism among the Mennonite Brethren. But as Kyle's essay notes, already in the 1950s there were indications of the resurgence of a more articulate Anabaptism. The 1960s would bring into focus a renaissance in Anabaptist-Mennonite theology that challenged the drift of the 1940 to 1960 period into American fundamentalism. While that topic is beyond the bounds of these essays, the recentering of the Mennonite Brethren Biblical Seminary during the 1960s and the collateral movements in the Board of Christian Literature and the Historical Commission, largely inspired by new Seminary faculty, mitigated the "instructional" concerns of the 1940 to 1960 period. The swift currents that carried the Mennonite Brethren along during the mid-century decades hardly abated in the years that followed. The need for negotiating troubling waters and for constructing new bridges would remain. Yet surely the mid-century experience also offered some hope that bridging was possible. Nothing better illustrates both the hope and the ability to negotiate through these difficulties than the three short autobiographies by Waldo Hiebert, David Ewert and J. B. Toews. Each is an intriguing story in its own right. The despair and hope they experienced were common to the pilgrimage of their people. In the ability of each of these individuals to fashion remarkable careers and provide sustained leadership to the church during and after these decades lies hope. They navigated turbulent waters. One hopes that the church can do so in the future as well.

I.
Church and State Issues

North American Mennonite Brethren and Issues of War, Peace and Nonresistance

Abe Dueck

A study of the response of the Mennonite Brethren Church in North America to questions of war, peace and nonresistance during the period 1940-1960 raises several interesting questions. Were there differences between Mennonite Brethren (MB) in the United States and Canada, or between the MB experience and that of other Mennonites in North America? Did Mennonite Brethren fit into the pattern of the wider Mennonite experience? Were there significant differences between the developments in the two countries? Did MB theology, attitudes and practices on issues of peace, war, violence and justice shift during the mid-century decades?

Several recent studies have proposed significant hypotheses regarding the experience and impact of World War II on Menonites in the U.S. and Canada. Paul Toews has analyzed the development of Mennonite peace theology in the U.S. from the inter-war period to 1944 and the impact of Civilian Public Service (CPS) on American Mennonites.[1] The pre-war period, he states, was characterized by controversies between those who advocated a separatist stance and those who favored dialogue with other pacifist bodies. When the war erupted, this debate faded into the background as energies were devoted to organizing the CPS system. In 1944 a "conceptual triumph" emerged with the publication of Guy F. Hershberger's *War, Peace and Nonresistance*. Hershberger, says Toews, defined a position that was nonpolitical but nevertheless made a contribution to the political order. "It was an important part of the larger Mennonite reorientation toward greater political and mission activism that accompanied the World War II experience."[2] The "ideological revitalization" and idealism associated with Hershberger, Harold S. Bender and others of the "Goshen school" became closely linked with the CPS experience. Toews refers to CPS as "the Mennonite university experience."[3] It became the mechanism for engagement with the world, particularly in inducing a mood of self-confidence, producing a missional and service activism and in accelerating the Mennonite ecumenical movement. Toews concludes that "servant activism" became the core of an ideologically revitalized Mennonite identity.[4]

Toews's study focuses almost entirely on the (Old) Mennonite Church and the General Conference Mennonite Church. He mentions only two Mennonite Brethren, P. C. Hiebert and P. S. Goertz, who "were hardly representative of the Mennonte Brethren."[5] Mennonite Brethren clearly were not particularly active in theologizing about issues of church and state and the related questions of peace and nonresistance during this period.

Ted Regehr suggests that the main hypothesis or theme of Canadian Mennonite history for the period from 1940 to 1960 is one of accommodation.[6] Both the Mennonites and the government of Canada sought to apply the lessons from the past (World War I and the Russian Mennonite experience) and work cooperatively toward a solution during the war years. This spirit of cooperation carried forward into the prosperous 1950s. Although Regehr's study is broader in scope and does not deal at length with issues of peace and war, his hypothesis relating to Canada seems to run contrary to Toews's relating to the U.S. Accommodation is not a concept that would easily have applied to the revitalization connected with the recovery of the Anabaptist vision.

John H. Redekop makes a strong case for substantial differences between Mennonites in Canada and the U.S. based on the different national contexts. He seeks to explain "why Anabaptist pacifism in Canada has become distinctive and, in particular, how and why it differs from dominant expressions of Anabaptist pacifism in the United States."[7] Although Redekop acknowledges that Mennonites in Canada do not form a monolith, he does not explore denominational distinctives or make specific references to Mennonite Brethren.

Leo Driedger and Donald Kraybill have also recently examined North American Mennonite peacemaking,[8] particularly the impact of modernization on historic nonresistance. They conclude that there has been a radical transformation in Mennonite peace theology. The old "plausibilty structures" became shattered for Mennonites who left their sectarian enclaves. "Ideological brokers" created new plausibility structures that permitted Mennonite peace theology to survive in new forms. In keeping with Toews's thesis, the authors affirm that the most significant shift occurred after World War II and that North American Mennonites have "moved across the spectrum from passive nonresistance to assertive peacemaking."[9] These changes were accompanied by the acceptance of new words—love, shalom, justice, responsibility, peacemaking—as "subjects" became "citizens."[10] The dominant theme of the 1940s was "Biblical Nonresistance," they suggest, whereas the dominant theme of the 1950s was "The Way of Love."[11]

I will not attempt to test the validity of these various interpretations as they relate to the Mennonite experience as a whole. Rather, I will attempt to demonstrate that the MB experience, while coinciding with the larger Mennonite experience in many ways, nevertheless had its own unique timing, substance, and regional characteristics.

THE NORTH AMERICAN CONTEXT
FOR MB PEACE THEOLOGY

Mennonite Brethren first came to the United States as part of a larger Mennonite migration to North America from Russia in the 1870s. The circumstances that precipitated the move related to the changing policies of the Russian government and involved the withdrawal of some privileges that the Mennonites had enjoyed. These related particularly to the control of schools and absolute exemption from state service. It did not take long until the Mennonites who remained in Russia were required to serve in forestry camps in place of military service.

The Mennonite Brethren who came to the United States, therefore, were part of a conservative group who found conditions in Russia too threatening to their religious principles.[12] However, their move to the U.S. instead of Canada has suggested to some that they were not as separatistic as their Mennonite counterparts who migrated to Canada. The Canadian government gave better guarantees of religious freedom and allowed Mennonites to establish closed settlements similar to the colonies in southern Russia.[13] In Canada these immigrants became known as *Kanadier*, to distinguish them from the *Russländer* who arrived in the 1920s. When the MB Church began in Manitoba late in the nineteenth century, the first converts came from these groups and some of the attitudes toward the state among them continued to be distinguishable from the *Russländer* later.

The 1870s immigrants predominantly shaped the U.S. Mennonite Brethren Church. The later Russian Mennonite experience did not have the same direct impact that it had on Mennonite Brethren in Canada, many of who immigrated in the 1920s. Furthermore, because U.S. policies and experiences with respect to war and alternative service were different from Canada's, Mennonite Brethren in the U.S. have either had to link with other Mennonites to find a workable policy or else to blend with segments of evangelical protestantism.

The larger Mennonite context in the U.S. points to another important difference between Mennonite Brethren in the U.S. and Canada. Mennonite Brethren in the U.S. have made up a much smaller percentage of the total Mennonite population than they have in Canada. In 1936 the total Mennonite membership in the U.S. was around 114,337.[14] The MB membership was 7,595, representing approximately 6.6 percent of the total. In Canada in 1940 MB membership was approximately 7,890, representing about 18.4 percent of the total Mennonite membership of 42,876.[15] Therefore, U.S. Mennonite Brethren have not been able to take leadership on issues of nonresistance to the extent that other Mennonites have.[16] In Canada, on the other hand, Mennonite Brerthren took a much more active role particularly in the negotiations with the government before and during World War II. It also should be remembered that Mennonites of all kinds made up a considerably larger percentage of the population as a whole in Canada than in the U.S.

WORLD WAR II

As Mennonites in the two countries faced the possibility of another world conflagration in the late 1930s, they did so against the backdrop of very different experiences in World War I and the interwar period. The World War I experience for conscientious objectors in the U.S. was a very difficult one. They were drafted into the army and it was left to the military to decide how to deal with them. While some were treated well, others were virtually forced into combatant roles or found themselves in prison where they received very cruel treatment. Mennonites did not want to repeat that experience, and in a series of meetings and conferences they began to develop alternative proposals that they could present to government.

Although World War I had not been as difficult for Mennonites in Canada, the legal situation was more confusing. The government had made various provisions for conscientious objectors or for specific groups of Mennonites. These included exemption from military service of Mennonites and other pacifist groups based on the Militia Act of 1793. This special Order in Council promised exemption from military service to Mennonites who immigrated from Russia in the 1870s (the *Kanadier*), and promises to the Mennonites who immigrated in the 1920s (the *Russländer*) that they were protected by existing legislation.[17] But it was not clear which Mennonites might qualify for exemption under particular provisions and whether complete exemption from state service or only exemption from combatant service would apply to certain groups.

By 1940, Canada was already at war. Britain had declared war against Germany on September 3, 1939, and Canada followed about a week later. The United States did not become actively involved until the attack by the Japanese at Pearl Harbor in December, 1941. Therefore Canada's direct involvement preceded that of the U.S. by over two years and Canadian Mennonites faced the practical question of their role considerably earlier.

In Canada an alternative service program began in the summer of 1941. Before long many Mennonite young men were active in various forestry camps and later in mental institutions, hospitals and eventually in a vast array of other assignments including agriculture. This Alternative Service Work (ASW) program continued until the summer of 1946.

In the U.S., the CPS program began in May 1941, even before the country had become involved in the war, and the program continued until April, 1947.[18] In both countries Mennonites during this time were preoccupied with issues pertaining to the establishment of policies of the respective programs and the implementation of those policies as well as educational and pastoral responsibilities.

The Cold War and the Korean War

Another world conflagration such as the two world wars did not erupt in the succeeding decades, as many had feared. World tension between the two superpowers and their allies, however, increased and developed into what became known as the "Cold War." In June 1950, new hostilities erupted into the Korean War that, although nominally under United Nations auspices, was essentially an American war. American Mennonites were therefore kept constantly on the alert. From 1951 to 1973 American Mennonite young men again faced a national conscription system. An alternative service system known as I-W permitted civilian work in lieu of military service. In 1951 Mennonite Central Committee also began the Pax (peace) program of voluntary overseas service. While the Pax program was open to Canadians, it was essentially tailored for Americans needing to fulfill alternative service obligations, and thus few Canadians served in the program.

Canada was less affected but was minimally involved in the Korean War. The cold war fear of communism was also evident among Canadian Mennonite Brethren, fed partially by the memories of experiences of the Russian Mennonites after the Revolution of 1917, and partially by the U.S. media and certain religious broadcasts that many Canadian Mennonite Brethren listened to avidly.

MB PEACE THEOLOGY AND PRACTICE AT MID-CENTURY

The statistical information regarding participation of Mennonites in the military and in alternative service programs in both countries remains meager. More extensive studies exist relating to the Mennonites in the U.S. during World War II than concerning Mennonites in Canada.

According to statistics cited by Hershberger, the total number of Mennonites in the U.S. drafted during the CPS period was 9,809. Of these, 4,536 were in CPS (46.2 percent), 3,876 in the military (39.5 percent), and 1,397 opted for non-combatant roles in the military (14.2 percent). The General Conference Mennonite Church had the highest percentage of young men in the military (combatant and non-combatant = 73.3 percent), and the Mennonite Brethren were not far behind at 63.4 percent. The Mennonite Church was considerably lower at 40.5 percent, and most of the other more conservative groups were below 10 percent.[19] Among Mennonite Brethren approximately 36.4

percent of the draftees selected CPS, 31.5 percent the regular military, and 31.9 percent non-combatant services in the military. It is more difficult to arrive at accurate statistics for Canada. Ted Regehr has estimated that approximately 7,500 (62.5 percent) Mennonite men were active in alternative service during World War II and approximately 4,500 (37.5 percent) were in the armed forces.[20] Although the categories in the two countries are not entirely analogous, it seems clear that a much higher percentage of Mennonites in Canada opted for alternative service than in the U.S. Conversely, more U.S. Mennonites opted for the military. The Russian experience was obviously very determinative for most Canadian Mennonites who immigrated in the 1920s. Unfortunately, a breakdown by denomination is not available. It appears that a higher percentage of Mennonite Brethren in Canada served in the military than was true for Mennonites as a whole. According to 1942 reports to the Ontario MB Conference, there were fifteen Mennonite Brethren in ASW camps and ten in active military service.[21] In 1943 there were twenty-five in the army, four in the air force, one in the navy and twenty-one in alternative service (i.e., 58.8 percent in combatant service).[22] Some young men had received "farm postponements," however, and would otherwise probably have increased the numbers in the alternative service category considerably.[23]

Statistics for the 1950s and 1960s are even more difficult to obtain or to interpret. Occasionally some numbers appear in district or area conference reports, but these are not comprehensive enough to warrant firm conclusions. Reports to the Central District (U.S.) indicate that in 1956 there were eighty-five Mennonite Brethren in I-W. In 1959 the numbers are as follows:[24]

Government service total: 74
Military service: 25
Alternative service (I-W):   49

Statistics are available for the U.S. Area Conference for the years 1957, 1959 and 1960, as indicated in Table 1:[25]

Table 1

Year	I-W Service	Military
1957	70	40
1959	59	30
1960	45	ca. 1/3

It appears that in peacetime at least one-third of drafted young men in the U.S. opted for military service.

There are no comparable statistics for Canada during the post-war period. Canada did not have conscription, although some Mennonite men continued to be active in the military forces.

It is interesting how the general surveys of attitudes of 1972, 1982, and 1989 compare with the data of actual practice for the 1940s and 1950s. Table 2 shows the MB responses to particular questions relating to war and alternative service in the two countries at the time of these surveys. The table demonstrates that U.S. MBs have been less committed to the peace position than Canadians have. It also shows that there has been a further erosion in the U.S. during the period covered by the surveys, whereas Canadian Mennonite Brethren have increased their commitment to peace.

Table 2[26]
MB Attitudes to Issues of War and Peace, 1972-79

	1972 US	1972 Can	1972 Comb	1982 US	1982 Can	1982 Comb	1989 Comb
Christians should take no part in war	42	66	54	39	70	54	56
Owning stock in war bonds is wrong	21	36	29	21	43	32	NA
Christians should actively promote peace	39	52	46	36	50	43	53
Would choose alternative service if drafted	47	49	48	41	48	45	50

As might be expected, Mennonite Brethren statements on war and peace in North America are clustered around the two world wars. Besides the publication of the Confession of Faith in 1916 and 1917 (in German and English respectively), there were only four statements issued before 1934, and these appeared between 1917 and 1922. None originated in the Northern District (Canada) and only one came from the General Conference.[27] Table 3 provides a breakdown of statements on peace and war at the various conference levels in the two countries between 1935 and 1982.[28]

Table 3
Mennonite Brethren Statements on Peace and War
in North America

Years	To 1934	1935-1939	1940-1944	1945-1949	1950-1954	1955-1959	1960-1964	1965-1969	1970-1982
Canadian Conf.	1	5	3	6	6	5	5	6	0
Canadian Provinces	2	17	36	11	11	8	5	2	1
Total Canadian	3	22	39	17	17	13	10	8	1
U.S. Conf.	0	0	0	0	0	0	0	0	2
U.S. Districts	1	7	2	6	1	3	0	2	2
Total U.S.	1	7	2	6	1	3	0	2	4
General. Conf.	0	2	1	2	2	1	0	1	3
Total North America	4	31	42	25	20	17	10	11	8

Several observations can be made based on these statistics. One is that there is a very strong cluster of statements beginning about 1935 and continuing to about 1949. After that the number of statements diminishes constantly until at least 1980. Second, the total number of statements by Canadian Mennonite Brethren is significantly higher than those by U.S. Mennonite Brethren, at least until 1970. As Appendix I illustrates, district and provincial conferences appear to have made fewer and fewer statements, while more were made at the national or bi-national conference levels.

The content of the statements does not reflect any radical shifts over the entire period or, more particularly, for the decades from 1940 to 1960. Neither is there clear evidence of significant differences between the U.S. and Canada, although some differences clearly surfaced during discussions leading to the adoption of the statements.

A recent series of discussions sponsored by Mennonite Central Committee sought to develop a typology of Mennonite peace theologies. This resulted in an identification of ten different types, ranging from historic nonresistance to liberation pacifism.[29] Based on this typology, it seems clear that the statements issued during the entire period mentioned above most closely resemble "Historic Nonresistance." Some of them reflect an inclination toward an "apolitical nonresistant" position. A pacifism that is political or humanistic and that envisions an idyllic world without war and violence is repudiated. Based on the themes identified by

Driedger and Kraybill, the theme of "biblical nonresistance" comes closest to characterizing the entire period. The main perceived threat identified by the statements, however, lies in the possibility of a complete abandonment of the nonresistant position rather than in the adoption of a different kind of peace position.

The primary vocabulary is that of "nonresistance" (*Wehrlosigkeit*) and "peace" (*Frieden*). The specific issues addressed repeatedly are conscription, military service, noncombatant service in the military (e.g., the medical corps), the military oath and military drill, defense or civilian bonds and alternative service under military or civilian supervision. The emphasis is on educating the young men, who clearly are seen to bear the main burden of expressing the Mennonite peace position, although this is more evident during and immediately after the war.

The differences between the U.S. and Canadian Mennonite Brethren were clear to some who participated in the discussions leading to the recommendations. At the General Conference sessions in Mountain Lake, Minnesota in 1948, the original recommendation received by the delegation was similar to the one adopted by the Canadian Convention earlier in the same year. It included the provision for excommunication of those who participated in military service.[30] The majority rejected this provision. Abraham H. Unruh remarked that a clear difference of opinion was evident between the Americans and the Canadians and that the Canadians were intent on retaining the stricter provision. He expected that this issue would lead to serious tensions in the future.[31]

The issue of service in the medical corps of the military or medical service in the arena of war but without military training was addressed on several occasions on both sides of the border already before and during World War II. In Canada B.B. Janz, who for a time was chairman of the Military Problems Committee of Western Canada, was the most outspoken advocate of an alternative service program that might include "forestry, first aid, ambulance and hospital work and farm or any national service of a non-military character."[32] John B. Toews has characterized Janz's stance as "one of the more radical among the Canadian Mennonites,"[33] which he formulated very much based on the Russian Mennonite experience. Janz was even willing to have the young men wear uniforms and serve under military authority, if their duties were restricted to acts of love and mercy. The more conservative Mennonites of Western Canada, however, wanted complete exemption from state service and this led to alienation between the two groups in western Canada. Furthermore, many Swiss Mennonites in Ontario wanted a more restricted alternative service program. Negotiations with the government continued for some time, but in January 1942 Janz was informed that all conscientious objectors would go to alternative service work camps and there would be no provision for a Mennonite ambulance corps. Nonetheless, some MB men enlisted in the medical corps of the military and generally did not become subject to church discipline.

At district conferences in the U.S. and at the General Conference sessions the issue of medical service did become a problematic one. In 1948 the various district conferences and the General Conference passed resolutions approving service in the medical corps of the military. Subsequently, however, a delegation went to Washington to discover what the terms and purposes of such service were. The response was clear: the government regarded such service as part of the broader war effort under military jurisdiction. The primary purpose of the medical corps was not to save life but to advance the cause of the war. The result was that the 1948 resolution was rescinded at the General Conference sessions in 1954. Subsequently (1957) the Canadian Conference also took a position against service in the medical corps because it appeared that the Canadian government's view of the medical corps was similar to that of the United States military.

The desire to distinguish pacifism from Mennonite nonresistance appeared in conference discussions at various times. Delegates at the Southern District Conference expressed concerns about attempts to establish a "warless world" as early as 1922. At the Northern District Conference in 1934, a group of Russian believers who had joined the Mennonite Brethren through evangelistic efforts in Saskatchewan brought a resolution asking for a condemnation of all wars because

> war did not resolve conflict, because it destroyed the moral foundations of society, because it left huge debts and many orphans, widows, cripples, and persons mentally ill, and because of the role in war played by capitalist industry and power-hungry diplomats.[34]

The resolution failed because "the Conference did not see its mission to proclaim anti-war resolutions." The Conference also spoke against cooperating with Quakers and other "popular movements which employ force."[35] Anything resembling a social-political agenda was therefore suspect. Historian Frank Epp noted that the Russian brethren were never heard from again.

Concerns about a socio-political agenda arose at various times in later statements. In 1957 the General Conference approved a major resolution pertaining to a theology of peace. One statement read as follows: "Biblical nonresistance is not pacifism; it arises from an entirely different motive and the two are propagated by two entirely different groups of people."[36]

Nevertheless, it condemned war as brutal and inhuman. "The fact that Jesus said 'there shall be wars and rumors of wars' cannot justly be construed to be His stamp of approval upon war."[37] The Conference's strong objection to a more active political stance probably set the stage for some serious criticism of MCC in the next several decades. The 1969 Canadian Convention dealt with mounting criticism of MCC because of its social, cultural and political involvement. About a decade later a special task force of the Board of Spiritual and Social Concerns evaluated MCC's mandate because of the continuing criticism directed against that organization's activities.[38]

During the 1950s the issues of civil defense and disarmament also were major concerns in society. Some of those concerns appear in Conference statements and in the periodicals. *The Canadian Mennonite*, which began publication in 1953, frequently carried articles and editorials concerning these issues. Although the editor, Frank H. Epp, was not a member of the Mennonite Brethren Church, the paper was widely read by MB intellectuals. It became a vehicle for a more activist socio-political agenda among Mennonite Brethren, including new forms of peace witness.

Mennonite Brethren did not have many trained theologians in the 1940s and 1950s who could articulate a peace theology to nurture the post-war generation of young people. The most significant voice in North America was probably John A. Toews, who was already active in ministry to young men in ASW camps in Canada in 1943. During the next several decades Toews was the most prolific writer and popular speaker on peace and nonresistance. He wrote articles in the *Zionsbote, Mennonitische Rundschau, Mennonite Observer, The Christian Leader*, and *The*

Voice, in addition to publishing several booklets on the topic. Particularly important for Mennonite Brethren on both sides of the border was his booklet, *True Nonresistance Through Christ.*[39] In 1958 the Canadian Conference decided that ten copies per one hundred members should be distributed to the churches and that churches should present them to baptismal candidates and otherwise make them available to members.[40] Several years later Toews produced another volume giving an account of alternative service in Canada during the war.[41]

Toews undoubtedly had learned much from the American Mennonites connected with Harold S. Bender. Although the most frequent citations in *True Nonresistance* came from Rutenbur's *The Dagger and the Cross,*[42] Toews frequently cited Bender, Hershberger and other Mennonite scholars.

Frank C. Peters was another bi-national MB leader affected by the "ideological transformation" of American Mennonites. Both his M.Th. and his Th.D. theses focused on Mennonites. In 1953 Peters gave several lectures at Tabor's annual Peace Conference, with Erland Waltner of the General Conference Mennonite Church and Milo Kaufman of the Mennonite Church.[43] Although Peters did not publish a great deal, he spoke quite frequently on issues of peace and nonresistance.

Among Mennonite Brethren in the U.S., there were none who published significant monographs on peace and nonresistance. *The Christian Leader* often carried articles about the draft, I-W service, and the teaching of nonresistance. Contributors to the *Leader* included Orlando Harms and Wesley Prieb. Dwight Wiebe became active as a leader in the I-W program in the late 1950s and carried a strong concern for the historic peace position.

CONCLUSION

Mennonite Brethren in North America did not experience the same type of "ideological reorientation" during and after the war as did the other major Mennonite groups, particularly those of Swiss origin. The reasons why this did not happen were different in the U.S. than in Canada. In the U.S., Mennonite Brethren were overwhelmed by other Mennonites who had seized the initiative because of their numbers and their more advanced education. Mennonite Brethren did not have the "theological brokers" during the middle decades to facilitate the transition into a new era. The Mennonite Church and the General Conference Mennonite

Church asked questions of their own identity in American society earlier. They had to face the threat of fundamentalism on the right and liberalism on the left earlier. Mennonte Brethren, on the other hand, often simply continued to nurture relationships with Baptists.

In Canada, Mennonite Brethren had a larger voice within the Mennonite community, but they had not generally completed the language and cultural transition that many Mennonites in the U.S. had. The expression of the peace witness was often simply carried over from the Russian experience without a keen sense that it needed rearticulation in the North American context. John B. Toews has referred to nonresistance in the Russian experience as "historically associated with its legality as a right and a privilege." Because of this perspective, it "did not become a deeply-rooted ethic."[44] The "commitment to peace remained a structural rather than an experimental one," he states. To some extent continuity with Russia probably diminished the creative potential of alternative service in Canada. Little new theologizing seemed necessary. That which did take place was still mostly in the German language and therefore not suited to inspire and energize the next generation.

Mennonite Brethren also did not attend universities, colleges and seminaries in North America in large numbers until after World War II, especially in Canada. The first MB institution in Canada to offer more advanced theological and liberal arts education was the Mennonite Brethren Bible College. It opened in 1944, initially with a faculty that had received most of its education in Russia. Much of the instruction was still in German. Almost a decade passed before the impact of North American Mennonite scholarship made itself felt in a significant way. Abraham H. Unruh's *Die Geschichte der Mennoniten-Bruedergemeinde*, published in 1955, did not draw on North American Mennonite scholarship. In the 1950s, John A. Toews and Frank C. Peters, both of whom taught at MBBC, came closest to translating the writings of Harold S. Bender and others within the Anabaptist Vision school of Mennonite historiography for a new generation of Mennonite Brethren in Canada. Neither, however, functioned as ideological brokers in the way that Hershberger, Yoder, or Burkholder did for the Mennonite Church. Nevertheless, in some ways the decade of the 1950s, at least in Canada, was analogous to the decade of the 1940s for other Mennonites in the U.S.

In neither country, the United States or Canada, could

Mennonite Brethren define themselves primarily in terms of nonresistance or the Anabaptist vision. Nonresistance could not serve Mennonite Brethren as a differentiating characteristic from other Mennonite groups. They already had established a strong base for working with other evangelical groups, particularly with Baptists but also with Plymouth Brethren and non-denominational fundamentalist groups. Many Mennonite Brethren in both Canada and the U.S. adopted a dispensationalist eschatology. In the U.S. this often came through militant and patriotic fundamentalist groups. The nonresistant principles of Mennonite Brethren individuals attending these fundamentalist schools were severely tested and often weakened. Canadian Mennonite Brethren of the 1920s migration, on the other hand, received their dispensational theology in Russia through contacts with institutions like the Blankenburg conferences, which were probably not as militant. It is clear from the writings of prominent dispensational preachers in Canada that their hermeneutic did not lead them to a disavowal of the nonresistant position. They still emphasized the relevance of the Sermon on the Mount.

It may be that Mennonite Brethren did not go through as many stages as the larger Mennonite bodies did. A generally more conservative theology forced many to choose between historic or biblical nonresistance and a complete rejection of nonresistance in favor of a more Lutheran two-kingdom perspective. They did not have the liberty to choose between all the options available to other Mennonites because of the work of ideological brokers.

Decades of Transition: North American Mennonite Brethren in Politics

John H. Redekop

While historians, theologians and sociologists continue to make impressive additions to the literature addressing Mennonite understandings of church-state relations, very little scholarly writing has appeared on practical political involvement. James Juhnke[1] has addressed the political acculturation of Kansas Mennonites, including Mennonite Brethren; a survey article appeared in 1983[2]; and recently Leland Harder has interpreted the findings—including the political components—of the Anabaptist Church Member Profile surveys of 1972 and 1989.[3] Nonetheless, the paucity of analysis persists.

The actual political situation, however, has changed and developed in remarkable ways and with very significant consequences. Certain causes, trends, realities, and general contours can be identified. While we cannot define sudden beginnings or sudden endings, the political life of North American Mennonite Brethren changed fundamentally—and apparently, permanently—during the two decades between 1940 and 1960.

In assessing this hypothesis it is necessary to make some comparisons to preceding and subsequent eras. Some of the available data therefore take us beyond the decades in question and beyond the strictly Mennonite Brethren scene to the larger Mennonite context, especially in Canada.

This study will not deal with the substantial Mennonite penetration of government bureaucracies nor the very extensive presence of Mennonites in the various forms of municipal government including school boards, hospital boards, and similar bodies. Nor will it assess the rapidly increasing Mennonite Brethren utilization, both individually and corporately, of government services or the expanding interaction and cooperation with government, both locally and at more senior levels. Similarly, it will not attempt systematic analysis of changed beliefs and attitudes, although some will be noted.

We will instead focus on three kinds of evidence. The first is an analysis of a political candidacy survey limited, unfortunately, to Canada. Next, we will examine two Mennonite Brethren periodicals: *The Christian Leader* and *Zionsbote*. We will also assess the *Mennonitische Rundschau,* which was not then a denominational periodical but was closely associated with the Mennonite Brethren. Finally, we will review the results of a random sample survey of political views and behavior among American and Canadian Mennonite Brethren old enough to have voted in the 1940s and 1950s. This survey may not substantiate any political shifts but will help us to assess voting behavior and attitudes during those decades. Given the time that has elapsed, we did not sample the views and voting practices of people who were old enough to have voted in the 1930s.

A critical question for this kind of sampling is how we define "Mennonite Brethren" and, more fundamentally, how do we define "Mennonite?"[4] Suffice it to say here that Mennonites in Canada and the United States, and traditional Mennonite communities in certain other countries, may best be understood as an ethnoreligious group with significant subgroups. The religious component rests on more than 450 years of history. Leo Driedger and other Mennonite sociologists have extensively documented the more recent ethnic dimension.[5] This chapter assumes a broad definition of Mennonite, including people who grew up Mennonite or have maintained at least some ethnic or religious connection with other Mennonites or who are first-generation Mennonites

MENNONITE BRETHREN POLITICAL
INVOLVEMENT: HISTORICAL BACKGROUND

Mennonite Brethren, who established themselves as an autonomous conference in 1860, may not have focussed on the 1527 Schleitheim Confession's insistence that "the sword" was "an ordering of God outside the perfection of Christ" and that "it does not befit a Christian to be a magistrate."[6] Their views, however, were similar to that position. At their first conference in North America, held in Nebraska in 1878, they decided "that brethren are not to serve in any government offices."[7] In 1888 the MB Conference, in dealing with the question of serving as a delegate to a national political convention, decided that "the conference does not want to form a definite resolution in this matter."[8] Two years later the MB conference passed a resolution that stated: "members of the church [should] refrain from participation and involvement in the contentions of political parties, but are permitted to vote quietly at elections, and may also vote for prohibition."[9]

For Canadian Mennonite Brethren the next major shift occurred with the July, 1917 enactment of the Wartime Elections Act. This act, in a climate of Canadian anti-German sentiment and of military crisis for Allied forces in Europe, excluded Mennonites from voting. Any Mennonites who voted would automatically lose their military exemption privileges.[10] This denial of the franchise was not rescinded until 1920.

Interviews with elderly Mennonite Brethren suggest that voting became widespread by the 1920s and 1930s. In 1943, faced with mounting resentment of German-speaking pacifists, the MB Conference adopted a resolution stating, in part, "we confirm our undivided loyalty to our country and our government." The term "country" apparently referred to both the United States and Canada.[11] The assertion of unqualified allegiance is startling and signals a major shift. While actual political involvement   was increasing rapidly, the MB Conference did not formally alter its stance until 1966 when it adopted a lengthy statement on political involvement.

While acknowledging that "political involvement can easily become an 'entanglement,'" the 1966 resolution said that Mennonite Brethren "believe that the Church and its members should be constructively critical of the political order, always ready to promote justice, respect for human dignity, and conditions of peace." In the concluding section it altered the official conference stance even more markedly: "We believe that it is proper for Christians to vote, to exert influence on governmental officials provided that neither means nor ends are un-Christian, and also under special conditions to stand for political office, if neither the attempt to gain the position nor the exercizing of its functions, requires a compromise of Christian ethics."[12] As we shall shortly see, this clarifying resolution came largely after the fact.

THE PARTICIPATION OF MENNONITES AS CANDIDATES IN CANADIAN ELECTIONS

While the definition of "Mennonite" created some problems, and additional research on some individuals remains to be done, findings thus far suggest that a total of 327 Mennonites ran for elective public office provincially and federally in Canada between the country's formation on July 1, 1867 and January 20, 1993. Two of them also contested seats in the colonial Upper Canada Assembly. This information comes mainly from the Canadian Parliamentary Guide[13] but also from newspapers, various directories, assorted versions of *Who's Who*, other reference materials, phone calls and interviews. Many people, such as the politically-active Penner family of Winnipeg, Gordon Snyder of Moose Jaw, Edward Good of Waterloo and Alberta's Henry Kroeger (born in Moscow during the Mennonite exodus in the 1920s), were excluded because they seemed to have had neither religious nor ethnic connections to the Mennonite community in their adult life. Significantly, because of their ethnic roots, I include a few who were candidates for the Communist or Marxist-Leninist parties. One intriguing chap, "Honest Don Bergen," contested a Winnipeg federal seat in 1980 and 1984 for the Rhinoceros Party, whose satirical and humorous platform was a spoof on the foibles and failures of the "respectable" parties.

The actual numbers of individuals, according to jurisdiction, are given in Table 1.

Table 1
Mennonite Participants in Canadian Elections
1867 to 1991

Federal level	95
Alberta	23
British Columbia	26
Manitoba	90
Ontario	26
Saskatchewan	67
Total	327

Because a few individuals contested elections at both federal and provincial levels, the actual number of people involved appears to be 315. Since many candidates contested more than one election, the number of candidacies is, of course, greater.

Table 2
Canadian Mennonite Political Candidacies by Jurisdiction 1854-1991

Jurisdiction	AB	BC	SK	MB	ON	Totals
Pre-Confederation					5	5
Provincial Candidacies, 1867-1991	28	41	99	136	38	342
Federal Candidacies by Province, 1867-1991	10	26	21	53	53	163
Totals	38	67	120	189	96	510

The *Parliamentary Guide* provides biographical statements for all winning candidates unless the successful candidate chose not to submit one. A few of the winners listed in Appendices A to F did not submit one. The self-descriptions are both fascinating and revealing and need to be published. Mennonite candidates describe themselves most frequently as Swiss, German, Swiss-German, Pennsylvania Dutch, Mennonite, Ukrainian, Canadian, or Dutch. The latter is particularly evident during and after the two World Wars.

Of the 315 Mennonite candidates, only four could be identified as belonging to a Mennonite church but not having a Mennonite ethnic identity or background: Deane Whiteway in Manitoba, Carol Gran in British Columbia, and Herbert Swan and Carol Teichroeb (a non-Mennonite who married a Mennonite named Teichgroeb) in Saskatchewan. The latter three served as provincial cabinet ministers. All except Carol Teichroeb were active in Mennonite Brethren congregations.

The religious identification or affiliation of the 315 candidates was diverse. While many listed themselves as Mennonite or Mennonite Brethren, others simply described themselves as Christian or Protestant. Some were or are members of other denominations such as United Church, Evangelical Free, Nazarene, Christian and Missionary Alliance, Baptist, and Pentecostal. Some changed affiliation while in office as did the Honourable Jake Epp—twice. In the 1961 *Parliamentary Guide* the Hon. David Boldt of Saskatchewan listed himself as Catholic. In the 1964 edition, this dominant politician from Rosthern appeared thus: "Rel. Mennonite." His predecessor as MLA (Member of the Legislative Assembly) for Rosthern, Gerhard Enns, while prominent in the Mennonite community, was a Swedenborgian by religion.

The inclusion of all identifiable Mennonites in this part of the research project needs to be explained. In the first place, some Mennonite Brethren simply listed themselves as "Mennonite," a category more readily understood in Ottawa and among the general readers of the reference sources. It is also the case that identifying the entire Mennonite cohort, as defined for this investigation, proved to be easier than identifying the Mennonite Brethren group within that cohort. Also, the Mennonite Brethren involvement as political candidates should be seen as part of a larger Mennonite trend, one in which the General Conference (or United Mennonites, now Conference of Mennonites in Canada) branch of Mennonites took the lead and still dominates.

The exact number of Mennonite Brethren involved cannot be determined precisely because for some individuals the available information, to date, is vague or insufficient. According to the criteria established for this project, I estimate the number to be about one-third of the total, that is, about 105. This diverse group includes successful candidates such as Peter A. Dueck (B.C.), Ray Ratzlaff (Alta.), Harold Martens (Sask.), John Penner (Sask.), Jake Epp (Man.), and John Reimer (Ont.). All are high profile politicians and all, except Reimer, served as cabinet members in either provincial or national governments. All have been very active in their MB congregations. The group also includes unsuccessful candidates such as Jack Suderman (B.C.), Werner Schmidt (Alta.), Peter J. Klippenstein (Sask.), Henry W. Redekopp (Man.), and David Wiebe (Ont.). All of them were or still are prominent MB church members.

The data covers such a long span of time in order to permit the comparison of candidacies during the 1940s and 1950s with previous and subsequent decades. Only then can we establish whether the two decades actually were "decades of transition." Tables 3 and 4 provide summarized data for the federal level. (Note that the first "decade" consists of twelve years.) Tables 5 and 6 provide parallel data, in aggregate form, for the five western provinces. (I could not locate any Mennonite candidates in the other five provinces and two territories, including the North West Territories, which until 1905 included the territory that became Saskatchewan and Alberta). To allow for better comparisons, post-1989 provincial data, provided in Appendices C, D, E, and F, do not appear in Tables 5 and 6.

Table 3
Mennonite Candidacies and Winners
in Federal Elections, 1867 to 1929

Decade Comparison	1867-79	1880-89	1890-99	1900-09	1910-19	1920-29
Total number of Mennonite candidacies	8	2	2	1	0	1
Number of federal elections	4	2	2	3	2	3
Average number of candidacies per election	2	1	1	.3	0	.3
Total number of wins	6	1	2	1	0	0
Average number of wins per election	1.5	.5	1	.3	0	0

The biographical notes of winners and other sources of information reveal the fact that until 1921 all federal Mennonite candidates ran for office in Ontario. All, furthermore, were of Swiss-German, Pennsylvania origin.

Table 4
Mennonite Candidacies and Winners in Federal Elections, 1930 to 1989

Decade Comparison	1930-39	1940-49	1950-59	1960-69	1970-79	1980-89
Total number of Mennonite candidacies	1	6	21	36	38	46
Number of federal elections	2	3	3	4	3	3
Average number of candidacies per election	.5	2	7	9	12.7	15.3
Total number of wins	0	0	4	5	12	12
Average number of wins per election	0	0	1.3	1.25	4	4

The data reveal some important trends. Following an almost total absence of Mennonite candidacies between 1900 and 1939—three candidacies in four decades—we move to six in the 1940s, despite the anti-Mennonite, war-related sentiments, and to twenty-one in the 1950s. The average number of candidacies per election and the total number of wins together with the average number of wins per election, quite low because of an understandable lag factor, underscore the trend. One reason for the increased number of candidacies is that Mennonites were greatly attracted by new parties, especially if they had a religious dimension. In the 1940s and 1950s five of the twenty-seven candidacies were for Social Credit, led by evangelical Christians, and fourteen were for the CCF (Cooperative Commonwealth Federation), which, during those early years, incorporated major elements of the Social Gospel. In the following twenty years, thirty-two of the seventy-four candidacies were for Social Credit and eleven for the NDP— on July 31, 1961 the CCF became the New Democratic Party— which had become more labor union-oriented.

Clearly, given the above data and in light of sustained political involvement after 1960, the two decades between 1940 and 1960 were consequential decades of political transition.

Table 5
Mennonite Candidacies and Winners in Provincial Elections, 1867 to 1929; Five Provinces*

Decade Comparison	1867-79	1880-89	1890-99	1900-09	1910-19	1920-29
Total number of Mennonite candidacies	0	3	2	12	8	2
Number of provincial elections	11	7	9	14	13	14
Average number of candidacies per election	0	.4	.2	.9	.6	.1
Total number of wins	0	2	2	7	3	0
Average number of wins per election	0	.3	.2	.5	.2	0

*Note: Ontario became part of Canada, July 1, 1867.
Manitoba joined July 15, 1870.
British Columbia joined July 20, 1871.
Alberta and Saskatchewan joined September 1, 1905.

The evidence is clear. Besides a few pioneering exceptions, Mennonite involvement in provincial elections was rather limited up to 1929. We should note, of course, that during the first sixty-two years of Canada's existence there were twenty-seven Mennonite candidacies at the provincial level including fourteen wins, a high rate of success.

Table 6
Mennonite Candidacies and Winners in Provincial Elections, 1930-1989*

Decade Comparison	1930-39	1940-49	1950-59	1960-69	1970-79	1980-89
Total number of Mennonite candidacies	7	7	36	64	67	95
Number of provincial elections	10	13	11	14	14	13
Average number of candidacies per election	.7	.5	3.3	4.3	4.8	7.3
Total number of wins	2	1	8	17	22	32
Average number of wins per election	.2	.1	.7	1.2	1.6	2.5

* For better comparison, the Ontario and Manitoba elections of 1990 and the Saskatchewan and British Columbia elections of 1991 do not appear in these aggregate data.

Concerning the aggregate provincial data presented in Table 6 we see trends paralleling those noted in the federal data. The one major difference seems to be that at the provincial level the real political transition occurred only in the 1950s rather than in both decades. Doubtless the impact of World War II was a major deterrent to success and perhaps it lingered longer where candidates, as in provincial elections, are well-known to the voters.

Again we see the major drawing power of the small parties, especially if those parties incorporated some Christian emphasis. As Canadian Mennonites became politically active, these parties held great fascination for them. Of the forty-three candidacies occurring between 1940 and 1959, twenty-one involved the Social Credit Party and ten the CCF.

In whatever way one interprets the provincial data, the basic trend is unmistakable. Before 1940 Mennonite provincial political candidacies were few and sporadic; after 1960 they were numerous: they increased nine-fold from the 1930s to the 1960s.

A REVIEW OF MENNONITE BRETHREN PERIODICALS

It can be assumed that into the 1960s many, if not most, Mennonite Brethren in Canada as well as many in the U.S. read the German-language weekly, *Zionsbote*. This would have been true especially in the early decades. Presumably most church, conference and other opinion leaders, probably older and better educated than average, read it carefully.

Reviewing issues from those years one notices that even beyond 1960, *Zionsbote* did not address political issues, let alone voting behavior. Nor did it spell out any Christian or denominational guidelines for political involvement.While acknowledging that I could not check every issue I can say that I could not locate a single editorial or article dealing with political life. This official organ of the Mennonite Brethren Church of North America did not deal with political life other than as a topic occurring in the Bible. During most of these years it carried mainly congregational and institutional reports, mission updates, serialized books, devotional articles, and denominational news. No matter how earth-shaking some international news might have been, or how great the significance of a Canadian or an American election, or even how extensive Mennonite Brethren voting and political candidacy had become, the *Zionsbote* had virtually no interpretive comment. At most, it seems to have briefly noted only a few events.

In 1937 the Mennonite Brethren Church of North America established *The Christian Leader*, its first English-language periodical. A survey of issues between 1937 and 1960 reveals that it frequently discussed questions about war and peace, nonresistance,[14] the state, alternative service, relief programs and race relations. At the same time, it skimmed over political issues, including voting. It provided no substantive conference guidance on political activism and no discussion of voting or other political issues during those years. Despite major evidence of widespread Mennonite Brethren voting and even other political activity, conference leaders, church leaders, educators, and theologians had nothing to say or were unwilling to say it.

The first noteworthy discussion of voting seems to have been editor Orlando Harms' editorial, "Our Government and We," which appeared September 20, 1960. In addressing the possible election of a Roman Catholic president in the United States, Harms wrote:

> In a democratic society it is possible for a people, many of whom are unregenerate, to elect people who are there by the permissive will of God rather than by His active will. This, however, places a great responsibility upon the Christians in that state to exercise their vote in behalf of the candidate they believe God would have and who would rule according to the

precepts of God's Word. . . . It is not our aim to tell people how to vote. This is a matter of personal liberty. We believe, however, that one should weigh the facts carefully, for aside from the individual, whether our next president is a Protestant or Catholic may have far-reaching implications for our nation for all time. . . . That vote may determine whether we maintain a "government by the people" under God or whether we will allow ecclesiastical totalitarianism to become even more forceful in our government than it is today. . . . Government is of God. Let us do our part to keep Him in first place.[15]

To the extent that Harms' call was a plea to vote for the Republican Richard M. Nixon, we can now say that he need not have worried. Appendix J shows that American MB voters voted overwhelmingly Republican in the 1940s and 1950s. I had moved to the U.S. in September 1960, and recall being taken aside and mildly "challenged" by some church leaders after a social occasion during which I, a non-American, had casually expressed some qualified support for John F. Kennedy's candidacy. I could find no other member of that congregation who shared my view.

Apparently the first three articles to deal explicitly with a practical political agenda and provide political guidance appeared in 1962, 1963 and 1964. The first was entitled, "Comments on the Anti-Communist Movement." The second asked, "Is the United States a Christian Country?" The third discussed "Evangelical Christianity and Political Ideology."[16] Not until 1965 did *The Christian Leader* in its annual subject index for the preceding year, have a heading entitled "Socio-Politics."[17] Perhaps, however, we should not be too critical. The four-volume *Mennonite Encyclopedia*, published from 1955-1959,[18] had no entries entitled, "Government," "Voting," "Politics," or "Political Involvement." An article entitled, "State, Anabaptist-Mennonite Attitudes Towards," did, however, address some of these matters.

The third periodical to be considered, the inter-Mennonite *Mennonitische Rundschau*, while not an official Mennonite Brethren publication, had a great influence on Mennonite Brethren, especially in Canada. Perusing issues from the 1930s one looks in vain for either guidance or analysis. One finds, instead, as a small section of the magazine, concise but wide-ranging news coverage of world events, including the occasional sympathetic treatment of Adolf Hitler and his activities.

For the Mennonite Brethren periodicals, and the Mennonite Brethren elites they represented, the years between 1940 and 1960 apparently did not constitute decades of political leadership or transition. There is a striking dearth of political analysis, guidance, or even description.

DATA FROM THE 1992 MENNONITE BRETHREN VOTERS SURVEY

In late 1992 I mailed out 331 questionnaires, soliciting responses from Mennonite Brethren in Canada and the U.S. who were old enough to vote in the elections between 1940 and 1960. A total of 118 questionnaires went out to twenty-six congregations in ten U.S. states. A total of 213 questionnaires were sent to forty-five congregations in the five most westerly Canadian provinces. I choose these congregations because they appeared to have many present attenders who were Mennonite Brethren in the 1940s and 1950s and were then eligible to vote. The number of questionnaires sent to a congregation varied from three to fourteen (see Appendix I).

I asked the pastors or their designates to prepare an alphabetical list of eligible—and sufficiently healthy—members, and to select respondents randomly by counting off the names appropriately (e.g., "If you have received ten envelopes and you have a list of twenty people, then select every second name.") The cooperation from church leaders and their secretarial staff was excellent. All churches cooperated, although two Canadian pastors informed me that they did not have any eligible or able respondents. In one such case I selected a substitute congregation and, in the other case, I added the questionnaires to those of a nearby congregation with many elderly people.

Table 7
Distribution of Voter Questionnaires

	Canada	U.S.	Total
Number of provinces or states	5	10	15
Number of congregations	44	26	70
Number of questionnaires sent out	213	118	331
Number of questionnaires returned	142	100	242
	(66.7%)	(84.7%)	(73.1%)
Number of usable questionnaires returned	137	98	235
	(64.3%)	(83%)	(71%)

Appendix H provides the aggregate data for the total survey. Appendix I isolates the Canadian data, Appendix J the U.S. data, Appendix K the data for female respondents, Appendix L the data for male respondents, and Appendices M to P provide additional data for Canadian and U.S. respondents, male and female. Unfortunately the many revealing and interesting comments are not appended but a few summary statements should be made.

When asked if they had voted during the 1940s and 1950s, some non-voters gave reasons for not having done so. One U.S. male wrote, "We were married in early 40s, so it was work 5 or 6 days, Church on Sunday. No Newspaper. No Politics." A Canadian female said, "I was young and uninformed." One Canadian female wrote: "Obedience to my husband. My husband was a liberal so I voted liberal." Almost all who said that they had not voted indicated that they subsequently had changed their mind. There were twenty-six comments by Canadians about supporting the Liberals because they let Mennonites enter Canada. One Canadian male observed, "It was under McKenzie King that the immigration of the 1920s took place. These immigrants were encouraged to vote 'liberal' out of gratitude. I consistently voted 'liberal'." Another elderly Canadian gentleman wrote: "Wasn't the 'mystery man' the Saviour of the Mennos?" Canadians also expressed gratitude for exemption from military service, for freedom, and the privilege of voting.

Comments from American respondents focused much more on supporting Republicans rather than Democrats, because the former party was more conservative, more in line with Christian beliefs, and better at keeping taxes down. The following comments from U.S. males are typical. "The other party always raised taxes." "Usually the Republican party is a bit more conservative than Democrats." One Oklahoma male wrote, apparently as a lament, "We hardly ever had Republican candidates."

Many respondents in both countries said that they had weighed the merits of candidates and policies rather than always voting for one party. Many also strongly affirmed the democratic system and expressed deep gratitude for being citizens of their respective countries.

Much could be said about Table 8 but a few items deserve special mention. First, in most respects the differences between Canadian and American Mennonite Brethren, or between men and

women, are not significant. Second, the number of Mennonite Brethren who say they voted in the 1940s and 1950s is very high. It is much higher than for the general electorate in either country but particularly in the U.S. where voter turnout is much lower than in Canada. Third, for Mennonite Brethren in these two decades, at least, voting was very much associated with good citizenship and gratitude to God. Fourth, the Canadian cohort had a much broader ideological spectrum than did the American. This reality for Canadians comes through strongly also in the political candidacy data. Fifth, the percentage of female respondents is lower than I had expected, especially given the longer female life expectancy. Perhaps some questionnaire distributors did not follow instructions very carefully, perhaps some females did not accept the questionnaires, and perhaps females were more reluctant than males to express themselves politically. I received some feedback to substantiate the last two possible explanations. Unfortunately the numbers for Question 6, which asked if respondents had changed their mind about voting since the 1950s, are somewhat misleading. Some respondents said that they had moved from being non-voters to voters. Most who said they had changed their mind, however, referred not to voting but to which party
they supported. Finally, the evidence strongly supports the conclusion that Canadian and American Mennonite Brethren took voting very seriously between 1940 and 1960. Perhaps political transition in this area came in the 1930s or even earlier.

Table 8

Summary of Voter Survey Data (in percentages; usable responses)
Note: Not all respondents answered all of the questions; a few checked more than one party.

Summarized Questions	All (N=235)	Can. (N=137)	US (N=98)	Male (N=163)	Female (N=72)	Can. Male (N=91)	Can. Female (N=46)	US Male (N=72)	US Female (N=26)
1. Voted in 1940s and 1950s Yes	94	93	95	95	92	96	89	94	96
No	5	5	4	3	8	2	11	4	4
2. Reasons for voting (1 or more)									
a) required by good citizenship	80	77	86	82	76	80	70	85	89
b) desire to support a party	46	56	33	47	44	57	52	33	31
c) expresses gratitude to God	71	68	75	71	71	68	67	74	77
d) expresses gratitude to government	37	39	35	37	35	43	33	33	39
e) all citizens should vote	75	70	82	76	72	70	70	83	77
3. Reasons for not voting (1 or more)									
a) not required for good citizenship	1	1	1	1	0	1	0	1	0
b) no party had appeal	1	1	1	1	0	1	0	1	0
c) expressed gratitude to God in non-political ways	2	2	2	2	2	1	2	2	0
d) expressed gratitude to government in other ways	1	0	2	1	0	0	0	2	0
e) took too much time, a bother	1	1	1	1	2	0	2	1	0
f) I did not know enough	3	4	2	1	7	0	11	2	0
4./5. Federal voting									
Democratic			8					10	4
Republican			84					83	85
CCF		2				3	0		
Liberal		59				63	52		
Progressive Conservative		44				44	44		
Social Credit		15				14	15		
Other		2	1			1	2	0	4

4./5. State/Provincial voting

Democratic			8					10	4
Republican			74					72	77
CCF		4				6	0		
Liberal		32				34	28		
Progressive Conservative		31				31	33		
Social Credit		36				36	35		
Other		2				1	4		

6. Have changed my mind about voting	Yes	14	17	9	12	17	14	22	10	8
	No	80	76	86	81	78	78	72	85	89

OBSERVATIONS

The Canadian Mennonite political candidacy data suggest that the 1940s and 1950s were indeed decades of political transition for Mennonite Brethren, at least in Canada. The voters survey results reinforce this conclusion, at least to the following extent. Following a period of limited Mennonite political activity in the U.S., and prohibition from voting in Canada by the Wartime Elections Act in 1917, the Mennonite Brethren of North America became avid voters by the 1940s. Commenting on the pre-WW II years James Juhnke writes that "The inter-war period was marked by continual Mennonite resistance to voting, failure of many Mennonites to seek public office, and a tendency to give special support to candidates who ran against the establishment."[19] The "resistance to voting" had vanished for Canadian and American Mennonite Brethren by the 1940s.

How can we account for the political changes and activism that we have noted, especially as documented for Canada? A variety of factors interacted to produce, or at least facilitate, the change. We must speak, therefore, of a confluence of events and factors.

The increasing shift, especially among the younger generation, from German to English made greater political involvement feasible. Simultaneously, by 1940 a more wide-ranging acculturation was underway, especially in the United States. Canadian acculturation began later but, once begun, the Canadian Mennonite integration into the polity was more rapid than the parallel experience in the U.S. because the Canadian Mennonites did not have to deny or seriously compromise their ethnoreligious heritage in order to become integrated into the polity. Even integration into society, as contrasted with polity, was easier and more rapid in Canada, which consciously reinforced multicultural reality. In such a context the ethnoreligious group and its individual members could join the mainstream simply by moving alongside the many other ethnic groups. Also, more Mennonite Brethren in Canada settled in enclaves than did American Mennonite Brethren. Importantly, that situation included major enclaves in Winnipeg and other major urban areas. These stronger enclaves helped propel first and second-generation Mennonite Brethren into politics and that fact, in turn, further stimulated voting.

We also must remember that Mennonites in the U.S. form a much smaller percentage of the total population than they do in Canada and, further, that among the American Mennonites the earliest and still dominant political norms have been set by the larger and more politically aloof Swiss-German Mennonites. In Canada the Dutch-Russian Mennonites, both General Conference and Mennonite Brethren, have set the dominant tone since the late 1920s. They had by then established a clear political identity apart from the Swiss-German Mennonites.

Further, in Canada much more than in the U.S., voting (especially for the Liberal Party) was seen as an expression of gratitude for being accepted as refugees. Deep-seated thankfulness will seek ways to express itself. Most Canadian Mennonites for at least a generation saw their migration to Canada as being made possible largely by a particular governmental decision. To a large extent they were right. That was not true in the U.S.

We also should note that Mennonite Brethren in Canada have identified more—and more positively—with government and less with the country itself. Many Canadian Mennonite Brethren, even as they moved into the political arena, could be aloof, even critical, of the country whose political system they were entering. In the U.S., conversely, the Mennonite Brethren, like Americans generally, came to identify more intensely with the country while remaining more aloof from the political parties and the more complicated "checks and balances" system of government.

In both countries the increased political involvement of the 1940s and 1950s was facilitated by rapid movement up the socio-economic ladder. The Great Depression, of course, both retarded progress and drastically altered individual and group priorities.

World War II and the accompanying prosperity, however, accelerated this socio-economic advancement very rapidly.

During and after both world wars, in both Canada and the U.S., Mennonite Brethren pacifism and the use of the German language produced animosity. After World War II this reality did not last long and the mainly financially successful, socially respected, and bilingual Mennonites in Canada were poised to undertake political activity. The American Mennonite Brethren followed a similar path but did so less dramatically. As the candidacy data document, this development took firm root in the 1950s, especially in Manitoba and Saskatchewan where the Mennonites were most numerous and had established substantial, almost homogeneous communities. It is surely noteworthy that in Saskatchewan constituencies Mennonites four times accounted for two out of three candidates; twice for three out of four; and three times, all in Rosthern, they fielded all of the candidates. Even more striking, in Manitoba the Mennonites three times accounted for two out of three candidates, twice for three out of four, once for three out of five, and four times (all in Rhineland) all of the candidates were Mennonites. Also in the 1988 federal election, three of six candidates in Provencher, Manitoba, were Mennonites.

Another significant factor in the Canadian political scene was the emergence of political parties with a substantial "Christian" emphasis. Mennonites were attracted, in significant numbers, to Social Credit and the Cooperative Commonwealth Federation—although these two had largely different orientations—and later to COR, Reform, and other "religious" parties. These parties, in turn, became agents of political acculturation. This phenomenon was largely absent in the U.S.

The Canadian political scene also produced more "public enterprise" politics, a much more extensive welfare state, and more joint private and government ventures than was the case in the U.S. These trends brought politics to Mennonites and Mennonites to politics. Most Canadian Mennonites, especially those of Dutch-Russian background, developed positive attitudes toward governments. One of the first descriptions of this attitude was published in 1976.[20] The fact that a more positive view of government had made major inroads in Canada and the U.S. is evident in the results of the 1972 Kauffman-Harder survey. For five Anabaptist groups, only 4 percent agreed with the statement, "The State (national, provincial and state government) is basically an evil force in the world, an opponent or enemy of the church and its program." Seventy-seven percent disagreed. For Mennonite Brethren the figures were 2 percent and 86 percent.[21]

The rapid and extensive politicization of Canadian Mennonites was also facilitated by the Canadian tradition, which still persists, of mixing Christianity and politics, at least superficially. Canadian Mennonites did not need to minimize their Christian assertiveness as they entered the political arena. The idea of a "wall of separation" is not part of the Canadian mileau. With the entrenchment of the Charter of Rights and Freedoms in 1982, a gradual and partial Americanization of the Canadian political system has, however, begun. Mark A. Noll has written that "the antistatism, individualism, populism, and egalitarianism that characterize American history have been decidedly less prominent in Canada. Where Canada has stressed the state and community values, the United States has featured the individual and laissez faire."[22] Given that some social, political, demographic and other factors are different in Canada than in the U.S., the fact that there was a different political development should come as no surprise. The Canadian confluence of factors and trends had no parallel in the U.S.

CONCLUSION

The political transition experienced by North American Mennonites, here documented especially for Canada, between 1940 and 1960 was widespread and lasting. It continues apace. Recently the Hon. Jake Epp was offered a Senate seat. He declined that offer. He was also invited to become the next Lieutenant-Governor of Manitoba.[23] He declined that as well. The initial, major shifts involved ordinary folk. The religious elites, the leaders, became followers. As the Mennonite Brethren periodicals reveal, the religious elites hardly even reported what the rank and file were doing or noted the socio-political dynamics involved. Thus the preachers kept on preaching nonresistance while many Canadian and American Mennonite Brethren strongly supported, and even became candidates for, parties that mainly proclaimed the opposite. Moreover, virtually nobody seems to have articulated how Christian nonresistance relates to partisan political involvement.

Most religious leaders, schooled in traditional ways, still viewed their religious followers as political subjects, who acquiesced, hopefully conditionally, rather than as citizens who participated. In any event, both religious leaders and followers did very little questioning, at least for the record. The citizenship stance and pronouncements of the elites remained mainly historical, theoretical and theological rather than practical and immediately relevant. Many emphasized nonresistance, albeit selective nonresistance, rather than selective participation and thus became spectators of the political evolution of their communities. For the most part events shaped ethics and practice preceded and informed policies.

The two decades in question certainly were decades of political transition, although in uneven ways. That conclusion holds true even if change in all areas is not equally demonstrable. Mennonite Brethren subjects had become citizens and the citizens were rapidly becoming politicized. The data suggest that this political transition is basic and permanent to the degree that the Canadian and American democracies remain stable and free.

The Mennonite Brethren community and institutional elites— religious, academic, and other—are now busily attempting to catch up with reality and to interpret it. Doubtless there will soon be more description, analysis, and guidance.

APPENDIX A

Mennonite Candidates for Election to the Canadian House of Commons Since Canadian Confederation, July 1, 1867

Parties

L   Liberal

Lab   Labour

C   Conservative [later became Progressive Conservative]

ND   New Democracy [Social Credit]

CCF   Cooperative Commonwealth Federation [A democratic socialist party. On July 31, 1961 the name changed to New Democratic Party]

PC   Progressive Conservative

NDP   New Democratic Party [A democratic socialist party]

Ind   Independent

CPC   Communist Party of Canada

M-L   Marxist-Leninist

SC   Social Credit

Comm   Communist

(N/A) Not available

Rhino Rhinoceros Party [A party of satire that spoofed the elites and advocates humorous, irrational policies; anarchic]

Lib   Libertarian [A very conservative party stressing limited government and individual freedom]

CRWP   Confederation of Regions Western Party

CHP   Christian Heritage Party

RP   Reform Party [A populist conservative-reform party led by Preston Manning, an evangelical Christian]

Provinces

AB	Alberta
BC	British Columbia
MB	Manitoba
ON	Ontario
SK	Saskatchewan

Election Dates (# of Mennonite Candidates)	Constituency	Candidate	Party	Votes	Rank
1st Aug. 7-Sept. 20, 1867 (2)	ON Grey N (Owen Sound)	George Snider	L	won by a margin of 256	1
	ON Waterloo N	Isaac Erb Bowman	L	was acclaimed	
2nd July 20-Sept. 3, 1872 (2)	ON Grey N (Owen Sound)	George Snider	L	won by a margin of 141	1
	ON Waterloo N	Isaac Erb Bowman	L	was acclaimed	
3rd Jan. 22, 1874 (2)	ON Grey N (Owen Sound)	George Snider	L	1,320	1
	ON Waterloo N	Isaac Erb Bowman	L	was acclaimed	
4th Sept. 17, 1878 (2)	ON Grey N	George Snider	L	1,394	2
	ON Waterloo N	Isaac Erb Bowman	L	1,279	2
5th June 20, 1882 (1)	ON Waterloo N	Isaac Erb Bowman	L	lost by a margin of 57	2
6th Feb. 22, 1887 (1)	ON Waterloo N	Isaac Erb Bowman	L	2,080	1
7th Mar. 5, 1891 (1)	ON Waterloo N	Isaac Erb Bowman	L	2,289	18th
June 23, 1896 (1)	ON Perth, S	Dilman Kinsey Erb	L	won by a margin of 218	1
9th Nov. 7, 1900 (1)	ON Perth, S	Dilman Kinsey Erb	L	2,171 (won by 10 votes)	1
		(Losing candidates are not listed.)			
10th Nov. 3, 1904		none			
11th Oct. 26, 1908 (some data is missing)		apparently none			
12th Sept. 21, 1911		none			

Election Dates (# of Mennonite Candidates)	Constituency	Candidate	Party	Votes	Rank
13th Dec. 17, 1917		none			
14th Dec. 6, 1921 (1)	MB Winnipeg N	Penner	Lab	565	4
15th Oct. 29, 1925		none			
16th Sept. 14, 1926		none			
17th July 28, 1930		none			
18th Oct. 14, 1935 (1)	SK Lake Centre	Peters	C	4,100	2
19th Mar. 26, 1940 (3)	SK Rosthern	Lepp	ND	2,381	3
	SK Swift Current	Thiessen	CCF	5,507	2
	ON Waterloo N	Honsberger	CCF	1,597	3
20th June 11, 1945 (1)	ON Lincoln (St. Catharines)	Allen E. Schroeder	CCF	4,540	3
21st June 27, 1949, (2)	ON Lincoln (St. Catharines)	Schroeder	CCF	5793	3
	MB Lisgar	Heppner	PC	5,684	2
22nd Aug. 10, 1953 (7)	BC New Westminster	Adrian	PC	3,083	4
	BC Burnaby-Richmond	**Erhart Regier**	CCF	**7,232**	1
	MB Provencher	Thiessen	PC	2,151	2
	ON Waterloo N	Janzen	PC	10,751	2
	SK Meadow Lake	Kelln	SC	1,817	3
	SK Rosetown-Biggar	Froese	SC	877	4
	SK Rosthern	Isaak Elias	SC	2,333	3
23rd June 10, 1957 (6)	**BC Burnaby-Coquitlam**	**Erhart Regier**	CCF	**10,947**	1
	BC Okanagan-Revelstoke	Dyck	CCF	1,455	4
	MB Springfield	**Jacob Schulz**	CCF	**5,949**	1
	ON Waterloo N	Honsberger	CCF	7,406	3
	SK Moose Jaw-Lake Centre	Kelln	SC	2,740	4
	SK The Battlefords	Klippenstein	SC	2,298	4
24th Mar. 31, 1958 (7)	**BC Burnaby-Coquitlam**	**Erhart Regier**	CCF	**12,917**	1
	BC Okanagan-Revelstoke	Dyck	CCF	1,859	4
	BC Vancouver-Kingsway	Froese	SC	1,642	4

Election Dates (# of Mennonite Candidates)	Constituency	Candidate	Party	Votes	Rank
	MB Provencher	Siemens	CCF	281	4
	MB Springfield	Jacob Schulz	CCF	4,962	2
	ON Waterloo N	Honsberger	CCF	5,148	3
	SK Prince Albert	Unruh	L	2,538	3
	(The Cons. candidate in Prince Albert was Prime Minister John Diefenbaker.)				
Dec. 15, 1958 by-election	MB Springfield	Jacob Schulz	CCF	3,400	3
25th June 18, 1962 (12)	BC Burnaby-Coquitlam	**Erhart Regier**	**NDP**	**19,050**	**1**
	MB Portage-Neepawa	**Siegfried John Enns**	**PC**	**11,125**	**1**
	MB Provencher	Loewen	SC	2,504	3
The first known	MB Springfield	Rempel	SC	1,669	4
competition between	MB Springfield	Jacob Schulz	NDP	4,960	3
Mennonites federally	MB Winnipeg N	DeFehr	SC	1,733	4
	ON Hamilton S	Lepp	SC	657	4
	ON Lincoln	Heppner	SC	5,262	3
	ON Waterloo S	Fast	SC	566	4
	ON Waterloo N	Honsberger	NDP	7,722	3
	SK Yorkton	Kelln	SC	5,453	4
	SK Saskatoon	Harder	SC	1,556	4
26th April 8, 1963 (8)	BC Fraser Valley	Erhart Regier	NDP	9,735	2
	MB Lisgar	Loeppky	SC	4,099	3
	MB Portage-Neepawa	**Siegfried Enns**	**PC**	**12,532**	**1**
	MB Winnipeg N Centre	Willms	SC	1,026	4
	ON Hamilton S	Lepp	SC	459	4
	ON Renfrew N	Brubacher	SC	1,712	3
	SK Humboldt-Melfort	Dueck	SC	983	4

Election Dates (# of Mennonite Candidates)	Constituency	Candidate	Party	Votes	Rank
27th Nov. 8, 1965 (10)	SK Rosthern	Froese	SC	1,213	4
	AB Acadia	Wiebe	SC	5,384	2
	AB Lisgar	Loeppky	SC	2,711	3
	MB Lisgar	Elias	Ind	237	5
	MB Portage-Neepawa	**Siegfried Enns**	**PC**	**13,043**	**1**
	MB Provencher	Barkman	L	5,243	2
	MB Winnipeg N	Willms	SC	776	4
	MB Selkirk	Epp	SC	678	4
	ON Algoma West	Erhart Regier	NDP	9,564	3
	SK Humboldt-Melfort-Tisdale	Dueck	SC	561	4
28th June 25, 1968 (6)	SK Rosthern	Dyck	SC	704	4
	BC Prince George-Peace River	Erhart Regier	NDP	6,894	3
	MB Dauphin	Dean Whiteway	SC	1,194	4
	MB Lisgar	George G. Elias	Ind	614	5
	MB Portage	Siegfried Enns	PC	8,025	2
	ON Thunder Bay	**B. Keith Penner**	**L**	**9,540**	**1**
29th Oct. 30, 1972 (11)	ON Waterloo	Herbert A. Epp	L	14,835	2
	AB Vegreville	Abram Goerzen	SC	642	4
	AB Palliser	Edwin Enns	SC	2,546	4
	BC Coast Chilcotin	John Pankratz	PC	7,601	3
	BC Prince George-Peace River	Al Kruger	SC	2,854	4
	BC Surrey-White Rock	Ben Schroeder	SC	998	4
	MB Lisgar	John Harms	SC	943	4
	MB Provencher	**Jake Epp**	**PC**	**11,262**	**1**
	MB Provencher	Jake Wall	SC	784	4
	MB Selkirk	Dean Whiteway (lost by 20 votes)	PC	17,852	2
	ON Middlesex	Ray Funk	NDP	6,643	3

Election Dates (# of Mennonite Candidates)	Constituency	Candidate	Party	Votes	Rank
30th July 8, 1974 (16)	ON Thunder Bay	B. Keith Penner	L	10,954	1
	AB Medicine Hat	Edwin Enns	SC	1,538	4
	BC Okanagan Boundary	John Dyck	L	19,390	2
	BC Surrey-White Rock	Benno Friesen	PC	21,540	1
	BC Surrey-White Rock	Leonard Friesen	NDP	13,025	3
	MB Lisgar	Frank Froese	NDP	1,278	3
	MB Lisgar	Jacob M. Froese	SC	1,164	4
	MB Provencher	Jake Epp	PC	13,405	1
	MB Provencher	Jake Wall	SC	613	4
	MB Selkirk	Dean Whiteway	PC	22,441	1
	MB Winnipeg S	Harold James Dyck	CPC	79	7
	ON Lincoln	Bill Andres	L	17,499	1
	ON London East	Ray Funk	NDP	8,949	3
	ON Thunder Bay	B. Keith Penner	L	11,435	1
	ON Timmins	John Cornelson	SC	472	4
	SK Saskatoon-Humboldt	Julius Friesen	NDP	11,826	2
	SK Swift Current-Maple Creek	Isaac Klaassen	SC	390	4
31st May 22, 1979 (11)	BC Surrey-White Rock-NDelta	Benno Friesen	PC	29,728	1
	BC Victoria	Dorothy Ratzlaff	M-L	89	4
	MB Provencher	Jake Epp	PC	17,391	1
	MB Provencher	Howard Loewen	L	7,698	3
	MB Winnipeg-Birds Hill	Dean Whiteway	PC	19,536	2
	MB Winnipeg-Birds Hill	Harold J. Dyck	Comm	64	4
	ON Cochrane	B. Keith Penner	L	12,910	1
	ON Kitchener	John Reimer	PC	23,230	1
	ON Niagara Falls	Jake Froese	PC	16,919	1
	ON St. Catharines	William Andres	L	15,138	2

Election Dates (# of Mennonite Candidates)	Constituency	Candidate	Party	Votes	Rank
32nd Feb. 18, 1980 (14)	ON Waterloo	Frank Epp	L	17,902	2
	BC Fraser Valley East	Jack Suderman	L	9,490	3
	BC Fraser Valley East	John Pankratz	Ind	2,057	4
	BC Surrey-White Rock-N Delta	Benno Friesen	PC	28,151	1
	MB Lisgar	Herman Rempel	NDP	3,353	3
	MB Lisgar	Geo. G. Elias	(N/A)	396	4
	MB Provencher	Jake Epp	PC	14,677	1
	MB Winnipeg-Birds Hill	John Froese	PC	13,385	2
	MB Winnipeg-Birds Hill	Honest Don Bergen	Rhino	322	4
	ON Cochrane	Keith Penner	L	15,280	1
	ON Kitchener	John Reimer	PC	17,990	2
	ON Niagara Falls	Jake Froese	PC	14,250	2
	ON St. Catharines	David Wiebe	L	17,173	3
	ON Toronto-Spadina	Don Redekop	Lib	227	5
	ON Waterloo	Frank Epp	L	20455	2
	(Epp lost to Rev. Walter McLean, PC, by 144 votes.)				
33rd Sept. 4, 1984 (17)	AB Medicine Hat	Wally Regehr	NDP	4,652	2
	AB Peace River	Ted Krause	CRWP	2,877	4
	BC Cariboo-Chilcotin	George H. Janzen	SC	335	5
	BC Surrey-White Rock-N Delta	Benno Friesen	PC	39,544	1
	MB Lisgar	Peter Hiebert	NDP	2,052	4
	MB Portage-Marquette	Abe Suderman	L	4,161	4
	MB Provencher	Jake Epp	PC	20,077	1
	MB Provencher	Wally Rempel	L	4,859	3
	MB Winnipeg-Birds Hill	Honest Don Bergen	Rhino	569	4
	ON Cochrane-Superior	Keith Penner	L	12,359	1
	ON Essex-Kent	Hugo Tiessen	L	9,268	2

Election Dates (# of Mennonite Candidates)	Constituency	Candidate	Party	Votes	Rank
	ON Kitchener	**John Reimer**	PC	26,710	1
	ON Niagara Falls	Earle G. Erb	SC	178	5
	ON **Thunder Bay-Nipigon**	**Ernie Epp**	NDP	13,901	1
	ON Toronto-Parkdale-High Park	John Friesen	NDP	8,232	3
	SK MacKenzie	Harold E. Schultz	CRWP	1,269	4
	SK Swift Current	Jack Wiebe	L	5,967	3
34th Nov. 21, 1988 (16)	AB Edmonton East	Bernie Sawatzky	(N/A)	88	7
	AB Peace River	Norman Dyck	NDP	7,839	2
	AB Wetaskiwin	David J. Reimer	CHP		
	BC Nanaimo-Cowichan	Ted Schellenberg	PC	5,296	3
	BC Okanagan-Centre	Werner Schmidt	RP	7,599	4
	BC **Surrey**	**Benno Friesen**	PC	26,319	1
	MB Brandon-Souris	Abe Neufeld	CHP	1,324	5
	MB Dauphin-Swan River	Peter J. Neufeld	RP	1,209	4
	MB Lisgar-Marquette	Geo. G. Elias	CRWP	495	6
	MB **Provencher**	**Jake Epp**	PC	19,000	1
3 of 6 candidates were Mennonite	MB Provencher	Wes Penner	L	11,121	2
	MB Provencher	John Wiebe	CRWP	357	5
	ON **Kitchener**	**John Reimer**	PC	22,400	1
	ON Thunder Bay-Nipigon	Ernie Epp	NDP	13,019	2
	SK MacKenzie	John Froese	RP	689	4
	SK Prince Albert-Churchill River	**Ray Funk**	NDP	17,915	1

APPENDIX B

Mennonite Candidates for the Alberta Legislature Since Alberta Joined Canada, September 1, 1905

Parties (For additional comment see Appendix A.)

C	Conservative (later became Progressive Conservative)
L	Liberal
NDP	New Democratic Party
SC	Social Credit
WCC	Western Canada Concept [a regional, conservative, quasi-separatist party]
Ind	Independent
RPA	Representative Party of Alberta [a splinter regional reform party]
PC	Progressive Conservative

	Election Dates	Constituency	Candidate	Party	Votes	Rank
1st	Nov. 9, 1905	**Rose Bud**	**Cornelius Hiebert**	C	**586**	1
2nd	Mar. 22, 1909	Didsbury	Cornelius Hiebert	C	156	3
(Apparently there were no Mennonite candidates in the next ten elections.)						
13th	June 29, 1955	Pembina	George Schultz	L	1708	2
14th	June 18, 1959	Ponoka	Erwin E. Schultz	L	860	3
15th	June 15, 1963	Calgary-W	Jack D. Peters	NDP	568	4
		Drumheller-Gleichen	Irene Dyck	NDP	720	2
16th	May 23, 1967	Edson	C. Neil Reimer	NDP	1656	3
		Peace River	**Robert Wiebe**	SC	**2850**	1
		Three Hills	**Ray Ratzlaff**	SC	**2762**	1
17th	Aug. 30, 1971	Edmonton-Belmont	Werner G. Schmidt	SC	4052	2

(Schmidt served as leader of the provincial Social Credit party.)

Election Dates	Constituency	Candidate	Party	Votes	Rank
	Edmonton Ottewell	Ronald Penner	SC	4188	2
	Three Hills	Ray Ratzlaff	SC	2970	2
		(Ratzlaff lost by 8 votes.)			
18th Mar. 26, 1975	Three Hills	K. Robert Friesen	NDP	220	3
	Calgary Currie	Edwin Enns	SC	939	2
	Grande Prairie	John Baergen	SC	1475	3
	Taber-Warner	Werner Schmidt	SC	2418	2
	Wetaskiwin-Leduc	Waldo Siemens	SC	2076	2
19th Mar. 14, 1979	**Edmonton-Gold Bar**	**Al P. Hiebert**	**PC**	**6044**	**1**
	Three Hills	Henry Goerzen	SC	2660	2
20th Nov. 2, 1982	Bonnyville	Eric E. Enns	WCC	715	3
	Edmonton-Gold Bar	**Al P. Hiebert**	**PC**	**7,195**	**1**
	Grande Prairie	Jake Paetkau	Ind	522	4
	Stony Plain	Dick Martens	Ind	80	7
21st May 8, 1986	Calgary-McKnight	Carol Reimer	L	1307	3
	Edmonton-Gold Bar	Al P. Hiebert	PC	4150	2
	Red Deer-N	Elvin Janzen	RPA	153	4
22nd Mar. 20, 1989	Medicine Hat	Wally Regehr	NDP	4088	3
	Ponoka-Rimbey	Ervan Stobbe	L	808	3

APPENDIX C

Mennonite Candidates for the British Columbia Legislature Since British Columbia Joined Canada, July 30, 1871

Parties (For additional comment see Appendix A and B.)

SC — Social Credit
L — Liberal
CCF — Cooperative Commonwealth Federation
SCon — Social Conservative
PC — Progressive Conservative
NRP — New Republic Party [a small reformist party]
WCC — Western Canada Concept [a regional, conservative, quasi-separatist party]
C — Conservative (also known as Progressive Conservative)

(Apparently there were no Mennonite candidates in the first 20 elections.)

Election Dates		Constituency	Candidate	Party	Votes	Rank
21st	June 15, 1949	N Okanagan	Lorne Shantz	SC	509	3
22nd	June 12, 1952	N Okanagan	Lorne Shantz	SC	5,447	
24th	Sept. 19, 1956	Chilliwack	Goossen	L	3118	2
		N Okanagan	Lorne Shantz	SC	4583	1
		S Okanagan	Ratzlaff	CCF	1663	2
		Vancouver Centre (a 2-seat district)	Giesbrecht	CCF	4393	4
25th	Sept. 12, 1960	N Okanagan	Lorne Shantz	SC	4553	1
		S Okanagan	Ratzlaff	CCF	2902	2

Election Dates	Constituency	Candidate	Party	Votes	Rank
26th Sept. 30, 1963	Victoria (a 2-seat district) (apparently none)	Reimer	NDP	3275	9
27th Sept. 12, 1966	Shuswap	Hildebrand	SCon	131	4
28th Aug. 27, 1969	**Chilliwack**	**Harvey Schroeder**	SC	**8712**	1
29th Aug. 30, 1972	Albernie	Allan Schroeder	PC	950	3
30th Dec. 11, 1975	**Burnaby-Edmonds**	Ray Loewen	SC	**8125**	1
	Chilliwck	**Harvey Schroeder**	SC	**13052**	1
	Mackenzie	Eric Paetkau	SC	6671	2
	Saanich and the Islands	Irene Block	PC	2842	3
	Okanagan S (a 2-seat district)	Frederick Bartell	NRP	141	7
31st May 10, 1979	**Chilliwack**	**Harvey Schroeder**	SC	**11236**	1
32nd May 5, 1983	Central Fraser Valley	Jacob Suderman	L	399	4
	Chilliwack	**Harvey Schroeder**	SC	**12255**	1
	Chilliwack	Scott Fast	NDP	7955	2
	Langley	Jake Martens	WCC	519	4
	Okanagan S	Frederick Bartell	Ind	165	5
	Rossland-Trail	Walter Siemens	SC	6581	2
33rd Oct. 22, 1986	Boundary-Similkameen	Wesley Nickel	NDP	6886	4
	Cariboo (a 2-seat district)	Peter Epp	PC	316	8
	Central Fraser Valley	**Peter Dueck**	SC	**16672**	1
	Chilliwack	Scott Fast	NDP	5804	2
	Langley (a 2-seat district)	**Carol Gran**	SC	**17252**	1
	Nelson-Creston	**Howard Dirks**	SC	**8189**	1

Election Dates	Constituency	Candidate	Party	Votes	Rank
	Okanagan S	Frederick Bartell	NRP	141	7
	(a 2-seat district)				
34th Oct. 17, 1991	**Matsqui**	**Peter Dueck**	SC	**8064**	1
	Langley	Carol Gran	SC	5054	3
	(a 2-seat district)				
	Nelson-Creston	Barry L. Neufeld	L	3047	3
	Nelson-Creston	Howard Dirks	SC	5035	2
	Peace River N	**Richard Neufeld**	SC	**5561**	1
	Peace River S	Marcheta Loeppky	L	3408	3
	Rossland Trail	Walter Siemens	SC	3190	3
	Skeena	**Helmut Giesbrecht**	NDP	**5472**	1
	Victoria Hillside	Elmer Wiens	L	7047	2

APPENDIX D

Mennonite Candidates for the Manitoba Legislature Since Manitoba Joined Canada, July 15, 1870

Parties (For additional comment see Appendix A and B.)

C	Conservative (also known as Progressive Conservative)
L	Liberal
L-P	Liberal Progressive [a regional version of Liberal]
Ind	Independent
CCF	Cooperative Commonwealth Federation
SC	Social Credit
NDP	New Democratic Party
ManPrg	Manitoba Progressive
PC	Progressive Conservative
COR	Confederation of Regions Party [a conservative, limited government party]
Comm	Communist
LPM	Libertarian Party of Manitoba
WIP	Western Independence Party

Election Dates	Constituency	Candidate	Party	Votes	Rank
(Apparently there were no Mennonite candidates in the first 10 elections.)					
11th Mar. 7, 1907	Rhineland	Cor. Bergman	C	321	2
(Apparently there were no Mennonite candidates in the next six elections.)					
18th June 16, 1932	Mountain	Ivan Schultz	L	3076	1
		(Schultz was first elected, by acclamation, in a by-election in "Mountain," Jan. 29, 1930.)			
	Morden and Rhineland	C.W. Wiebe, M.D.	L-P	2837	1

	Election Dates	Constituency	Candidate	Party	Votes	Rank
19th	July 27, 1936	(incomplete records)				
20th	April 22, 1941	Morden-Rhineland	L. Kruger	Ind	109	4
21st	Oct. 15, 1945	(incomplete records)				
22nd	Nov. 10, 1949	Gilbert Plains	Jacob Schulz	C	1268	2
23rd	June 8, 1953	Carillon	K.T. Kroeker	SC	1065	2
		Dufferin	G. Loeppky	SC	1329	2
		Emerson	J.J. Friesen	SC	220	3
		Ethelbert	H. Dyck	SC	225	4
		Iberville	C.F. Rempel	SC	374	4
		Portage La Prairie	B.H. Rempel	SC	784	3
24th	June 16, 1958	**Elmwood**	**Steve Peters**	CCF	**2375**	1
		Rhineland	A. Enns	SC	758	3
25th	May 14, 1959	Carillon	Peter J. Thiessen	PC	1791	2
		Elmwood	**Steve Peters**	CCF	**2782**	1
		Kildonan	C.K. Huebert	L-P	1972	3
		In a by-election held in Rhineland on Nov. 26, 1959 the results were:				
			Jacob M. Froese	SC	**1300**	1
			David K. Friesen	L-P	1075	2
26th	Dec. 14, 1962	Carillon	Peter J. Thiessen	PC	1278	2
		Carillon	**Leonard Barkman**	L	**2116**	1
		Elmwood	**Steve Peters**	NDP	2024	1
		Kildonan	**John DeFehr**	SC	N/A	1
	All 3 of the candidates were Mennonites	**Rhineland**	**Jacob M. Froese**	SC	**1511**	1
		Rhineland	A.J. Thiessen	PC	1478	2
		Rhineland	J.H. Penner	L	791	3
27th	July 7, 1966	**Carillon**	**Leonard Barkman**	L	**2352**	1
		Kildonan	Henry W. Redekopp	SC	1331	4
		Osborne	Howard J. Loewen	L	2141	3

Election Dates	Constituency	Candidate	Party	Vote	Rank
	Pembina	Frederick Hamm	SC	878	3
	Rhineland	**Jacob M. Froese**	SC	**1676**	1
	Rhineland	Alf Loewen	L	696	3
	Rock Lake	Jacob Harms	SC	505	3
	Rockwood-Iberville	**Harry J. Enns**	PC	**2091**	1
	Souris-Lansdowne	Irene Bauman	NDP	238	4
	Turtle Mountain	Peter H. Sawatsky	SC	690	3
28th June 25, 1969	Emerson	Jacob Wall	SC	237	4
	Lakeside	**Harry J. Enns**	PC	**2532**	1
	La Verendrye	**Leonard Barkman**	L	**1933**	1
	La Verendrye	Elmer Reimer	NDP	721	3
	Morris	Henry W. Funk	SC	231	4
	Osborne	Win Loewen	L	965	3
	Pembina	David Harms	SC	521	3
3 of the 4 candidates were Mennonites	**Rhineland**	**Jacob M. Froese**	SC	**1981**	1
	Rhineland	Henry D. Hildebrand	PC	1853	2
	Rhineland	Jacob W. Heinrichs	NDP	181	4
	St. Matthews	Rudy Peters	L	1119	3
	(Of 185 candidates, 11 were Mennonites.)				
29th June 28, 1973	Fort Garry	Henry Janzen	L	4331	2
	Fort Rouge	Samia Friesen	NDP	3614	2
	Lakeside	**Harry J. Enns**	PC	**2969**	1
2 of the 3 candidates were Mennonites	**La Verendrye**	**Robert Banman**	PC	**2912**	1
	La Verendrye	Leonard Barkman	L	2387	2
	Pembina	Paul Klassen	NDP	1013	3
All 5 of the candidates were Mennonites	**Rhineland**	**Arnold Brown**	PC	**2903**	1
	Rhineland	Jacob M. Froese	SC	1587	2
	Rhineland	Jacob Heinrichs	NDP	1002	3

Election Dates	Constituency	Candidate	Party	Votes	Rank
	Rhineland	Henry Friesen	L	578	4
	Rhineland	John Epp	Ind	52	5
	Rossmere	Alfred Penner	PC	6239	2
	(Penner ran against Premier Ed Schreyer, NDP, who received 6827 votes.)				
	Seven Oakes	Carl Zawatsky	PC	4921	2
	Seven Oaks	Henry Froese	L	1386	3
	(Of 187 candidates, 14 were Mennonites.				
	They ran in 8 of the 57 electoral districts.)				
30th Oct. 11, 1977	Emerson	**Albert Driedger**	**PC**	**3125**	**1**
	Lakeside	**Harry J. Enns**	**PC**	**3987**	**1**
	La Verendrye	**Robert Banman**	**PC**	**4914**	**1**
	La Verendrye	Robert Rempel	L	924	3
	Minnedosa	John Martens	NDP	2311	2
	Pembina	Vic Epp	L	1141	2
All 4 of the candidates	**Rhineland**	**Arnold Brown**	**PC**	**3610**	**1**
were Mennonite	Rhineland	Jacob M. Froese	SC	813	4
	Rhineland	Ray Hamm	L	943	3
	Rhineland	Jacob Heinrichs	NDP	1001	2
	Rossmere	Henry P. Krahn	PC	8516	2
	Seven Oaks	Carol Zawatsky	PC	6777	2
31st Nov. 17, 1981	Emerson	**Albert Driedger**	**PC**	**4376**	**1**
	Emerson	Jack Thiessen	ManPrg	116	4
	Gladstone	Abe Suderman	L	737	3
	Inkster	Bill Dueck	PC	1561	2
	Interlake	C.N. (Neil) Dueck	PC	2181	2
	Lakeside	**Harry J. Enns**	**PC**	**5055**	**1**
	Lakeside	John Hubert	ManPrg	107	4
	La Verendrye	**Robert Banman**	**PC**	**4418**	**1**

Election Dates	Constituency	Candidate	Party	Votes	Rank
	Rhineland	**Arnold Brown**	**PC**	**4116**	**1**
	Rhineland	Jacob M. Froese	ManPrg	349	3
	Rossmere	**Vic Schroeder**	**NDP**	**5776**	**1**
	Rossmere	Merv Unger	ManPrg	142	4
	St. Johns	Henry Koslowski	L	674	3
	Sturgeon Creek	John Epp	L	732	3
	(Of 195 candidates, 14 were Mennonites. They won in 5 of 57 districts.)				
32nd Mar. 18, 1986	Arthur	Peter J. Neufeld	COR	1198	2
	Emerson	**Albert Driedger**	**PC**	**4758**	**1**
	Kirkfield Park	Irene Friesen	L	1932	3
	Lakeside	**Harry J. Enns**	**PC**	**4303**	**1**
2 of 3 candidates	**La Verendrye**	**Helmut Pankratz**	**PC**	**3618**	**1**
were Mennonites	La Verendrye	Walter Hiebert	L	734	3
3 of 5 candidates	Pembina	Abe Giesbrecht	COR	944	2
were Mennonites	Pembina	Eduard Hiebert	NDP	913	3
	Pembina	Lynn Rempel	L	849	4
	Radisson	**Arnold Brown**	**PC**	**3037**	**1**
	Rossmere	**Vic Schroeder**	**NDP**	**4613**	**1**
	Rossmere	Harold Neufeld	PC	4086	2
	Seven Oaks	Harold Dyck	Comm	65	4
	(Of 216 candidates, 14 were Mennonites. They won in 5 of 57 districts.)				
33rd April 26, 1988	Elmwood	Russ Letkeman	LPM	113	4
3 of 4 candidates	**Emerson**	**Albert Driedger**	**PC**	**5027**	**1**
were Mennonites	Emerson	Kurt Penner	NDP	1407	3
	Emerson	Jake Wall	COR	366	4
	Gladstone	Brian Hildebrandt	COR	759	3
	Kirkfield Park	Irene Friesen	L	5014	2
	Lakeside	**Harry J. Enns**	**PC**	**4475**	**1**

Election Dates	Constituency	Candidate	Party	Votes	Rank
	Lakeside	Eduard Hiebert	NDP	972	3
2 of 3 candidates	**La Verendrye**	**Helmut Pankratz**	**PC**	**4377**	1
were Mennonites	La Verendrye	C.E. Goertzen	L	2948	2
	Niakwa	**Herold Driedger**	**L**	**8576**	1
	Pembina	Abe Giesbrecht	COR	499	3
	Portage La Prairie	Darlene Hamm	L	2812	2
All 3 candidates	**Rhineland**	**Jack Penner**	**PC**	**5166**	1
were Mennonites	Rhineland	Walter Hiebert	L	1059	2
	Rhineland	Reg Loeppky	NDP	341	3
	Riel	John Hiebert	COR	121	4
	River E	Michael Dyck	NDP	3019	3
	River E	Neil Friesen	WIP	233	4
	Rossmere	**Harold Neufeld**	**PC**	**3950**	1
	Rossmere	Vic Schroeder	NDP	3424	2
	St. Vital	Trevor Wiebe	LPM	46	5
	Sturgeon Creek	Len Sawatzky	NDP	903	3

(Of 230 candidates, 23 were Mennonite.
They ran in 15 of 57 districts and won 6 seats.)

34th Sept. 11, 1990	Elmwood	Vic Toews	PC	3035	2
	Emerson	**Jack Penner**	**PC**	**4529**	1
	Lakeside	**Harry J. Enns**	**PC**	**3719**	1
	Lakeside	Eduard Hiebert	NDP	1248	3
	Niakwa	**Jack Reimer**	**PC**	**4950**	1
	Pembina	Bert Siemens	NDP	652	3
	Portage La Prairie	Darlene Hamm	L	2329	2
	Rossmere	**Harold Neufeld**	**PC**	**3893**	1
	Seine River	Herold Driedger	L	4418	2
	St. James	Len Sawatsky	NDP	2586	3

Election Dates	Constituency	Candidate	Party	Votes	Rank
		Candidate	Party	Votes	Rank
	St. Norbert	Andrew Sawatsky	NDP	1011	3
	Steinbach	**Albert Driedger**	**PC**	**5540**	**1**
	Steinbach	Cornelius Goertzen	L	1171	2
	Wolesley	**Jean Friesen**	**NDP**	**3265**	**1**

(Of 199 candidates, 14 were Mennonites.
They ran in 12 of 57 districts and won 6 seats.)

APPENDIX E

Mennonite Candidates for the Ontario Legislature Since Ontario Became Part of Canada, July 1, 1867

Parties (For additional comment see Appendix A.)

L	Liberal
C	Conservative (also known as Progressive Conservative)
Ind	Independent
CCF	Cooperative Commonwealth Federation
SC	Social Credit
FC	Family Coalition [a family-oriented conservative party]
PC	Progressive Conservative

Election Dates	Constituency	Candidate	Party	Votes	Rank
1854	N Waterloo	Isaac Erb Bowman	L		1
		(He represented this constituency for 13 years in the Upper Canada and, after Canadian Confederation, he served as a member of House of Commons for 24 years.)			
Assembly the federal 1863	Grey N	George Snider	L		2
		(He failed to win a seat in the Upper Canada Assembly but served 15 years as a member of the federal House of Commons.)			

(Apparently there were no Mennonite candidates in the first four elections after Confederation.)

Election Dates	Constituency	Candidate	Party	Votes	Rank
5th Feb. 27, 1883	Waterloo N	Elias Weber			
		Bingeman Snider	L	1569	1
		(He was first elected in a by-election on June 27, 1881.)			
6th Dec. 28, 1886	Waterloo N	E.W.B. Snider	L	by acclamation	1
7th June 11, 1890	Waterloo N	E.W.B. Snider	L	2205	1

	Election Dates	Constituency	Candidate	Party	Votes	Rank
8th	1894	(apparently none)				
9th	March 1, 1898	Bruce N	Charles M. Bowman	L	2464	1
10th	May 29, 1902	Bruce N	Charles M. Bowman	L	2477	1
		Norfolk N	Dr. Snider	C	1704	1
			(In a January 7, 1903 by-election, called for an unknown reason, Snider lost.)		1764	2
11th	Jan. 25, 1905	Bruce N	Charles Bowman	L	2162	1
		Huron E	Bowman	C	2070	2
		Norfolk N	Dr. Snider	C	1588	2
12th	May 11, 1908	Bruce N	Charles Bowman	L	2282	1
13th	Dec. 11, 1911	Bruce N	Charles Bowman	L	2182	1
14th	June 29, 1914	Bruce W	Charles Martin Bowman	L	2153	1
		Perth S	D.K. Erb	L	2165	2
		Waterloo N	Helkiah Martin	N/A	595	3
		Waterloo S	Helkiah Martin	N/A	762	3
			(Candidates could run in more than one district.)			
15th	Oct. 20, 1919	Waterloo N	Walter Snider	N/A	2974	3
16th	June 25, 1923	Waterloo N	E.O. Weber	Ind	1853	3
17th	Dec. 1, 1926	none				
18th	Oct. 30, 1929	none				
19th	June 19, 1934	none				
20th	Oct. 6, 1937	Lincoln	Schroeder	CCF	1975	3
21st	Aug. 4, 1943	Lincoln	Schroeder	CCF	7438	2
22nd	June 7, 1948	none				
23rd	Nov. 22, 1951	none				
24th	June 9, 1955	Ottawa S	Schroeder	CCF	826	3
		Wellington S	Bowman	CCF	2634	3
25th	June 11, 1959	none				

Election Dates		Constituency	Candidate	Party	Votes	Rank
26th	Sept. 25, 1963	Cochrane N	Raymond Braun	L	3887	2
		Lincoln	Frank Dyck	NDP	4235	3
		Lincoln	Ed Goertzen	SC	753	4
27th	Oct. 17, 1967	none				
28th	Oct. 21, 1971	Waterloo N	John Dietrich Koop	Ind	359	4
29th	Sept. 18, 1975	Brant-Oxford-Norfolk	Don Harder	PC	6424	2
		Eglinton	Donald Redekop	Ind	256	5
30th	June 9, 1977	**Waterloo N**	**Herb Epp**	L	**13556**	1
31st	March 19, 1981	Ottawa S	Robert Dyck	L	8832	2
		Waterloo N	**Herb Epp**	L	**12843**	1
		Brock	Bill Andres	L	9081	2
32nd	May 2, 1985	**Waterloo N**	**Herb Epp**	L	**16458**	1
33rd	Sept. 10, 1987	**Waterloo N**	**Herb Epp**	L	**16792**	1
34th	Sept. 6, 1990	Brantford	Dave Neumann	L	13644	2
		Kitchener-Wilmot	Carl Zehr	L	10787	2
		Niagara Falls	Art Klassen	FC	702	5
		St. Catharines-Brock	Ed Klassen	FC	873	5

APPENDIX F

Mennonite Candidates for the Saskatchewan Legislature Since Saskatchewan Joined Canada, September 1, 1905

Parties (For additional comment see Appendix A.)

L	Liberal
C	Conservative (also known as Progressive Conservative)
SC	Social Credit
CCF	Cooperative Commonwealth Federation
NDP	New Democratic Party
WCC	Western Canada Concept Party
PC	Progressive Conservative

	Election Dates	Candidate	Constituency	Party	Votes	Rank
1st	Dec. 4, 1905	**Gerhard Ens**	**Rosthern**	L	628	1
2nd	Aug. 14, 1908	**Gerhard Ens**	**Rosthern**	L	474	1
3rd	July 11, 1912	H.M. Klassen	Morse	C	548	2
		Gerhard Ens	**Rosthern**	L	718	1
4th	June 26, 1917		none			
5th	June 9, 1921		none			
6th	June 2, 1925	S. Adrian	Arm River	C	1491	2
7th	June 6, 1929		none			
8th	June 19, 1934		none			
9th	June 8, 1938	W.H. Schroeder	Last Mountain	SC	902	4
		Henry P. Tiesen	Morse	CCF	1808	2
		Rev. P. Peters	Rosthern	SC	228	3

Election Dates	Constituency	Candidate	Party	Vote	Rank
	Saskatoon (a 2-seat district) 10th	J.I. Klassen	SC	4339	6
June 15, 1944	**Rosthern**	**P.J. Hooge**	**L**	**2199**	1
11th June 24, 1948	Last Mountain	G. Kelln	SC	1219	3
	Watrous	Martin Kelln	SC	1092	3
12th June 11, 1952	Last Mountain	Martin Kelln	SC	915	4
	Rosthern	J. Thiessen	CCF	2333	2
	Rosthern	P.P. Lepp	SC	908	3
	Shellbrook	E. Unruh	L	3246	2
13th June 20, 1956	Last Mountain	Martin Kelln	SC	2223	3
	Notukeu-Willowbunch	E. Lautermilch	CCF	2580	2
	Rosthern	**Isaak Elias**	**SC**	**3096**	1
	Shellbrook	**John Thiessen**	**CCF**	**2596**	1
	Swift Current	R.C. Dahl	L	3276	2
	The Battlefords	A. Dyck	L	2664	2
	The Battlefords	Peter J. Klippenstein	SC	934	3
	Wadena	E.A. Schmor	SC	1900	3
	Weyburn	G.T. Froese	SC	1170	3
14th June 8, 1960	Biggar	H. Neufeld	SC	258	4
	Hanley	I. Thiessen	L	2217	2
	Kelsey	E. Boschman	SC	1477	3
	Kelvington	P. Pankratz	SC	1135	3
	Last Mountain	Martin Kelln	SC	2035	2
	Morse	Peter Harder	SC	606	3
	Pelly	G.C. Peters	PC	290	4
3 of the 4 candidates were Mennonites	**Rosthern**	**David Boldt**	**L**	**2280**	1
	Rosthern	Isaak Elias	SC	2033	2
	Rosthern	T. Ratzlaff	CCF	1533	3

Election Dates	Constituency	Candidate	Party	Votes	Rank
	Shellbrook	**John Thiessen**	**CCF**	**2244**	1
	Shellbrook	G.T. Froese	SC	877	4
	Swift Current	Ben Letkeman	SC	979	4
15th April 4, 1964	Last Mountain	Martin Kelln	SC	1382	3
All 3 candidates were	**Rosthern**	**David Boldt**	**L**	**2873**	1
Mennonites	Rosthern	G.G. Guenther	CCF	1949	2
	Rosthern	E. Isaac	SC	1239	3
	Shellbrook	John Tiessen	CCF	2259	2
16th Oct. 11, 1967	Biggar	P. Wiebe	PC	1334	3
	Elrose	D. Loewen	NDP	2957	2
	Notukeu-Willowbunch	Allen W. Engel	NDP	2216	2
	Regina S W	D. Braun	PC	1084	3
Only 2 candidates,	**Rosthern**	**David Boldt**	**L**	**2950**	1
both Mennonites	Rosthern	G.G. Guenther	NDP	1466	2
17th June 23, 1971	**Notukeu-Willowbunch**	**Allen W. Engel**	**NDP**	**2542**	1
	Rosetown	Robert D. Loewen	NDP	2953	2
Only 2 candidates,	**Rosthern**	**David Boldt**	**L**	**2795**	1
both Mennonites	Rosthern	A.R. Friesen	NDP	2572	2
18th June 11, 1975	**Saskatoon City Park**	**Beverly Milton Dyck**	**NDP**	**2590**	1
	Assiniboia-Gravelbourg	Allen W. Engel	NDP	3012	2
	Athabasca	Ben Siemens	L	1175	2
	Morse	**John E.N. Wiebe**	**L**	**2517**	1
	Morse	Harold Martens	PC	1847	3
	Rosthern	A.R. Friesen	NDP	2030	3
	Saskatoon-Eastview	**Glen Penner**	**L**	**3175**	1
	Saskatoon-Eastview	Larry Fast	PC	1418	3
	Saskatoon-Mayfair	**Beverly Milton Dyck**	**NDP**	**3467**	1
	Saskatoon-Nutana	Bruno F. Reimer	L	2280	2

	Election Dates	Constituency	Candidate	Party	Votes	Rank
19th	Oct. 18, 1978	Assiniboia-Gravelbourg	Allen W. Engel	NDP	3126	1
	2 of the 3 candidates	Morse	Harold Martens	PC	2203	2
	were Mennonites	Morse	Jack Wiebe	L	2024	3
		Rosetown-Elrose	Herbert Swan	PC	3587	1
20th	Apr. 26, 1982	Saskatoon-Mayfair	Beverly Milton Dyck	NDP	3587	1
		Assiniboia-Gravelbourg	Allen Engel	NDP	2875	1
		Morse	Harold Martens	PC	3565	1
		Redberry	Wayne Ratzlaff	WCC	303	3
		Regina Rosemount	Gordon Dirks	PC	5271	1
		Rosetown-Elrose	Herbert Swan	PC	4802	1
		Rosthern	Chris Banman	NDP	1889	2
		Rosthern	James Boschman	N/A	188	4
		Swift Current	Henry Banman	WCC	787	3
		The Battlefords	Vernon Loeppky	WCC	249	4
21st	Oct. 20, 1986	Assiniboia-Gravelbourg	Allen W. Engel	NDP	2395	2
	3 of the 4 candidates	Morse	Harold Martens	PC	3694	1
	were Mennonites	Morse	Al Harder	L	605	3
		Morse	Burton Rempel	WCC	74	4
		Prince Albert-Duck Lake	Eldon Lautermilch	NDP	4448	1
		Regina Rosemount	Gordon Dirks	PC	3828	2
		Rosetown-Elrose	Herbert Swan	PC	4276	1
	2 of 3 candidates	Rosthern	Bill Z. Neudorf	PC	5700	1
	were Mennonites	Rosthern	Edgar Epp	NDP	3348	2
		Swift Current	John Penner	NDP	3785	2
22nd	Oct. 21, 1991	Bengough-Milestone	Laurie Unruh	L	1662	3
	2 of the 3 candidates	Morse	Harold Martens	PC	2672	1
	were Mennonites	Morse	Carl Siemens	NDP	2086	2

Election Dates
2 of the 3 candidates were Mennonites

Constituency	Candidate	Party	Votes	Rank
Prince Albert-Northcote	Eldon Lautermilch	NDP	5372	1
Prince Albert-Northcote	Terry Wiebe	PC	983	3
Rosetown-Elrose	Berry Wiens	NDP	2631	1
Rosthern	Bill Z. Neudorf	PC	4182	1
Saskatoon-Idylwyld	Roland Loewen	L	2537	2
Saskatoon-River Heights	Carol Teichroeb	NDP	5039	1
Swift Current	John Penner	NDP	4373	1
Regina-Churchill Downs	John Bergen	PC	671	3
Turtleford	Jerry Spenst	PC	2030	2

(Harold Martens and John Penner, PC and NDP, are both members of the Mennonite Brethren Bridgeway Community Church in Swift Current. Of 207 candidates, 12 were Mennonites.

They ran in 10 of the 66 electoral districts and won in 6.)

APPENDIX H
Aggregate Voter Survey Data
QUESTIONNAIRE
N = 235   Mennonite Brethren Voting Behavior, 1940-1960

NOTE: Please read all of the questions before you check off any answers. [ignore the numbers in parentheses; they only identify the questions for tabulation purposes.]

QUESTION 1.   Was it your practice to vote in national and provincial/state elections in the 1940s and 1950s?

        Yes 221 (1)   No 11 (2)
        Comments:

Please answer Question 2 or Question 3.

QUESTION 2.   If you voted, why did you vote? You may check off one or more of the following reasons. You may also write in your own reason or reasons.
(a)   Christians should be good citizens and this includes voting. 189 (3)
(b)   I wanted to support a particular political party. 108 (4)
(c)   Voting is a way of expressing gratitude to God for the fact that I could live in a free country. 166 (5)
(d)   Voting is a way of expressing gratitude to government. 88 (6)
(e)   If at all possible, all citizens should vote. 176 (7)
(f)   I had some other reason. (8)

QUESTION 3.   If you did not vote, why did you not vote? You may check off one or more of the following reasons. You may also write in your own reason or reasons.
(a)   Christians should be good citizens but good citizenship does not include voting. 2 (9)
(b)   None of the political parties appealed to me. 2 (10)
(c)   I was grateful to God that I could live in a free country but I expressed my gratitude in non-political ways. 4 (11)
(d)   I expressed my gratitude to government in other ways. 2 (12)
(e)   Voting took too much time and was too much of a bother. 2 (13)
(f)   I did not know enough about politics in order to vote. 7 (14)
(g)   I had some other reason. (15)

Please answer Question 4 or Question 5 if you voted.

QUESTION 4.   **FOR AMERICAN RESPONDENTS** (who voted)
    Usually I voted for the following political party in national elections.
    Democratic 8 (16)   Republican 82 (17)   Other 1 (18)
    Comment
    Usually I voted for the following political party in state elections.
    Democratic 8 (19)   Republican 72 (20)   Other 2 (21)
    Comment

QUESTION 5. **FOR CANADIAN RESPONDENTS** (who voted)
    Usually I voted for the following party in federal elections.
    CCF 3 (22) Liberal 81 (23) Progressive Conservative 60 (24)
    Social Credit 20(25) Other 2 (26)
    Comment
    Usually I voted for the following party in provincial elections.
    CCF 5 (27) Liberal 44 (28) Progressive Conservative 43 (29)
    Social Credit 49 (30)
    Comment

QUESTION 6. Whatever your opinion was about voting in the 1940s and 1950s,
    have you since that time changed your mind about voting?
    Yes 32 (31) No 188 (32)
    Comment

QUESTION 7. In what year were you born?
    (33) Are you male 162 (34) female 72 (35)

QUESTION 8. In what province or provinces, or what state or states, did you live in
    the 1940s and 1950s? (36)
    Comment

QUESTION 9. In what province or state do you live now? (37)

Thank you very much for your help. If you want to you may sign your name.

John H. Redekop, 298 Ferndale Place
Waterloo, Ontario, CANADA N2J 3X9   December 10, 1992

Have you any other comments?

APPENDIX I
Aggregate Canadian Survey Data
QUESTIONNAIRE
N = 137   Mennonite Brethren Voting Behavior, 1940-1960

NOTE: Please read all of the questions before you check off any answers.

QUESTION 1. Was it your practice to vote in national and provincial/state elections in the 1940s and 1950s?
Yes 128 (1)   No 7 (2)
Comments:

Please answer Question 2 or Question 3.

QUESTION 2. If you voted, why did you vote? You may check off one or more of the following reasons. You may also write in your own reason or reasons.
(a)   Christians should be good citizens and this includes voting. 105 (3)
(b)   I wanted to support a particular political party. 76 (4)
(c)   Voting is a way of expressing gratitude to God for the fact that I could live in a free country. 93 (5)
(d)   Voting is a way of expressing gratitude to government. 54 (6)
(e)   If at all possible, all citizens should vote. 96 (7)
(f)   I had some other reason. (8)

QUESTION 3. If you did not vote, why did you not vote? You may check off one or more of the following reasons. You may also write in your own reason or reasons.
(a)   Christians should be good citizens but good citizenship does not include voting. 1 (9)
(b)   None of the political parties appealed to me. 1 (10)
(c)   I was grateful to God that I could live in a free country but I expressed my gratitude in non-political ways. 2 (11)
(d)   I expressed my gratitude to government in other ways. 0 (12)
(e)   Voting took too much time and was too much of a bother. 1 (13)
(f)   I did not know enough about politics in order to vote. 5 (14)
(g)   I had some other reason. (15)

Please answer Question 4 or Question 5 if you voted.

QUESTION 4. **FOR AMERICAN RESPONDENTS** (who voted)
Usually I voted for the following political party in national elections.
Democratic (16) Republican (17) Other (18)
Comment
Usually I voted for the following political party in state elections.
Democratic (19) Republican (20) Other (21)
Comment

QUESTION 5. **FOR CANADIAN RESPONDENTS** (who voted)
Usually I voted for the following party in federal elections.
CCF 3 (22) Liberal 81 (23) Progressive Conservative 60 (24)
Social Credit 20 (25) Other 2 (26)
Comment
Usually I voted for the following party in provincial elections.
CCF 5 (27) Liberal 44 (28) Progressive Conservative 43 (29)
Social Credit 49 (30)
Comment

QUESTION 6. Whatever your opinion was about voting in the 1940s and 1950s,
have you since that time changed your mind about voting?
Yes 23 (31) No 104 (32)
Comment

QUESTION 7. In what year were you born?
(33) Are you male 91 (34) female 46 (35)

QUESTION 8. In what province or provinces, or what state or states, did you live in
the 1940s and 1950s? (36)
Comment

QUESTION 9. In what province or state do you live now?   (37)

Thank you very much for your help. If you want to you may sign your name.

John H. Redekop, 298 Ferndale Place
Waterloo, Ontario, CANADA N2J 3X9   December 10, 1992

Have you any other comments?

APPENDIX J
Aggregate U.S. Survey Data
QUESTIONNAIRE
N = 98   Mennonite Brethren Voting Behavior, 1940-1960

NOTE: Please read all of the questions before you check off any answers.

QUESTION 1.   Was it your practice to vote in national and provincial/state elections in the 1940s and 1950s?
Yes 93 (1)   No 4 (2)
Comments:

Please answer Question 2 or Question 3.

QUESTION 2.   If you voted, why did you vote? You may check off one or more of the following reasons. You may also write in your own reason or reasons.
(a)   Christians should be good citizens and this includes voting. 84 (3)
(b)   I wanted to support a particular political party. 32 (4)
(c)   Voting is a way of expressing gratitude to God for the fact that I could live in a free country. 73 (5)
(d)   Voting is a way of expressing gratitude to government. 34 (6)
(e)   If at all possible, all citizens should vote. 80 (7)
(f)   I had some other reason. (8)

QUESTION 3.   If you did not vote, why did you not vote? You may check off one or more of the following reasons. You may also write in your own reason or reasons.
(a)   Christians should be good citizens but good citizenship does not include voting. 1 (9)
(b)   None of the political parties appealed to me. 1 (10)
(c)   I was grateful to God that I could live in a free country but I expressed my gratitude in non-political ways. 2 (11)
(d)   I expressed my gratitude to government in other ways. 2 (12)
(e)   Voting took too much time and was too much of a bother. 1 (13)
(f)   I did not know enough about politics in order to vote. 2 (14)
(g)   I had some other reason. (15)

Please answer Question 4 or Question 5 if you voted.

QUESTION 4.   **FOR AMERICAN RESPONDENTS** (who voted)
Usually I voted for the following political party in national elections.
Democratic 8 (16) Republican 82 (17) Other 1 (18)
Comment
Usually I voted for the following political party in state elections.
Democratic 8 (19) Republican 72 (20) Other 2 (21)
Comment

QUESTION 5. **FOR CANADIAN RESPONDENTS** (who voted)
    Usually I voted for the following party in federal elections.
    CCF (22) Liberal (23) Progressive Conservative (24)
    Social Credit (25) Other (26)
    Comment
    Usually I voted for the following party in provincial elections.
    CCF (27) Liberal (28) Progressive Conservative (29) Social Credit (30)
    Comment

QUESTION 6. Whatever your opinion was about voting in the 1940s and 1950s,
    have you since that time changed your mind about voting?
    Yes 9 (31) No 84 (32)
    Comment

QUESTION 7. In what year were you born?
    (33) Are you male 72 (34) female 26 (35)

QUESTION 8. In what province or provinces, or what state or states, did you live in
    the 1940s and 1950s? (36)
    Comment

QUESTION 9. In what province or state do you live now?   (37)

Thank you very much for your help. If you want to you may sign your name.

                John H. Redekop, 298 Ferndale Place
                Waterloo, Ontario, CANADA N2J 3X9   December 10, 1992

Have you any other comments?

APPENDIX K
Aggregate Female Survey Data
QUESTIONNAIRE
N = 72   Mennonite Brethren Voting Behavior, 1940-1960

NOTE: Please read all of the questions before you check off any answers.

QUESTION 1. Was it your practice to vote in national and provincial/state elections
in the 1940s and 1950s?
Yes 66 (1)   No 6 (2)
Comments:

Please answer Question 2 or Question 3.

QUESTION 2. If you voted, why did you vote? You may check off one or more of the
following reasons. You may also write in your own reason or reasons.
(a)   Christians should be good citizens and this includes voting. 55 (3)
(b)   I wanted to support a particular political party. 32 (4)
(c)   Voting is a way of expressing gratitude to God for the fact that I could live in a
free country. 51 (5)
(d)   Voting is a way of expressing gratitude to government. 25 (6)
(e)   If at all possible, all citizens should vote. 52 (7)
(f)   I had some other reason. (8)

QUESTION 3. If you did not vote, why did you not vote? You may check off one or
more of the following reasons. You may also write in your own reason or
reasons.
(a)   Christians should be good citizens but good citizenship does not include
voting. 0 (9)
(b)   None of the political parties appealed to me. 0 (10)
(c)   I was grateful to God that I could live in a free country but I expressed my
gratitude in non-political ways. 1 (11)
(d)   I expressed my gratitude to government in other ways. 0 (12)
(e)   Voting took too much time and was too much of a bother. 1 (13)
(f)   I did not know enough about politics in order to vote. 5 (14)
(g)   I had some other reason. (15)

Please answer Question 4 or Question 5 if you voted.

QUESTION 4. **FOR AMERICAN RESPONDENTS** (who voted)
Usually I voted for the following political party in national elections.
Democratic 1 (16) Republican 22 (17) Other 1 (18)
Comment
Usually I voted for the following political party in state elections.
Democratic 1 (19) Republican 20 (20) Other 1 (21)
Comment

QUESTION 5. **FOR CANADIAN RESPONDENTS** (who voted)
Usually I voted for the following party in federal elections.
CCF 0 (22) Liberal 24 (23) Progressive Conservative 20 (24)
Social Credit 7 (25) Other 1 (26)
Comment
Usually I voted for the following party in provincial elections.
CCF 0 (27) Liberal 13 (28) Progressive Conservative 15 (29)
Social Credit 16 (30)
Comment

QUESTION 6. Whatever your opinion was about voting in the 1940s and 1950s,
have you since that time changed your mind about voting?
Yes 12 (31) No 56 (32)
Comment

QUESTION 7. In what year were you born?
(33) Are you male 0 (34) female 72 (35)

QUESTION 8. In what province or provinces, or what state or states, did you live in
the 1940s and 1950s? (36)
Comment

QUESTION 9. In what province or state do you live now?   (37)

Thank you very much for your help. If you want to you may sign your name.

John H. Redekop, 298 Ferndale Place
Waterloo, Ontario, CANADA N2J 3X9   December 10, 1992

Have you any other comments?

APPENDIX L
Aggregate Male Survey Data
QUESTIONNAIRE
N = 163 Mennonite Brethren Voting Behavior, 1940-1960

NOTE: Please read all of the questions before you check off any answers.

QUESTION 1. Was it your practice to vote in national and provincial/state elections in the 1940s and 1950s?
Yes 155 (1)   No 5 (2)
Comments:

Please answer Question 2 or Question 3.

QUESTION 2. If you voted, why did you vote? You may check off one or more of the following reasons. You may also write in your own reason or reasons.
(a) Christians should be good citizens and this includes voting. 134 (3)
(b) I wanted to support a particular political party. 76 (4)
(c) Voting is a way of expressing gratitude to God for the fact that I could live in a free country. 115 (5)
(d) Voting is a way of expressing gratitude to government. 63 (6)
(e) If at all possible, all citizens should vote. 124 (7)
(f) I had some other reason. (8)

QUESTION 3. If you did not vote, why did you not vote? You may check off one or more of the following reasons. You may also write in your own reason or reasons.
(a) Christians should be good citizens but good citizenship does not include voting. 2 (9)
(b) None of the political parties appealed to me. 2 (10)
(c) I was grateful to God that I could live in a free country but I expressed my gratitude in non-political ways. 3 (11)
(d) I expressed my gratitude to government in other ways. 2 (12)
(e) Voting took too much time and was too much of a bother. 1 (13)
(f) I did not know enough about politics in order to vote. 2 (14)
(g) I had some other reason. (15)

Please answer Question 4 or Question 5 if you voted.

QUESTION 4. FOR AMERICAN RESPONDENTS (who voted)
Usually I voted for the following political party in national elections.
Democratic 7 (16) Republican 60 (17) Other 0 (18)
Comment
Usually I voted for the following political party in state elections.
Democratic 7 (19) Republican 52 (20) Other 1 (21)
Comment

QUESTION 5. **FOR CANADIAN RESPONDENTS** (who voted)
Usually I voted for the following party in federal elections.
CCF 3 (22) Liberal 57 (23) Progressive Conservative 40 (24)
Social Credit 13 (25) Other 1 (26)
Comment
Usually I voted for the following party in provincial elections.
CCF 5 (27) Liberal 31 (28) Progressive Conservative 28 (29)
Social Credit 33 (30)
Comment

QUESTION 6. Whatever your opinion was about voting in the 1940s and 1950s, have you since that time changed your mind about voting?
Yes 20 (31) No 132 (32)
Comment

QUESTION 7. In what year were you born?
(33) Are you male 163 (34) female 0 (35)

QUESTION 8. In what province or provinces, or what state or states, did you live in the 1940s and 1950s? (36)
Comment

QUESTION 9. In what province or state do you live now?   (37)

Thank you very much for your help. If you want to you may sign your name.

> John H. Redekop, 298 Ferndale Place
> Waterloo, Ontario, CANADA N2J 3X9   December 10, 1992

Have you any other comments?

APPENDIX M
Canadian Female Survey Data
QUESTIONNAIRE
N = 46   Mennonite Brethren Voting Behavior, 1940-1960

NOTE: Please read all of the questions before you check off any answers.

QUESTION 1.   Was it your practice to vote in national and provincial/state elections in the 1940s and 1950s?

Yes 41 (1)   No 5 (2)
Comments:

Please answer Question 2 or Question 3.

QUESTION 2.   If you voted, why did you vote? You may check off one or more of the following reasons. You may also write in your own reason or reasons.
(a)   Christians should be good citizens and this includes voting. 32 (3)
(b)   I wanted to support a particular political party. 24 (4)
(c)   Voting is a way of expressing gratitude to God for the fact that I could live in a free country. 31 (5)
(d)   Voting is a way of expressing gratitude to government. 15 (6)
(e)   If at all possible, all citizens should vote. 32 (7)
(f)   I had some other reason. (8)

QUESTION 3.   If you did not vote, why did you not vote? You may check off one or more of the following reasons. You may also write in your own reason or reasons.
(a)   Christians should be good citizens but good citizenship does not include voting. 0 (9)
(b)   None of the political parties appealed to me. 0 (10)
(c)   I was grateful to God that I could live in a free country but I expressed my gratitude in non-political ways. 1 (11)
(d)   I expressed my gratitude to government in other ways. 0 (12)
(e)   Voting took too much time and was too much of a bother. 1 (13)
(f)   I did not know enough about politics in order to vote. 5 (1
(g)   I had some other reason. (15)

Please answer Question 4 or Question 5 if you voted.

QUESTION 4.   **FOR AMERICAN RESPONDENTS** (who voted)
Usually I voted for the following political party in national elections.
Democratic (16) Republican (17) Other (18)
Comment
Usually I voted for the following political party in state elections.
Democratic (19) Republican (20) Other (21)
Comment

QUESTION 5. **FOR CANADIAN RESPONDENTS** (who voted)
Usually I voted for the following party in federal elections.
CCF 0 (22) Liberal 24 (23) Progressive Conservative 20 (24)
Social Credit 7 (25) Other 1 (26)
Comment
Usually I voted for the following party in provincial elections.
CCF 0 (27) Liberal 13 (28) Progressive Conservative 15 (29)
Social Credit 16 (30)
Comment

QUESTION 6. Whatever your opinion was about voting in the 1940s and 1950s,
have you since that time changed your mind about voting?
Yes 10 (31) No 33 (32)
Comment

QUESTION 7. In what year were you born?
(33) Are you male (34) female 46 (35)

QUESTION 8. In what province or provinces, or what state or states, did you live in
the 1940s and 1950s? 36)
Comment

QUESTION 9. In what province or state do you live now?   (37)

Thank you very much for your help. If you want to you may sign your name.

John H. Redekop, 298 Ferndale Place
Waterloo, Ontario, CANADA N2J 3X9   December 10, 1992

Have you any other comments?

APPENDIX N
Canadian Male Survey Data
QUESTIONNAIRE
N = 91   Mennonite Brethren Voting Behavior, 1940-1960

NOTE: Please read all of the questions before you check off any answers.

QUESTION 1.   Was it your practice to vote in national and provincial/state elections
in the 1940s and 1950s?
Yes 87 (1)   No 2 (2)
Comments:

Please answer Question 2 or Question 3.

QUESTION 2.   If you voted, why did you vote? You may check off one or more of the
following reasons. You may also write in your own reason or reasons.
(a)   Christians should be good citizens and this includes voting. 73 (3)
(b)   I wanted to support a particular political party. 52 (4)
(c)   Voting is a way of expressing gratitude to God for the fact that I could live in a
free country. 62 (5)
(d)   Voting is a way of expressing gratitude to government. 39 (6)
(e)   If at all possible, all citizens should vote. 64 (7)
(f)   I had some other reason. (8)

QUESTION 3.   If you did not vote, why did you not vote? You may check off one or
more of the following reasons. You may also write in your own reason or
reasons.
(a)   Christians should be good citizens but good citizenship does not include
voting. 1 (9)
(b)   None of the political parties appealed to me. 1 (10)
(c)   I was grateful to God that I could live in a free country but I expressed my
gratitude in non-political ways. 1 (11)
(d)   I expressed my gratitude to government in other ways. 0 (12)
(e)   Voting took too much time and was too much of a bother. 0 (13)
(f)   I did not know enough about politics in order to vote. 0 (14)
(g)   I had some other reason. (15)

Please answer Question 4 or Question 5 if you voted.

QUESTION 4.   **FOR AMERICAN RESPONDENTS** (who voted)
Usually I voted for the following political party in national elections.
Democratic (16) Republican (17) Other (18)
Comment
Usually I voted for the following political party in state elections.
Democratic (19) Republican (20) Other (21)
Comment

QUESTION 5. **FOR CANADIAN RESPONDENTS** (who voted)
   Usually I voted for the following party in federal elections.
   CCF 3 (22) Liberal 57 (23) Progressive Conservative 40 (24)
   Social Credit 13 (25) Other 1 (26)
   Comment
   Usually I voted for the following party in provincial elections.
   CCF 5 (27) Liberal 31 (28) Progressive Conservative 28 (29)
   Social Credit 33 (30)
   Comment

QUESTION 6. Whatever your opinion was about voting in the 1940s and 1950s,
   have you since that time changed your mind about voting?
   Yes 13 (31) No 71 (32)
   Comment

QUESTION 7. In what year were you born?
   (33) Are you male 91 (34) female 0 (35)

QUESTION 8. In what province or provinces, or what state or states, did you live in
   the 1940s and 1950s? (36)
   Comment

QUESTION 9. In what province or state do you live now?   (37)

Thank you very much for your help. If you want to you may sign your name.

John H. Redekop, 298 Ferndale Place
Waterloo, Ontario, CANADA N2J 3X9   December 10, 1992

Have you any other comments?

APPENDIX O
U.S. Female Survey Data
QUESTIONNAIRE
N = 26   Mennonite Brethren Voting Behavior, 1940-1960

NOTE: Please read all of the questions before you check off any answers.

QUESTION 1.   Was it your practice to vote in national and provincial/state elections in the 1940s and 1950s?
Yes 25 (1)   No 1 (2)
Comments:

Please answer Question 2 or Question 3.

QUESTION 2.   If you voted, why did you vote? You may check off one or more of the following reasons. You may also write in your own reason or reasons.
(a)   Christians should be good citizens and this includes voting. 23 (3)
(b)   I wanted to support a particular political party. 8 (4)
(c)   Voting is a way of expressing gratitude to God for the fact that I could live in a free country. 20 (5)
(d)   Voting is a way of expressing gratitude to government. 10 (6)
(e)   If at all possible, all citizens should vote. 20 (7)
(f)   I had some other reason. (8)

QUESTION 3.   If you did not vote, why did you not vote? You may check off one or more of the following reasons. You may also write in your own reason or reasons.
(a)   Christians should be good citizens but good citizenship does not include voting. 0 (9)
(b)   None of the political parties appealed to me. 0 (10)
(c)   I was grateful to God that I could live in a free country but I expressed my gratitude in non-political ways. 0 (11)
(d)   I expressed my gratitude to government in other ways. 0 (12)
(e)   Voting took too much time and was too much of a bother. 0 (13)
(f)   I did not know enough about politics in order to vote. 0 (14)
(g)   I had some other reason. (15)

Please answer Question 4 or Question 5 if you voted.

QUESTION 4.   **FOR AMERICAN RESPONDENTS** (who voted)
Usually I voted for the following political party in national elections.
Democratic 1 (16) Republican 22 (17) Other 1 (18)
Comment
Usually I voted for the following political party in state elections.
Democratic 1 (19) Republican 20 (20) Other 1 (21)
Comment

QUESTION 5. **FOR CANADIAN RESPONDENTS** (who voted)
Usually I voted for the following party in federal elections.
CCF (22) Liberal (23) Progressive Conservative (24)
Social Credit (25) Other (26)
Comment
Usually I voted for the following party in provincial elections.
CCF (27) Liberal (28) Progressive Conservative (29) Social Credit (30)
Comment

QUESTION 6. Whatever your opinion was about voting in the 1940s and 1950s, have you since that time changed your mind about voting?
Yes 2 (31) No 23 (32)
Comment

QUESTION 7. In what year were you born?
(33) Are you male (34) female 26 (35)

QUESTION 8. In what province or provinces, or what state or states, did you live in the 1940s and 1950s? (36)
Comment

QUESTION 9. In what province or state do you live now?   (37)

Thank you very much for your help. If you want to you may sign your name.

John H. Redekop, 298 Ferndale Place
Waterloo, Ontario, CANADA N2J 3X9   December 10, 1992

Have you any other comments?

APPENDIX P

U.S. Male Survey Data
QUESTIONNAIRE
N = 72   Mennonite Brethren Voting Behavior, 1940-1960

NOTE: Please read all of the questions before you check off any answers.

QUESTION 1.   Was it your practice to vote in national and provincial/state elections in the 1940s and 1950s?
Yes 68 (1)   No 3 (2)
Comments:

Please answer Question 2 or Question 3.

QUESTION 2.   If you voted, why did you vote? You may check off one or more of the following reasons. You may also write in your own reason or reasons.
(a)   Christians should be good citizens and this includes voting. 61 (3)
(b)   I wanted to support a particular political party. 24 (4)
(c)   Voting is a way of expressing gratitude to God for the fact that I could live in a free country. 53 (5)
(d)   Voting is a way of expressing gratitude to government. 24 (6)
(e)   If at all possible, all citizens should vote. 60 (7)
(f)   I had some other reason. (8)

QUESTION 3.   If you did not vote, why did you not vote? You may check off one or more of the following reasons. You may also write in your own reason or reasons.
(a)   Christians should be good citizens but good citizenship does not include voting. 1 (9)
(b)   None of the political parties appealed to me. 1 (10)
(c)   I was grateful to God that I could live in a free country but I expressed my gratitude in non-political ways. 2 (11)
(d)   I expressed my gratitude to government in other ways. 2 (12)
(e)   Voting took too much time and was too much of a bother. 1 (13)
(f)   I did not know enough about politics in order to vote. 2 (14)
(g)   I had some other reason. (15)

Please answer Question 4 or Question 5 if you voted.

QUESTION 4.   **FOR AMERICAN RESPONDENTS** (who voted)
Usually I voted for the following political party in national elections.
Democratic 7 (16) Republican 60 (17) Other 0 (18)
Comment
Usually I voted for the following political party in state elections.
Democratic 7 (19) Republican 52 (20) Other 1 (21)
Comment

QUESTION 5. **FOR CANADIAN RESPONDENTS** (who voted)
Usually I voted for the following party in federal elections.
CCF (22) Liberal (23) Progressive Conservative (24)
Social Credit (25) Other (26)
Comment
Usually I voted for the following party in provincial elections.
CCF (27) Liberal (28) Progressive Conservative (29) Social Credit (30)
Comment

QUESTION 6. Whatever your opinion was about voting in the 1940s and 1950s, have you since that time changed your mind about voting?
Yes 7 (31) No 61 (32)
Comment

QUESTION 7. In what year were you born?
(33) Are you male 72 (34) female 0 (35)

QUESTION 8. In what province or provinces, or what state or states, did you live in the 1940s and 1950s? (36)
Comment

QUESTION 9. In what province or state do you live now? (37)

Thank you very much for your help. If you want to you may sign your name.

John H. Redekop, 298 Ferndale Place
Waterloo, Ontario, CANADA N2J 3X9   December 10, 1992

Have you any other comments?

II.
Theological
Autobiography

David Ewert

L et me tell you very briefly where I was in 1940 and how I got there. In the winter of 1926, when I was almost four years old, we landed in Canada. I had a brother one year older and a sister who was a baby in mother's arms. My father carried a little bundle of bedding. We arrived penniless with a big debt to the Canadian Pacific Railroad. It was frightfully cold when we got off the train in Herbert, Saskatchewan in November. We had nowhere to go and did not know anyone.

Jobs were not available and so after knocking about that first winter, my father got a job working for a farmer. Through an advertisement in the *Mennonitische Rundschau* my parents heard of opportunities in northern Ontario, at Risor. Several Mennonite immigrant families had gone there to cut trees for the pulp and paper industry. And so in late fall 1927 we moved into the deep forest of northern Ontario, near Kapiskasing.

After two years in this wilderness, my parents realized that this was no place to bring up a family, and so we headed west. First we lived in Linden, Alberta; then in Grassy Lake, in southern Alberta; always working for farmers. Finally, we were able to make a down payment on a CPR farm in Coaldale, Alberta, on condition that we grow sugar beets. When we came to Coaldale I was misplaced into grade two with my older brother. Until I got married and began my teaching ministry, my address was Box 64, Coaldale, Alberta.

With the outbreak of the war in 1939, I entered the Coaldale Bible School at age sixteen. Here I spent three wonderful years under the tutelage of men such as Jacob H. Quiring, John A. Toews, and Bernhard W. Sawatzky.

Sawatzky took a personal interest in me and helped me to regain some self-confidence. Since humility was seen as the epitome of piety in those days (B. B. Janz, our church leader, would on occasion come to town with his jacket tied up with binder twine), we had been duly knocked down in our youth. Some of us needed to be delivered from despising ourselves. Mr. Sawatzky helped me to regain some self-confidence.

Doctor A. H. Unruh was considered the prince of preachers at that time in Canadian churches and preached in Coaldale repeatedly. So for my fourth year of Bible schooling I went to Winkler, Manitoba to study under him.

I spent summers on the farm, with much time to reflect and to day-dream. We had next to nothing to read in those years. Before I entered Bible school, I enjoyed sports, but in my first year there I learned that sports were not conducive to godliness and so gave that up.

Radio was still taboo in our church when I grew up, but with the outbreak of the war, people were anxious to hear the news, and so most families bought radios. That opened up another world to us. We never missed listening to the Old Fashioned Revival Hour of Charles E. Fuller. Also we could hear Leslie E. Maxwell of Prairie Bible Institute speak every Sunday morning on the Victory Broadcast. Sometimes Ruth Miller, who had been one of Maxwell's teachers in Kansas, preached the sermon, much to the consternation of my mother. Listening to Mr. Maxwell's messages on the victorious Christian life, led to a fifth year of biblical studies at Prairie Bible Institute in Three Hills, Alberta.

Many of my friends spent four to five years in conscientious objector camps during the war. I, however, was spared the draft and spent those five years in biblical studies. The studies were narrowly focused and, as I think of them now, lacked some depth. But these were the formative years of my life, and provided the background for my life's calling to be a teacher of the Scripture.

It came as a grand surprise to me in 1944 when I received an invitation to teach in the La Glace Bible School in northern Alberta. I accepted the challenge with fear and trembling. When I learned that the La Glace community probably would not accept a single young man of twenty-one as a Bible teacher, Lena Hamm and I settled that question by getting married.

For seven years we were involved in Bible school teaching. We didn't always get a salary in those years. In Hepburn we got thirty dollars a month and housing. Bible schools ran for only six months of the year and so we had to pick up odd jobs in summer to earn our daily bread. For us the summer was usually broken up further by university summer schools. But we felt so privileged to be involved in Christian education that, to my knowledge, we never complained and carefully tithed our meager income.

Higher education was generally suspect when I grew up. It was often equated with "the wisdom of the world" of which Paul speaks in 1 Corinthians. However, I rejected that attitude and earned a B.A. at a secular university, the University of British Columbia. On one occasion when my father-in-law saw some of my text-books he could only exclaim: *"Gefährlich, gefährlich!"* ("Dangerous, dangerous!").

I also earned an M.A. and a B.D., as well as an M.Th. in those years, but by then we lived in Winnipeg. In 1953 we joined the faculty of Mennonite Brethren Bible College. Benjamin B. Janz, our church leader, and a member of the Board of General Welfare and Public Relations, wanted us to go to Brazil for a Bible teaching ministry. We had applied to our mission board for service abroad. The board decided to send us to Europe to work among Mennonite refugees. Mr. H. H. Janzen, president of MBBC and member of our mission board, had voted in favor, but on his return from Hillsboro, he gave us a call to join the faculty of MBBC. His letter and the letter from A. E. Janzen of the mission board, arrived on the same day. In a split second we made our decision to teach at MBBC. For twenty-five years our lives revolved around what is now Concord College.

I should mention, also, that teaching was only one aspect of our life during these years. Our churches regularly invited Bible teachers from Mennonite Brethren schools to preach all over Canada. Three-day Easter and Christmas Bible conferences almost became institutionalized, and we participated in these for many years.

Next to my parents and the ministers of our church in Coaldale (we had twelve of them), my Bible school teachers had the greatest influence on my life. My spiritual mentor in the Coaldale Bible School was B. W. Sawatzky. He modelled the Christian life for me, taught me how to outline sermons, took me along in preaching missions, and awakened gifts in me that I didn't think I had.

Doctor A. H. Unruh of Winkler helped me to become more human. Somehow I had come to understand piety as seriousness, and Unruh demonstrated for us that naturalness, and even a sense of humor, did not militate against godliness. He explicitly told us that we needed to be converted not only to Christ but also to our humanity. After all, there is a difference between being human and being sinful.

Another man who profoundly affected my life was L. E. Maxwell of Prairie Bible Institute. Some may find this hard to believe, but he showed me as no other the continuity of God's salvatory plan for humankind in the Scripture and weaned me away from dispensationalism, though he never mentioned John Nelson Darby by name. I shall remain forever grateful for the

lecture in which he severely criticized the views of Lewis Sperry
Chafer, of Dallas Seminary, and then flung Chafer's book, *Grace*,
across the podium. He taught us that people were always saved by
grace through faith and so helped us to see the unity of Old and
New Testaments.

At Luther Seminary in St. Paul, Minnesota, where I did my
M.Th., I received my introduction to European theology. Here I
was profoundly influenced by Dr. Rozentals, formerly professor of
New Testament at the University of Riga, who had come to America
as a refugee. He offered (among other courses) a course on the
Apocalypse of John so moving that I, like the Seer of Patmos, was
reduced to tears.

At Prairie Bible Institute I had unconsciously come under the
influence of Fundamentalism (our churches were still German-
speaking during my Bible school years, and did not get caught up
in the Liberal/Fundamentalist controversy). At Wheaton College I
learned of a wider and more open Evangelicalism. Dr. Berkeley
Mickelson, New Testament professor at Wheaton, became for me a
model in exegesis and hermeneutics, as did Dr. Kenneth Kantzer,
although he to a lesser degree.

Many issues we faced during the 1940s and 1950s were
cultural in nature, although we did not see them that way then. By
making them theological issues, some of them became the
occasions for acute conflict. Most Mennonite Brethren among
whom I moved were immigrants who had come to Canada in the
1920s. Threatened by the new culture, they tried very hard to
maintain the values of their European past.

Crucial among these was the German language. In some
homes English was strictly forbidden, though that was the
language the children spoke in school. This caused deep rifts in
some families. I spent Saturdays in German school for several
years, and loathed it deeply. We young people were eager to shake
off our European past and to identify with our Canadian friends at
school.

Nevertheless, when Lena and I became parents, we spoke only
German to our children, for by then we thought it would be an
advantage for them to be bilingual. However, when the children
went off to school, they soon turned to English and we decided not
to make an issue of it. Lena and I, however, to this day have our
evening prayers in German.

The language conflict in church was often more acute than in the home, because the faith of our parents was somehow bound up with their mother tongue. For us as teenagers it sounded a bit comical to hear leading churchmen explain, that with the loss of German we also would lose our faith. The language change also created problems for our school. In the early years of MBBC (begun in 1944) a major concern at the annual college board meetings was, how many courses were taught in German compared to those in English. When I began to teach at MBBC in 1953, I still had to teach some classes in German. A language change is, of course, no laughing matter, for few things run as deep in a person's psyche as language.

But there were other tensions caused by clashes in cultural mores. There were certain European patterns of behavior that parents expected their children to perpetuate. Women were to dress conservatively, and sometimes a preacher who—as it was then said—was not afraid to speak the truth, aimed his wrath at the sisters who wore short-sleeved dresses. Also, it was thought bad form for women to wear their hair short, because of, what I consider a misinterpretation of 1 Corinthians. Once at the Canadian Conference, when I was moderator, I was taken aback when a woman got up and asked what we were going to do about the fact that she had been excommunicated years ago for cutting her hair. At Prairie Bible Institute girls were strictly forbidden to cut their hair. Since I worked on the garbage crew as part of my work, it was enlightening to find piles of hair in the dustbins, just before graduation, in time for going home. Evidently the truth had not sunk in.

The wearing of jewelry was generally taboo, particularly since, according to the book of Judges, the Midianites had worn earrings. (That Eleazar gave Rebekah a nose ring, weighing half a shekel, was overlooked.) I recall B. B. Janz reminding the congregation that he preferred a marriage without a wedding ring.

Another question that troubled us greatly was how to relate to our non-Mennonite neighbors—designated as the "world." In school we were with other ethnic groups, but after school we had next to no contact with them. We were constantly warned against friendship with the world and it would not have occurred to us to invite non-Mennonite neighbors (or even General Conference Mennonites) to our home.

This became a serious theological problem for us when our teachers in Bible school encouraged us to witness to our faith in our community. Our efforts at missions had to be kept at a safe distance from the local church. One outlet for us was to teach Daily Vacation Bible School in country schools away from our community. Even if we had wanted to invite a neighbor-friend to church it would have been pointless, for our services in the 1940s were still in German. A few efforts were made to begin Sunday evening services in English in the local high school, but the church leadership stopped them rather quickly.

When our teacher, J. A. Toews, ventured to say in a sermon that it was not our duty as a church "*den Kulturwagen zu ziehen*" ("to pull the wagon of culture"), but that it was our calling to evangelize, he found himself in trouble with B. B. Janz—not a comfortable position in which to be. I might add that there was great interest in foreign missions in my growing-up years. That, however, called only for prayer and giving; the church did not have to receive these converts.

Looking at it now from a sociological point of view, I have great sympathy with our parents and our ministers. They saw so much of what was precious to them in their European culture go by the board. A mild parallel might be the loss that some of us feel so keenly today as we lose the hymnody that nourished our souls in the past.

Our families had come through the trauma of the revolution in Russia. Most of them had lost everything and the beginnings in Canada were hard. That may explain the strong emphasis on "the better land" in the world to come. Our favorite hymns were "*Heimat lieder*" ("Songs of heaven"), and I memorized many of them in my youth. Also, much of the preaching had an apocalyptic note in it, creating much fear. As a child I feared the night, since Christ was to come as a thief in the night. When informed on one occasion that the Mount of Olives had already split in three, we were sure the end of the world was near.

One often-debated question was the security of the believer. "Eternal security" was considered a heresy. We knew nothing about Calvinism or Arminianism, but we knew that the warnings of Scripture had to be taken seriously. This often led to a lack of assurance and robbed us of much joy and peace.

Sanctification was very central in the church's teaching, and at times it was understood as perfectionism. Since none of us measured up, we often felt like giving up. It was clearly stated that we were saved by grace, but the strong emphasis on holy living and good deeds caused us to wonder whether we would be able to stand in the final judgment or whether, like the five foolish maidens, we would find the door shut.

Conversion was generally understood as a crisis experience, and those who had come into the kingdom in a more gentle way, not kicking and screaming, would have to do a lot of explaining before a six-hundred-member congregation when it came to baptism.

One of the dangers we were frequently warned against was the teaching of evolution. One of the reasons for establishing Mennonite high schools was to keep young people from imbibing this heresy. It was not recognized at the time that the social sciences and literature, in which human values are constantly debated, were actually more dangerous.

One theological issue that earned me personally much criticism was my failure to uphold the dispensational approach to the Bible. Some thought I had become a modernist because I no longer held to a pretribulation rapture. In fact I was Anabaptist in this regard. I took the Sermon on the Mount seriously, which Scofield had relegated to the coming millennium. I didn't have to speculate on who or what the treasure in the field or the pearl of great price was, because I interpreted all the parables of Jesus as Kingdom parables. The most bitter attacks came when it was discovered that I put little stock in political developments in modern Israel, which is largely godless; and when I pointed out that the line in the New Testament is no longer drawn between Jew and Gentile, but between people of faith and unfaith.

We also faced ecclesiological changes. Immigrant Mennonite Brethren churches transplanted their accustomed worship styles from Russia to Canada. All churches put great emphasis on congregational singing and on choirs, although B. B. Janz tried to stop the change from *Ziffern* to notes—"*die kleinen Dinge mit Häckchen, die lass bleiben*" ("Leave those little markings with hooks alone"). Lengthy prayer sessions usually opened the Sunday morning services. The pulpit was central. In Coaldale we always had two sermons for adults (Sunday school was for children). Most of our preachers had little or no theological training (except the Bible school teachers). They nonetheless preached amazingly well, although our hearts did sink when certain ministers got their turn.

Minister B. B. Janz often asked young men to lead the prayer meeting. If they showed gifts in public speaking, he might ask them to preach the first of two sermons. Should there be a fiasco, the second preacher could correct all the blunders the first speaker made. The result (and perhaps it was not even planned) was that a score of teachers and preachers from Coaldale later served our churches and schools all over Canada.

Churches were generally "congregational" when it came to decision making. The church council served as a clearing house, and prepared the agenda for the business meetings. The congregation made the decisions on matters great and small. This was very time-consuming, but created a great *esprit de corps*. Often, too, it led to fiery debates over minutiae. I was a member of the church council when the question was first raised in our church whether we should have a salaried pastor. It took many years before the church agreed to pay its leading minister.

Church membership was taken seriously and discipline practiced regularly. Some members were excommunicated for trivial reasons and that was reprehensible. But where would one find a church today that excommunicates a member because of greed? Our church did, and won the brother back, too. Baptismal candidates usually received a long list of rules that the church expected them to observe. Much as these were later ridiculed, they did give new members clear parameters for daily living. The danger of equating true piety with the observance of such an ethical code was, of course, always present.

In retrospect one smiles at some of the foibles and failures of our churches in the 1940s and 1950s. Some things that seemed so crucial then have now become non-issues. Personally, I am glad we could leave behind some things that caused us so much grief. However, I must say to the credit of our leaders during those decades, that they took their calling seriously. There was a vitality about church life that is often lacking today. Most of our leaders who served the church during those decades lie buried in the Coaldale cemetery. In spite of their shortcomings, I would join the writer to the Hebrews: "Remember your leaders, those who spoke the word of God to you; consider the outcome of their way of life, and imitate their faith."

III.
Economic
Developments

The Economic Transformation of Canadian Mennonite Brethren

T. D. Regehr

The 1940s and 1950s were years of exceptionally rapid change for Canadian Mennonite Brethren. In 1940 Mennonite Brethren, like most other Canadian Mennonites, still lived in relatively isolated rural communities and were occupationally tied to agriculture and small town agricultural service activities.[1] They still adhered to a separatist lifestyle, but tended to define the evidence of separation from "the world" in cultural and social, rather than in economic or technological terms.

Some other Mennonite groups took these concerns more seriously than did the Mennonite Brethren. Old Order Mennonites and the Old Order Amish in Ontario, for example, thought the technology associated with automobiles and electricity might involve dangerous compromises with unbelievers.[2] They also insisted on distinctive forms of dress, particularly for the women. The Northwest Mennonite Conference, a regional conference of the Mennonite Church in Alberta and Sasktachewan, issued warnings about Christians becoming unequally yoked with unbelievers in the Prairie Wheat Pools and other agricultural supply management schemes. The Old Colony Mennonites in Saskatchewan and Manitoba placed great emphasis on separatist educational models. Mennonite Brethren, however, were more likely to identify the old Methodist favorite quintet of sins— alcohol, smoking, card playing, dancing and movies—as the most visibile evidence of worldliness. Pool halls were added to the list of places to be avoided in response to unique local circumstances in some communities.

The comparative willingness of Mennonite Brethren to accept close economic links with the outside world was partially rooted in their unique historical experiences in Canada, and resulted in support for a curious array of different kinds of economic organizations.

UNIQUE ASPECTS OF MENNONITE BRETHREN ECONOMIC HISTORY AND IDENTITY.

Mennonite Brethren patterns of economic integration and assimilation in Canada were based, in part at least, on their unique and more sharply differentiated economic experiences in the 1920s, 1930s and the early war years. Two factors were particularly important.

The first unique aspect of the Canadian Mennonite Brethren economic identity at mid-century was due to the simple fact that immigrants who came from the Soviet Union in the 1920s gained an influence and dominance in Canadian Mennonite Brethren communities, congregations and conferences unmatched in any other Mennonite or Canadian immigrant group. The membership statistics given in the various Mennonite Brethren Conference Yearbooks are not altogether reliable, but they do suggest some obvious trends. Taken decade by decade, sharp increases in membership in the Northern District of the Mennonite Brethren Conference of North America are obvious.

Table 1[3]

Canadian Mennonite Brethren Membership, by Decade.

Year	Membership
1920	1790
1930	3870
1940	7877
1950	10,710
1960	13,952
1970	16,880
1980	21,892
1990	27,336

It should be noted how small the membership in Canadian Mennonite Brethren churches was before the immigration of the 1920s. Almost all the new members were new immigrants, or the children of members.[4] Much has been written about the aggressive congregational and conference leadership styles of these immigrants, but very little thus far about the leadership they provided in abandoning many separatist Mennonite economic organizations and their acceptance of virtually complete integration into Canadian economic affairs.

The economic experiences of the Mennonite immigrants of the 1920s were, in some respects, uniquely difficult and disruptive. The immigrants came from a variety of economic backgrounds in the

Soviet Union, but almost all hoped or expected to establish themselves as agriculturalists or in agricultural service industries in Canada.[5] From an economic point of view, they arrived in Canada at a very bad time. Those wishing to establish themselves in farming had to borrow large sums at high interest rates to purchase farm land and machinery at the inflated prices of the late 1920s.[6] Advice and assistance from the Canadian Pacific Railway (CPR) and the Canada Colonization Association[7] protected Mennonite land purchasers from the worst excesses of the late 1920s. However, they purchased much land and equipment at prices that left very little when drought and low commodity prices in the 1930s devastated the farm economy. When the transportation debt owed to the CPR was included, the debts incurred by Mennonite immigrants in the 1920s created enormous difficulty in the 1930s and early 1940s.

At the 1939 annual meeting of Mennonite settlers in Alberta, Rev. Aaron A. Toews of Namaka expressed the disappointment, frustration, and hopelessness of the immigrant farmers who tried, in the drought and depression-plagued 1930s, to discharge the onerous obligations they had accepted in the 1920s. Toews praised the generous and helpful support the immigrants had received from the Canadian Pacific Railway, the Canada Colonization Association, and private land vendors, but then pointed out that

> if, today, we contemplate the naked truth, recognizing how most of the settlers are desperately struggling to maintain their impoverished situation, and realizing how many have already given up any hope of ever obtaining a clear title to their own soil and home, in spite of the hard work already done, one must ask in astonishment: "How is this possible? Why must experienced agriculturalists with unparalleled hard work and perseverence, who should be well on the road to prosperity, face such an uncertain future and such drastically restricted economic prospects. Where can we find an explanation for such a dilemma?"[8]

Toews lamented that these economic problems were particularly difficult for the young people. Many young Mennonites had already been lost or estranged from their own people and joined the ranks of the unemployed and restlessly discontented proletariat. His conclusion, while theologically sound, was hardly inspiring:

> So, what shall we do now? Shall we become discouraged and fold our hands in our laps. No! that would be unworthy of

Christians and Mennonite farmers! We must again put our
hand to the plow, but look heavenward from whence all
earthly blessings come. Then we can move forward with
courage and confidence. The world belongs to the
courageous. But, if in spite of our best efforts, it has been
determined that we remain poor, we should repeat with the
Apostle Paul: "Having food and raiment, let us be content
therewith." The word of God further admonishes us to "Seek
first the Kingdom of God and its righteousness, and all these
things will be added unto you."[9]

This was not a welcome message for discouraged farmers' sons
considering the advantages of enlistment in the Canadian armed
forces or of better paid off-farm wartime employment. It is true that
the general agricultural situation improved during the war years,
but not equally for all farmers. To the surprise of most Canadian
agricultural experts and farmers, who expected a sharp increase in
the demand for wheat, wartime demand for cereal grains fell
sharply in 1940. British, and later American food policies required
much less wheat and much larger quantities of bacon, cheese, eggs,
beef, chickens and turkeys.[10] Farmers with the necessary
technological expertise and capital to invest in hog, dairy, poultry
and beef operations prospered. Those who lacked the necessary
financial resources to diversify their operations and instead stayed
with grain, found the early 1940s as difficult as the 1930s.[11]

The Mennonite immigrants of the 1920s who had gone heavily
into debt to acquire their farms, stock and equipment in the 1920s
had neither the savings nor the credit to diversify their operations
during the war years. As a result, farm failures among them were very
high. Many of those leaving the farms for active or alternative service
or off-farm wartime employment had neither the resources nor the
incentive to return to farming after the war.[12] The many post-war
Mennonite immigrants were even less likely to have or obtain the
capital necessary to establish themselves on farms of their own.
Mennonite farmers on well established farms with only moderate
debts were able to weather the depression and early wartime crises.
Such farmers prospered if they switched their operations to meet
changing market conditions early in the war or had good grain
crops after 1943. But those who had come to Canada in the 1920s
and begun farming with heavy debt loads had a terrible time.
Canadian Mennonite Brethren, as already indicated, were
disproportionately represented in this latter category.

A second factor further aggravated the situation for the

Mennonite Brethren. They had a much larger proportion of their members in British Columbia, Alberta and Saskatchewan than did any of the other Mennonite groups. Again the available conference statistics, although not entirely accurate, give a clear picture of the disproportionate western distribution of Mennonite Brethren members.

Table 2[13]
Canadian Mennonite Brethren membership, by province

Year	Total Mem.	B.C.	Alta.	Sask.	Man.	Ont.	Que.	Mar.
1920	1,790	--	--	1,425	365	--	--	--
1930	3,870	--	221	2,166	1,483	--	--	--
1940	7,877	1,131	873	2,800	2,268	805	--	--
1950	10,710	3,343	1,048	2,130	2,664	1,525	--	--
1960	13,952	4,453	1,199	2,276	3,853	2,171	--	--
1970	16,880	5,660	1,456	2,495	4,445	2,778	46	--
1980	21,892	7,861	1,974	3,034	5,240	3,457	326	--
1990	27,336	11,320	2,294	3,240	5,866	3,825	691	64

The significance of these numbers lies in the fact that the agricultural economies of the western provinces were much more volatile than those of the Central Canadian provinces, or even of Manitoba. Farmers in the western provinces depended heavily on international export markets for their livelihood. That had also been the case in Ontario and Quebec in the first half of the nineteenth century, and in Manitoba early in the twentieth century, but urbanization and industrialization had created major local and domestic markets for agricultural products. By the middle of the twentieth century most of the farm produce grown in Ontario was consumed locally while Quebec had become a net importer of wheat and many other agricultural products. Even in Manitoba, the city of Winnipeg provided an important local market for local farmers, and Mennonites were among the first to supply that market with dairy and poultry products.

During the depression, Ontario Premier Mitch Hepburn, a farmer himself, established many provincial agricultural supply management and marketing boards. These boards sought to protect Ontario farmers from the worst and most violent international price fluctuations.[14] As long as the bulk of the Ontario grown produce was sold to consumers in the province, these provincial schemes provided stability, predictability and reasonable returns for the farmers. During the war that stability and predictability was further strengthened for eastern Canadian farmers by the tight controls established by the Wartime Prices and Trade Board for all products grown and consumed in the country.

Winnipeg markets cushioned the impact of international market fluctuations for many Manitoba farmers. Those further west, however, had to sell most of their produce on wildly fluctuating— and in the 1930s severely depressed—international markets.[15] After the outbreak of war, the Wartime Prices and Trade Board concerned itself both with the returns farmers needed to remain in business and the impact any price increases for agricultural products would have on domestic consumer prices. At various times the Board recommended small federal subsidies for agricultural producers so as to hold down food prices and thus control inflationary pressures. But those subsidies never completely protected western farmers from international price fluctuations. While the subsidies met the needs of well established farmers, those in a financially overextended state had difficulty keeping their farming operations financially afloat. The Wartime Prices and Trade Board policies were designed to keep established farmers—particularly those willing to diversify their operations—in business. The Board also accepted the fact that its pricing policies would force many marginal or heavily indebted farmers off the land and into active military service or employment in the booming but understaffed war industries.[16]

The Mennonite Brethren were particularly vulnerable. More of their members than any other group had entered Canadian agriculture in the late 1920s. Additionally, more of their members than any other Mennonite group lived in the western provinces where farmers were particularly vulnerable to the vicissitudes of international commodity markets. The agricultural crisis of the 1930s, and the sharp and unexpected shifts in agricultural market conditions during the early years of the war, therefore hit them particularly hard.

MENNONITE ECONOMIC INSTITUTIONS
AND PROBLEMS IN THE 1940S

The economic problems facing Canadian Mennonite Brethren at mid-century were, for the reasons just stated, exceptionally difficult. Survival, not economic or theological ideology, governed their economic activities during the difficult years and continued to do so even after conditions improved in the mid and late-1940s. The result was that Canadian Mennonite Brethren became fully integrated into the economic life of the nation. Old notions of economic separation from "the world" were abandoned with the acceptance of new nationally and internationally integrated economic structures and marketing arrangements.

One revealing indicator of the failure to integrate Mennonite Brethren economic thinking with other aspects of their faith may be seen in the lack of any discussion of economic issues in *The Voice*, for many years the official academic publication of the Mennonite Brethren Bible College in Winnipeg. Even more notable is a sharp decline in references to economic matters in the local and community reports published in the *Mennonitische Rundschau* after the war. The seemingly deliberate avoidance of economic matters reminds me of the harsh reaction of one Mennonite Brethren leader when he heard that I was studying economics at the university. Why, he wondered, would anyone want to study the theology of Mammon?

Four types of economic institutions and organizations operated in most Canadian Mennonite communities before 1940. These were privately owned farms and small businesses, mutual aid organizations, secular cooperatives, and larger horizontally or vertically integrated corporations. All four had important separatist tendencies before 1940, but became fully integrated in the next two decades. Mennonite Brethren, with their uniquely difficult pre-war and early war economic experiences, offered less resistance to that integration than most other Canadian Mennonite groups. Mennonite Brethren leaders had been active and influential in several private and community economic initiatives before 1940. However, they provided very few guidelines for their members in the conduct of economic affairs after the war.[17]

The basic economic unit in Canadian Mennonite communities was the privately owned and independently operated family farm or small agricultural service business. These farms and small businesses required much hard work, but small capital investments. The scale of operation was generally quite small, and success depended on the reputation, the integrity, and the practical good sense of the operator. J. Winfield Fretz, in his 1989 study of Mennonites in Waterloo, Ontario, argued that

farming above all other occupations or professions provided
an ideal environment in which to carry out the church and
family ideals. Closeness to nature, in a setting where all family
members could take part in the work and enjoy the fruits of
their labor, has always appealed to Mennonites. Farming was
also historically favorable to the concept of the believers
church and its adherence to a policy of separation from the
world.[18]

Farming and agricultural service businesses were a wholistic
way of life in which the individual operator, the community and the
church came together, each with a recognized function. After 1945,
however, farming became more mechanized, requiring much
larger capital investments, and leaving other family, community and
church members formerly engaged in manual labor to earn their
livilihood elsewhere. Farming and rural service ventures became
more businesslike. Some Mennonite groups, of course, prescribed
specific measures to prevent the loss of their old separatist, rural
and agricultural way of life.[19] Mennonite Brethren leaders provided
no official guidelines and set no official limits to the size or
complexity of their members' business ventures.

During the more prosperous years after 1943 the relative
influence of capital and labor became more sharply differentiated
on many Mennonite farms. This was even more true in Mennonite
business ventures. Some successful Mennonite capitalists[20] in the
1940s and 1950s tried hard to preserve what they believed were the
best features of the old family farm or small family business.
Employees in Mennonite business firms were often described as
members of an extended family where everyone did what they
could to advance the common good and then, presumably, shared
in the resulting benefits. Several large businesses owned by
Mennonite Brethren in Winnipeg, for example, had morning
devotions for the workers on the shop floor, or appointed a
chaplain to look after the spiritual needs of the workers. Employers
boasted about the number of hours they spent working side by side
with their employees in the shop. It was generally assumed that in
hard times employers and employees alike would make sacrifices
to ensure the success of the business. But prosperity quickly
resulted in tensions if the reward or profits were not shared as
equitably as the hardships.

The gulf between capital and labor only rarely caused serious
trouble for Mennonite Brethren businessmen and workers before
1960. There were a few serious incidents, but when compared with

the employer-employee relations problems in Mennonite schools, conferences, missions and congregations, these seemed manageable. However, the fundamental tensions of modern, industrial and urban economic relations were also manifesting themselves in factories and businesses owned and operated by Mennonite Brethren. Conference and congregational leaders provided little or no guidance in such matters, and serious embarassments seemingly became inevitable. Some successful large scale Mennonite Brethren farming and business operators were exemplary in their business dealings. Others abused the power inherent in their control of major capital resources to exploit and intimidate their workers. Regretably, members of this latter group were very rarely disciplined or denied positions of influence and power in Mennonite Brethren congregations and conferences. One looks in vain for evidence of any sensitivity on such matters by senior conference leaders. The Board of Reference and Counsel, for example, spent a considerable amount of time and energy in dealing with a former pastor and Bible school teacher who had abused his position of authority for sexual gratification, but I have not found a single critical reference to members found guilty by labor relations boards or the courts of exploiting their employees. Special donations to the foreign missions budget protected even the greediest and most unscrupulous employers from any form of Mennonite Brethren church discipline. There were sometimes admonitions about the ways in which individuals spent or squandered their wealth, but almost never about the ways in which they had accumulated it.

All the larger Canadian Mennonite communities at mid-century had not only privately owned small independent agricultural and service ventures, but also important village or community based mutual aid organizations. These had been established to deal with some major problems in health care and basic social welfare cases, and usually had explicitly stated "Christian" objectives. They were to provide help and relief to the needy, the helpless and the suffering, regardless of ability to pay. The administration of orphans' trust funds, local hail and fire assistance, limited insurance plans, health care, relief work and other necessary social programs were established in many rural and agricultural Mennonite communities whose members did not wish to become "unequally yoked with unbelievers" in such endeavors.

These various Mennonite mutual aid organizations in Canada

during World War II were described in 1943 when J. Winfield Fretz, a Mennonite sociologist who had just completed a dissertation on the topic, was commissioned by Mennonite Central Committee to visit Canada to explore the possibilities of post-war Mennonite colonization. Fretz provided some of the most detailed information now available on economic conditions and circumstances in Mennonite communities across Canada.[21] He believed that mutual aid organizations should be based on "Christian principles" that he called "brotherhood economics." Christians, in Fretz's view, should not accept economic practices that conformed to the practices and ideology of the outside world. They should instead "move in an opposite direction." Essentially he envisioned a separatist—if not isolationist—and self-sufficient model of Mennonite mutual aid, which he defined thus in a 1947 pamphlet on the subject:

> A basic assumption underlying this pamphlet and the accompanying emphasis on mutual aid among Mennonites is that the Mennonite Church desires to continue teaching and practicing doctrines of separation of church and state; of non-resistance, of non-conformity to a secular world and of simplicity of living. This assumption must be accepted in order to appreciate the purpose of this pamphlet which is to encourage the development of a program of Christian mutual aid among Mennonites. This emphasis is a conscious effort to move in an opposition direction to the secular currents of our time. It assumes that the church, as a brotherhood . . . will seek to meet its economic and social needs through mutual assistance on the part of its people. . . . As Christians we hardly realize how far we have discarded the laws of Christ in favor of the laws of the market. In fact, many make no distinction between the two. The aim of this pamphlet is to help Christian people discover ways of aiding one another in Christ. Christian mutual aid is a program aimed to spiritualize our economic practices; to put a soul into our vocation and daily work.[22]

In his pamphlet Fretz argued that there was a clear difference between Christian mutual aid societies and secular cooperative organizations. "Mutual aid societies," he suggested, "may be characterized by the intimate nature of the relationships of the members and generally have as their primary motivation a religious or fraternal basis. Co-operative organizations are all too generally economically motivated and entirely secular in nature."[23] The well known and highly respected Mennonite scholar, Harold S. Bender, who wrote the introduction for this pamphlet, insisted that Fretz was "squarely within the authentic historic tradition of the Anabaptist-Mennonite movement with its spirit of Christian stewardship, mutual burden bearing, and practical brotherly love."[24]

There were many Mennonite mutual aid programs in which Canadian Mennonite Brethren participated and provided leadership in 1943, but Fretz and Bender were unduly influenced by the economic institutions established by their own conference and by the Old Order groups in the United States. Many Canadian Mennonite economic organizations that they regarded as mutual aid schemes in fact operated as the kind of cooperatives that Fretz tried very carefully to differentiate from true mutual aid programs. In addition, most of the Mennonite mutual aid programs in Canada did not operate as Fretz and Bender thought they ought to operate. Fretz argued that

> a practical program of mutual aid within the church is one of the most effective ways of counter-acting the threat of statism in America. Statism is a religion not unlike emperor worship of early Roman days. The state sets itself up as the ultimate authority, demands absolute obedience, and in time of war requires the equivalent of worship in its zeal for evidences of patriotism. . . . People who are dependent on the state for bread and butter, health, education, and economic security from the cradle to the grave will in the long run also tend to look to it for guidance and direction in other matters. As the state increases in importance, the church will decrease. Economic security apart from the church may mean spiritual indifference to the church. A program of mutual aid motivated by the Love of Christ will encourage men to look for guidance and direction to Christ and His followers rather than to Caesar. It is a way of testifying that Mennonites still believe in the separation of church and state.[25]

Canadian Mennonite Brethren did not impose this strong anti-statist ideology on their mutual aid organizations. The first major test came with the introduction of the Canadian family allowance plan in 1944. Some Ontario Mennonites and members of the Northwest Conference of the Mennonite Church rejected this intrusion of the state into matters that they believed should remain the concern of the church.[26] Some Mennonite Brethren also felt uneasy about the family allowances, but the government aid was not rejected in any coordinated manner.

The broad range of Canadian social development and welfare

policies that were a key element in the Canadian post-war reconstruction program were introduced with considerable sensitivity and political skill. Established welfare and mutual aid programs and organizations, such as church administered hospitals, old people's homes, child care facilities, and other mutual aid programs, could remain under private or denominational management and still receive government assistance if they met minimum government standards and requirements. The government policy was designed primarily to meet the unique conditions of Roman Catholic charitable institutions in Quebec, but charitable and mutual aid institutions elsewhere in Canada also could qualify for government funding. It usually took some time, and a financial crisis or the need to improve or expand facilities, often in response to a critical report from the fire inspector, before Canadian Mennonite charitable and mutual aid organizations accepted government money, but the opportunity to build and operate improved facilities proved almost irresistible. Thus, by 1960, few of the large and expensive charitable institutions administered and supported by Canadian Mennonites could survive without government grants, subsidies and concessions given either directly to the institution or to those receiving and paying for the services rendered there. Acceptance of government money, even when administrative control remained with the sponsoring Mennonite agency, made many of the largest Mennonite mutual aid institutions pseudo-public facilities. These institutions still provided the charitable services for which they had been established, but, far from reinforcing the separation of church and state, they became important instruments of economic integration.[27]

Besides the Mennonite charities and mutual aid organizations and institutions there were several other Mennonite-organized and promoted economic institutions that J. Winfield Fretz also identified as mutual aid organizations. These were, however, secular cooperatives established to serve the selfish and secular economic objectives of the members. The rhetoric of "brotherhood economics" can be found in the founding documents of some of these cooperatives, but membership was never congregationally based. It was not restricted to those who were members of a Mennonite Brethren, or even of a Mennonite church.[28] There was, moreover, no deliberate attempt "to move in an opposite direction to the currents of our time." Instead, the larger and more important

Canadian Mennonite cooperatives explicitly accepted and tried to maximize benefits to their members while operating according to the laws of the market.

Most agricultural cooperatives organized and administered by Canadian Mennonites were established for the same reasons that workers banded together in labor unions. Individually farmers had little or no influence on national or international market conditions. If, however, they banded together to process and market their products they could, collectively, exert considerable influence and force buyers to pay higher prices and to treat the growers or producers more generously. Similarly, consumers could band together to buy and distribute larger shipments of necessary supplies, thereby taking advantage of bulk purchases and avoiding the markups of various middlemen. Mennonite Brethren were not only prominent, but in fact dominated, the affairs of several of the largest Mennonite agricultural cooperatives. Since these cooperatives are less well understood, and became the subject of bitter controversy, their operation will be explained in detail.

Developments at Yarrow, British Columbia and Coaldale, Alberta are particularly revealing because in those communities Mennonite Brethren were the largest and most influential group. Both communities were established in the mid-1920s with exceptionally strong separatist overtones, and in spite of opposition from the Canadian Mennonite Board of Colonization at Rosthern.

At Yarrow a seven hundred-acre tract of land was purchased from a local land developer in 1927. Frustrated or failed prairie grain farmers were invited to purchase small tracts of that land at exorbitantly high prices but on exceptionally easy repayment terms. The original plan was to lay out villages and to establish local forms of government and economic organizations, all closely following separatist Russian Mennonite settlement and governance models. The community elected its own governing committee, chaired by a Mennonite Brethren, whose functions were similar to those of the *Schultze* in the Russian Mennonite communities. The chairman was expected to deal essentially on a government-to-government basis with outside government officials, and for a time did so. J. Winfield Fretz reported that

> in such local affairs as road work, bridge building and relief
> this committee deals entirely with the outside agencies. For

instance, during the depression when Mennonites opposed the receiving of relief for their members this committee went to the municipal officials and asked for permission to construct its own roads, build its own bridges and in general take care of its public utilities and be paid its proper share out of the public treasury. The government accepted this proposal and the funds were used to provide employment for those Mennonites who most needed it.[29]

The Yarrow settlers faced desperate poverty in the early years of the settlement. Their affairs improved in the late 1930s when a new variety of raspberry was developed that produced exceptionally well on their wet and heavy land.[30] At last the settlers had a saleable agricultural product. Unfortunately for them, Japanese berry growers in the Fraser Valley were already producing more berries than the Vancouver and prairie markets could absorb. The Japanese growers had established their own cooperative marketing organization, the Pacific Co-operative Union, which worked hard to develop new markets and to limit production to avoid disastrous price competition.

The entry of Mennonite berry growers into the market led to the organization of a parallel Mennonite berry handling, processing and marketing agency, the Yarrow Growers' Co-operative. Reasonably amicable relations were established between the Yarrow Growers' Co-operative and the Pacific Union Co-operative as both sought new markets. In 1938 that search ended in the signing of major contracts with British importers who were looking for berries suitable for the manufacture of jam. The Yarrow raspberries, packed in barrels in Sodium dioxide, were particularly well suited for that purpose, and the British contracts became the most important and profitable market for the Yarrow growers, particularly after the Japanese berry farmers were evacuated to the interior in 1942.

The Yarrow Growers' Co-operative extended its operations into a wide range of loosely related producer and consumer services. Its most important function was to process and market the locally grown berries at the best market price possible. When federal price controls set unacceptably low price ceilings for berries, the Yarrow Growers' Co-operative joined with other likeminded organizations to lobby and participate in public demonstrations demanding federal production subsidies. The forcible evacuation of the Japanese berry growers in 1942 left the field wide open for the Mennonite berry growers. The Yarrow

Growers' Co-operative rapidly expanded until it marketed nearly 70 percent of the berries grown in the lower Fraser Valley.

The success of the Yarrow Growers' Co-operative in the mid-1940s was due to its complete economic and political integration into the wartime economy of Canada. Old separatist notions of "brotherhood economics" were abandoned although there were still occasional polite references to those ideals. The Yarrow Growers' Co-operative prospered as a secular organization with essentially selfish economic objectives. As long as economic survival was the overriding concern, organizations like the Yarrow Growers' Co-operative, which provided growers with a better return for their produce, received strong support. But the Yarrow Growers' Co-operative came to a bad end in 1948. That year the Canadian government refused to provide additional export credits to British importers of berries for the manufacture of jam. Loss of the British market, and the failure or inability to make alternative marketing arrangements, led to the collapse of the Yarrow cooperative. It had rendered a necessary service during the war and immediately after, but it was too small and weak to cope with international market problems in the post-war era. After its collapse the local growers organized smaller and less ambitious marketing cooperatives linked to more powerful, influential, and obviously non-Mennonite processing and marketing companies and agencies.[31]

Agricultural producer cooperatives such as the Yarrow Growers' Co-operative were never separatist economic organizations. Instead they served as a transitional device facilitating the complete economic integration of Mennonites into the mainstream of Canadian economic life.

The situation was similar in the Mennonite community at Coaldale which, according to CPR officials, "was unique in that it was more completely planned in advance of settlement than any of the other Mennonite communitities with which he [T. O. F. Herzer of the Canadian Pacific Railway] was associated."[32] One of the important Mennonite-dominated farm producer cooperatives established at Coaldale was a cheese factory that processed and sold cheese and other dairy products.[33] Southern Alberta had few established cheese factories before the 1920s, and Mennonite organized cheese factories in the 1930s and 1940s were able to control local cheese markets,[34] much as the Northern Alberta Dairy Pool did further north. The success of the Coaldale Co-operative

Cheese Factory during the war years was due largely to the milk and cheese contracts signed with the administrators of the large prisoner of war camps at Lethbridge and Medicine Hat, each of which held ten thousand prisoners.[35] In addition, the Coaldale cheese factory supplied local and district markets. It also served as the center around which a host of other economic, social and cultural activities developed. An egg grading station, lumber, oil and gas retail outlets, a credit union, a German lending library, a government-sponsored cold storage plant,[36] the offices for various mutual aid organizations designed to help people in ill health or who had suffered hail, storm or fire losses, and eventually a local milk delivery system, all came to be concentrated on the grounds of the cheese factory. But in its primary functions the Coaldale Mennonite Co-operative Cheese Factory and the other Mennonite cheese factories in southern Alberta were economically and politically integrated and operated according to the laws of the markets.

In both Yarrow and Coaldale, as well as in many other Canadian Mennonite communities, there were not only Mennonite organized cooperatives, but also other more broadly based cooperative schemes. The Canadian Pacific Railway took the initiative in developing both the large irrigation system and in building a sugar refinery to process sugar beets that were to be grown on the irrigated land in southern Alberta. The main motives of the railway company in establishing and promoting these ancillary enterprises was to sell its lands and to generate more traffic. The company therefore organized a cooperative system that allowed the local irrigation and sugar beet farmers to participate with appointed railway officials in these ancillary ventures. The long term objective was to convert these ventures into locally owned, administered and self-sustaining cooperative operations. The Mennonites were offered eighty-acre irrigation farms, complete with basic buildings and equipment. No down payment was required, but the new farmer had to agree to plant and deliver to the credit of the CPR the produce of ten acres of sugar beets, thus repaying the $80 per acre purchase price of the land on terms directly linked to the productive capacity of the land. The CPR and the settlers it established on its irrigation lands formed a unique economic partnership. Here was an effective model of cooperation far removed from traditional separatist Mennonite mutual aid models. The CPR and Mennonite colonists were yoked together to achieve mutually beneficial but very different economic objectives.

More typical were the various broadly based cooperative agricultural products marketing schemes. The milk producers of the lower Fraser Valley had established an effective milk pool. This pool was similar to the wheat pools on the prairies, and to many other agricultural commodity supply management, marketing and pooling schemes, promoted by ubiquitous California lawyer, farm and labor activist, Aron Sapiro. Mennonite dairy farmers cooperated and participated in the supply managed milk pool of the Fraser Valley Milk Producers Association, particularly after the removal of Japanese dairy farmers opened up lucrative quotas for the Mennonite farmers. Poultry farmers in British Columbia joined a similar program. All these agricultural commodity marketing cooperatives were entirely secular and fully integrated into the local economic, social and political environment although Aron Sapiro, a California Jew, sometimes sounded very much like some prairie proponents of a social gospel.

In the post-war years almost all of the smaller agricultural cooperatives found direct competition with large vertically and horizontally integrated corporations difficult. A number sold out to the larger operators, some of which were privately owned, while others, notably the prairie wheat pools and the huge cooperative dairies, retained a cooperative structure but operated in the marketplace like other large companies. In other cases the smaller cooperatives sought refuge under the protective umbrella of the Federated Co-operatives Ltd., or sold out to one of the larger integrated agricultural corporations. The old, single commodity agricultural cooperative organizations in which Canadian Mennonites had participated with great enthusiasm and in which they had achieved some phenomenal economic success, were generally too small or too narrowly specialized to meet the needs of the increasingly integrated corporate world of the 1950s.

In most Canadian Mennonite communities the cooperatives existed side by side with privately owned business ventures. Vertical or horizontal integration became an important survival and growth strategy for many large and rapidly growing corporations. Mennonite Brethren readily did business with—and sometimes became partners in or promoters of—such corporations. The laws of the market, not some concept of "brotherhood economics," dictated the policies and strategies of these integrated corporations. Mennonite Brethren conference proceedings offered no guidance on how members might reconcile the laws of the market with notions of brotherhood economics. They did not even suggest that there might have been some inconsistency between the two. Economic morality did not receive the same kind of attention as sexual morality from Mennonite Brethren leaders.

CONCLUSION

Private ownership of farms and small rural and agricultural service businesses, Mennonite mutual aid (charity) organizations, secular cooperatives, and large privately owned and managed entrepreneurial undertakings were all important economic institutions in Mennonite Brethren communities at mid-century. But the relative importance and the way in which each functioned changed rapidly in the two decades of the mid-century. Farming became increasingly mechanized and capital intensive, and therefore required better business skills. Meanwhile, the increased importance of capital in privately owned Mennonite businesses widened the gaps between those controlling that capital and the workers they employed. Charitable and mutual aid organizations became more dependent on government welfare policies and subsidies. The Mennonite dominated agricultural cooperative ventures provided vital economic services during the difficult depression and war years. However, they either had to expand, diversify their operations, or merge with much larger enterprises to meet the major economic problems of a post-war era dominated increasingly by larger horizontally and vertically integrated corporations.

The net result of these changes was that the old separatist and isolationist economic institutions gave way to new integrated ways of dealing with economic problems. Mennonite Brethren offered little resistance, and their intellectual and church leaders paid little attention to this rapid integration into the economic systems of the world. Missions, evangelism, and advanced education, not economic organizations or ideologies, dominated conference and congregational deliberations.

At mid-century Mennonite Brethren still spoke, wrote, preached and worried a great deal about worldliness. They ceased, however, to define it in economic terms, unless discretionary funds that could and should be used to support missions, the college, and other congregational and conference projects, were wasted on "worldly" pleasures and amusements. How members bought and sold what they produced or needed was their affair, but there were stern conference prohibitions against the purchase of television sets and other undesireable influences of the outside world. Stated bluntly, Mennonite Brethren in Canada at mid-century defined worldliness in social and cultural, but not in economic terms.

Mennonite Brethren Economic Developments in the United States

Calvin Redekop

The decade of the 1940s has been described as a turning point in the history of the United States. The American frontier had disappeared, and the influence of agriculture, employing less than half the population as early as 1880, was decreasing rapidly. By 1940, 17.4 percent were in the agricultural labor force while by 1960 only 6 percent remained.[1] The dominance of the small village as the commercial center was undergoing massive reduction as thousands of rural villages/towns simply disappeared. Agriculture clearly was in a transition from the basic rural institution with dramatic decreases in rural employment creating the needs for occupational opportunity elsewhere. The agricultural culture had become a part of "industrial America."[2]

The great depression, signaled by the stock market crash of 1929, was the second major event of historical proportions influencing the 1940s and 1950s. The resulting massive unemployment, exacerbated by drought and dust storms that afflicted much of the Midwest from Texas to Saskatchewan, affected farmers especially. Many farm families were uprooted and shunted to other parts of the nation to find means for subsistence.

Near poverty conditions affected almost every segment of the American population during the depression. Unemployment, only 4.2 percent in 1928, jumped to 23.6 percent four years later in 1932, then deceased to 14.6 percent by 1940, and was only 5.5 percent in 1960. In 1935, the average income per person was $474. In 1945, just ten years later, it had almost tripled to $1223. By 1960 it had risen to $2,219.

A third and equally important event in the decade of the 1940s was World War II. The war provided employment and increased wages in a rapidly growing industrial economy. It also opened new employment opportunities for women. The percentage of women in the labor force rose from 22 percent in 1930 to 32.5 percent in 1960, a 45 percent increase in thirty years. The war also expanded greatly the need for industrial and farm production, putting great stress on mechanization and technical advancement.

By 1960 the situation had changed dramatically. The economic stimulus resulting first from the "New Deal," the war and the postwar recovery reached its apex during the 1960s. Productivity was at its peak, evidenced by a U.S. public debt that was lower in 1960 ($1,572 per capita) than any year since 1943, but that by 1965 had begun a meteoric rise continuing until today ($10,534 per capita in 1988). Another significant cause and effect was the rise in population during the two decades. In 1940 there were 131.5 million people in the United States. By 1960 there were 179.3 million people—an increase of almost forty million in twenty years.

MENNONITE ECONOMIC LIFE IN THE LARGER CONTEXT

The predominantly rural Mennonites had been in this country barely two generations, and were still in the "homesteading" and settlement mode long after the indigenous population was beginning to move to urban areas. Mennonites were establishing church communities in remnants of the frontier and opening up new agricultural areas well into the 1940s.[3]

This constant movement that characterized many midwestern Mennonite families was substantial, as shown in Table 1. Abraham H. Unruh's brief descriptions of various Mennonite Brethren congregations and settlements provide a fascinating insight into the process of moving westward and "settling down" in the new frontier.[4]

The congregational statistics prior to 1960 indicate the relative rural-urban concentrations and residences of MB populations, and the relative strength of more urban congregations toward the end of the 1940-1960 period. The table also shows the general socio-economic and occupational status through the farming and business (e.g., retail shops, garages, implement sales) via the "Dominant Economic Rank" column that indicates the rank.

Table 1

U.S. Mennonite Brethren congregations surviving in 1960[5]

Congregation/ Location	Date founded	Type of community	Dominant economic rank[6]
Ebenfeld: Hillsboro, Kans.	1874	Rural	Farm
Henderson, Nebr.	1876	Rural	Farm/Bus
Carson: Delft, Minn.	1877	Rural	Farm
Mountain Lake, Minn.	1877	Town	Farm/Bus

Congregation/ Location	Date founded	Type of community	Dominant economic rank[6]
Buhler, Kans.	1879	Rural	Farm
Hillsboro, Kans.	1881	Town	Farm/Bus
Silver Lake: Marion, S.Dak.	1889	Rural	Farm
Okeene, Okla.	1889	Rural	Farm
Joes, Colo.	1892	Rural	Farm
Steinreich, Kans.	1893	Rural	Farm
Corn, Okla.	1893	Town	Farm/Bus
Fairview, Okla.	1893	Rural	Farm
Enid, Okla.	1893	Rural	Farm
Post Oak: Indiahoma, Okla.	1894	Rural	Mission
North Enid: Enid, Okla.	1897	Rural	Farm/Bus
Munich, N.Dak.	1897	Rural	Farm
Harvey, N.Dak.	1898	Rural	Farm
McClusky, N.Dak.	1902	Rural/Town	Farm/Bus
Hooker, Okla.	1904	Rural	Farm
Reedley, Calif.	1904	Town	Farm/Bus
Johns Lake, N.Dak.	1904	Rural	Farm
Bessie, Okla.	1905	Rural	Farm
Dallas, Oreg.	1905	Town	Farm/Bus
Adams, Okla.	1905	Rural	Farm
Balko, Okla.	1906	Rural	Farm
Minneapolis, Minn.	1907	City	Business
Lodi, Calif.	1908	Town	Business
Sawyer, N.Dak.	1909	Rural	Farm
Rosedale: Bakersfield, Calif.	1910	Rural/Town	Farm
Bakersfield, Calif.	1910	Town	Bus/Farm
Dorrance, Kans.	1912	Rural	Farm
Inola, Okla.	1912	Rural	Farm
Madera, Calif.	1913	Rural/Town	Farm/Bus
Collinsville, Okla.	1913	Town	Farm
Tampa, Kans.	1915	Rural	Farm
Chicago, Ill.	1915	City	Mission
Lustre, Mont.	1917	Rural	Farm
Shafter, Calif.	1918	Town	Farm/Bus
Grant, Nebr.	1919	Rural	Farm
Ingalls, Kans.	1922	Rural	Farm
Livingston/Winton, Calif.	1922	Rural/Town	Farm/Bus
Orland, Calif.	1923	Rural	Farm
Cimmaron, Kans.	1924	Town	Farm/Bus
Dinuba, Calif.	1925	Town	Farm/Bus
City Terrace: Los Angeles, Calif.	1926	City	Bus
Ulysses, Kans.	1928	Town	Farm/Bus
Larslan, Mont.	1929	Rural	Farm
Birch Bay, Wash.	1937	Rural	Farm

Congregation/ Location	Date founded	Type of community	Dominant economic rank[6]
Lawton, Okla.	1937	Rural	Farm labor
Los Ebanos, Tex.	1938	Town	Business
Salem, Oreg.	1940	City	Business
San Jose, Calif.	1942	City	Business
Bethany: Fresno, Calif.	1942	City	Business
Wichita, Kans.	1943	City	Business
Grulla, Tex.	1948	Rural	Farm
Pine Ridge, S.Dak.	1948	Rural	Mission
Sunset Gardens: Fresno, Calif.	1952	City	Business
West Park: Fresno, Calif.	1952	City	Business
Lakota, S.Dak.	1953	Rural	Mission
Martin Box, Ark.	1953	Town	Bus/Farm
Siloam Springs, Ark.	1953	Town	Business
Weatherford, Okla.	1953	Town	Farm/Bus
Open Bible: Wichita, Kans.	1954	City	Business
Harvey City: Harvey, N.Dak.	1954	Town	Farm
Minot, N.Dak.	1955	Town	Farm/Bus
Wolf Point, Mont.	1955	Town	Farm/Bus
Denver, Colo.	1955	City	Business
Butler Avenue: Fresno, Calif.	1957	City	Business
Tulsa, Okla.	1957	City	Business
Arleta, Calif.	1957	City	Business
Wasco, Calif.	1958	Town	Bus/Farm
Seattle, Wash.	1958	City	Business
Santa Clara, Calif.	1958	City	Business
Newton, Kans.	1958	Town	Business
Lincoln, Nebr.	1959	City	Business
Garden City, Kans.	1959	Rural	Farm/Bus

The congregations formed as the result of westward migrations or mission work, but that no longer existed in 1960 are described in Table 2. Close study of the time of formation and locations of the congregations and their termination provides considerable information on the rapid changes and turmoil involved in new settlements on the frontier and the search for new economic opportunities that played a very large part in the life of the congregations.

Table 2
Congregations Created and Disbanded by 1960[7]

Location	Date founded	Date closed
Woodson, Kans.	1876	1892
Springfield, Kans.	1877	1960
Parker, S.Dak..	1877	1912
Sutton, Nebr.	1878	1928
Hastings, Nebr.	1878	1929
Culbertson, Nebr.	1879	1955
Goessel, Kans.	1880	1926
Medford, Okla.	1889	1909
Jansen, Nebr.	1890	1946
Portland, Oreg.	1891	1937
North Dallas, Oreg.	1891	1896
Marion, Kans.	1894	1899
Wittenberg, N.Dak.	1894?	1899
Westfield, Tex.	1897	1899
Boone County, Nebr.	1897	?
Medford, Okla.	1899	1909
Gotebo, Okla.	1902	1942
Hitchcock, Okla.	1902	1919
Lahoma, Okla.	1902	1919
Pueblo, Colo.	1902	1914
Eldorado, Nebr.	1903	1950
Loveland, Colo.	1905	1948
Caddo, Okla.	1905	1919
Westheim, N.Dak.	1905	1923
Durham, Kans.	1906	1934
Nolan, Mich.	1907	1919
Escondido, Calif.	1908	1924
Velva, N.Dak.	1909	1936
Carpenter, S.Dak.	1910	1912
Henrietta, Tex.	1910	1915
Goodrich, N.Dak.	1910	1931
Menno, S.Dak.	1910	1912
Tampa, Kans.	1912	1959
Herrington, Kans.	1912	1925
Wasco, Calif.	1912	1916
Dogdon, N.Dak.	1912	1928
Inola, Okla.	1912	1955
Vinita, Okla.	1913	1919
Donald, Oreg.	1913	1915
Gladwin, Mich.	1914	1947
Littlefield, Tex.	1915	1923
Inman, Kans.	1916	1926
Stark, N.Dak.	1916	1936

Location	Date founded	Date closed
Chinook, Mont.	1916	1923
Norheim, Mont.	1917	1936
Hoffnungsfeld, N.Dak.	1917	1923
Volt, Mont.	1917	1948
Kingwood, Okla.	1918	1928
Lake Charles, La.	1920	1923
Cleveland, N.Dak.	1921	1925
Colby, Kans.	1922	1943
Detroit, Mich.	1923	1933
Tuttle, N.Dak.	1924	1936
Los Angeles, Calif.	1924	1957
Keenesburg, Colo.	1927	1934
Mildred, Minn.	1929	1949
Coldwater, Tex.	1929	1943
Ponemha, Minn.	1941	1948
Elk City, Kans.	1943	1944
Victor, Calif.	1949	1958

The casualty rate is startling. Of a total of 168 congregations begun between 1874 and 1960, ninety-four survived, a 56 percent survival rate, (conversely a 44 percent death rate). Further, the effects of migrations, basically westward, depleting the original states (Kansas, Oklahoma, North Dakota, Nebraska) appear clearly in the table. Kansas led with the termination of fifteen congregations, followed by Oklahoma with eleven, while North Dakota lost ten, followed by Nebraska with seven, Texas with five, and South Dakota with four congregations closed. Mennonite Brethren during this era witnessed a massive amount of family and community mobility westward that continued for several decades. Table 3 shows the geographical distribution, as of 1953.

Table 3
Mennonite Brethren population by state, 1953[8]

Central States		Western States	
Kansas	1764	California	3644
Nebraska	278	Oregon	340
Minnesota	420	Washington	218
North/South Dakota	363	Montana	130
Colorado	72		
Texas	42		
Total	5041	Total	4154
Grand Total:			9195

A tabulation of the populations of the three U.S. districts across the time span under study in Table 4 provides us with further information.

Table 4
Conference Population, 1935-1962[9]

Year	Central Dist.	Southern Dist.	Pacific Dist.	Total
1935	1,524	3,950	1,909	7,383
1938	1,497	3,743	2,473	7,393
1941	1,433	4,154	2,988	8,575
1944	1,431	4,237	3,379	9,047
1947	1,417	4,337	3,839	9,590
1950	1,464	4,345	4,138	9,947
1953	1,493	4,534	4,470	10,497
1956	1,546	4,761	4,753	11,060
1959	1,559	4,740	5,283	11,582
1962	2,235	4,980	5,916	13,221
Total gain	52%	26%	209%	79%
Yearly average	1.9%	.97%	7.7%	2.9%[10]

Table 4 shows the relative shift of population to the West Coast, and provides information on the relative loss or gain by emigration from one conference and region to the others. Using the total average percentage of growth as the norm, and assuming that the conferences did not differ significantly in their evangelistic efforts and birth and death rates, the Central District contributed 27 percent of its "theoretical estimated" growth to the Pacific District, while the Southern District contributed 43 percent of its "theoretical estimated" growth to the Pacific District.

The westward migration of Mennonite Brethren slowed by 1950. The occupational categorization of congregations in Table 1 suggests further that the establishment of the family farm in new lands had largely ended, and that the base of economic livelihood henceforth would be directed toward business or agri-business. This process was already beginning to take place by 1920 in several larger early MB settlements, especially Mountain Lake, Minnesota; Hillsboro, Kansas; Dallas, Oregon; Corn and Enid, Oklahoma; and Reedley and Bakersfield, California. The same seems true for the occupational and professional distributions, although the evidence is very sparse.

THE 1940-1960 PERIOD AND ECONOMIC ACTIVITY

Since there is little information available regarding the more specific economic activities of Mennonite communities during the 1940-1960 period,[11] it is relevant to analyze the subject from a community and congregational perspective, in order to place available statistics into context. Unfortunately, few community studies are available.[12] Two case studies of MB communities, both of which were among the first to be settled in North America, do offer at least some preliminary perspectives.

Mountain Lake, Minnesota

The town of Mountain Lake was platted in May 1872 and incorporated in 1886; Mennonites began arriving in 1873. The resident population grew rapidly, but began to level off in the 1940s as Table 5 reveals.

Table 5
Mountain Lake, Hillsboro and Reedley Population Statistics[13]

Year	Mt. Lake	Hillsboro	Mt. Lake MB	Hillsboro MB	Reedley MB
1895	595	750	100	20	—
1900	959	750	175	75	—
1910	1,081	745	225	140	—
1920	1,309	1,660	338	540	636
1930	1,388	1,650	340	560	500
1940	1,740	1,750	—	700	931
1950	1,733	1,980	287	825	1,340
1960	1,933	2,200	268	780	1,340
1970	1,965	2,800	223	845	1,347
1980	2,277	1,950	198	780	1,339

Three groups of Mennonite Brethren settled in the Mountain Lake area, all some distance from the emerging town itself. One was situated some miles between Mountain Lake and Bingham Lake (1877); another was located some miles south and west of town (1887), and the third group (Carson) settled near Delft. The "South Church" moved to the south edge of Mountain Lake in 1901, though most of the members remained on farms south of town.[14]

The available evidence of the non-farming business sector suggests that General Conference Mennonites managed and owned most of the businesses since a higher proportion of them lived in or near the town. However, by 1930, some Mennonite Brethren had moved to town and become active in business activities. By 1940, many small service centers within a fifteen-mile radius of Mountain Lake had for all practical purposes died, or become residential centers for farm laborers.

Table 6 provides the list of businesses and their proprietors in Mt. Lake, for two periods.

Table 6
Mountain Lake Business Proprietorships[15]

Type of business	Total[16] 1936	Total 1962	GC 1936	GC 1962	MB 1936	MB 1962
Auto dealers/garages	6	2	5	2	1	0
Bakers/Barbers	3	3	0	0	0	0
Bankers/Insurance/Real estate	6	8	5	6	1	0
Blacksmiths/Welding/Body shops	4	5	1	3	1	1
Builders/Contractors/ Carpenters/Finishers	10	11	7	6	2	2
Dentists/Medical doctors/ morticians/druggists	11	9	9	5	0	1
Dray/trucking/well drilling	3	4	2	4	0	0
Electricians	1	2	1	1	0	1
Feed/seed/mills/greenhouses	3	3	1	0	2	0
Harness/shoe repair	1	1	2	0	0	1
Hotels	1	0	1	0	0	0
Implement dealers/lumber yards	4	6	3	2	1	1
Jewelers	2	1	1	0	1	1
Lawyers	1	1	1	0	1	0
Manufacturing/sheet metal	1	3	1	0	0	1
Oil/gas delivery/service stations	5	7	4	4	0	0
Photographers	1	1	1	0	0	0
Plumbers	1	1	2	0	0	0
Publishers	1	1	0	1	0	0
Restaurant proprietors	4	6	1	0	0	0
Stores: hardware/grocery/ clothing/furniture/general	19	12	15	8	0	0
Theater	1	0	1	1	0	0
Totals	89	87	64	43	10	9

The proportion of Mennonite (GC and MB)/non-Mennonite businesses decreased between 1936 and 1962.[17] The MB gained slightly over the GC during the twenty-six-year period.

Three cooperatives were operating in Mountain Lake in 1936: a grain elevator (1901), a creamery (1895), and an oil/gas cooperative (1933).[18] By 1960, only the oil/gas cooperative remained. The initiative for the cooperative movement came mostly from several General Conference Mennonite leaders; the MB involvement seems to have been more passive. Mutual aid societies had also been initiated, including the "Mennonite Aid Society," a burial aid society, and the "Canada and States Mutual Insurance" company. [19]

Hillsboro, Kansas

Hillsboro was first organized in 1871, and by 1874 thirty-five Russian Mennonite families settled there. There were several groups of Mennonite Brethren among the immigrants. One group settled at Ebenfeld, south of Hillsboro, another at Lehigh in 1884, and yet another group near Johannestal, before moving to Hillsboro in 1881.

Many Mennonite Brethren settled in the surrounding area and also in Hillsboro and thus created a "critical mass" that increased the relative strength of the MB presence. Mountain Lake had a slightly larger population for a time, but the emergence of the Mennonite Brethren Publishing House, the establishment of Tabor College in 1908, and the location of the Foreign Mission Board headquarters there resulted in Hillsboro becoming the leading midwestern MB center. There was thus considerable migration of Mennonite Brethren to and from Hillsboro, especially to the West, during much of Hillsboro's history (See table 6). The Mennonite Brethren population proportion of the Hillsboro community, as Mountain Lake, can be inferred from Table 6.[20]

Since the percentage of membership change within the Hillsboro congregation is around the average population growth of the general population at the time, there must have been massive out-migration to other areas, since there was a continuing influx of migrants from Russia until the 1920s. With two General Conference congregations in the town along with the MB congregation, and with the Ebenfeld congregation several miles to the south, it must be concluded that Hillsboro was a "Mennonite town."

The developing economic and business activities must have been strongly influenced by the Mennonite Brethren, as the following table suggests. Of course their interaction with other Mennonites groups and non-Mennonites must have influenced them in turn.[21]

Table 7
Hillsboro Business Proprietorships[22]

Type of business	Total[23] 1945	Total 1960	GC 1945	GC 1960	MB 1945	MB 1960
Auto dealers/parts/repairs	6	10	2	6	1	4
Barbers	0	2	0	0	0	1
Bankers/insurance/finance	5	7	1	2	3	0
Beauty parlors	0	3	0	1	0	1
Body shops	0	1	0	0	0	1
Broom makers	1	0	1	0	0	0
Cafe/restaurant proprietors	0	4	0	2	0	0
Carpenters/builders	0	9	0	2	0	4
Dry cleaners	0	2	0	2	0	0
Electricians	0	3	0	0	1	2
Farm equipment	0	2	0	0	0	1
Flour milling	1	0	0	0	0	0
Grain dealers	1	1	0	0	0	0
Hatcheries	1	1	0	0	1	0
Home furnishings	1	1	0	0	0	0
Hotels/motels	1	1	1	0	0	0
Implements	0	2	0	0	0	0
Jewelers	1	2	1	0	0	1
Laundry	0	1	0	0	0	0
Lockers	0	1	0	0	0	1
Lumber/building materials	1	4	0	0	0	2
Machine shops	2	0	0	0	1	0
Co-ops: oil/creamery/grain/ electrical/credit unions	2	5	1	0	0	3
Dairies	1	3	0	0	1	2
Manufacturing	1	2	0	0	0	2
Meat markets	2	0	1	0	1	0
Doctors/dentists/other medical	9	11	1	1	7	5
Painters	0	2	0	0	0	1
Plumbers	0	3	0	0	0	2
Photographers	0	1	0	0	0	0
Produce brokers	1	0	0	0	1	0
Appliance repair	0	4	0	0	1	3
Oil/gas/service stations	3	8	1	2	2	4
Stores: hardware/variety/grocery/ general/book/floral	10	18	1	3	5	2
Shoe repair	1	1	0	0	0	0
Trucking	0	2	0	0	1	1
Welding	1	3	0	0	1	2
Veterinary	0	1	0	0	0	0
Total	52	122[24]	11	21	26	45

The number of establishments increased between the two periods with certain types of businesses ceasing while others have emerged.[25] One of the most interesting observations about these Mennonite communities is that many more substantive economic industries such as processing and sales of dairy, and grain products; and services, such as oil and gasoline began as cooperatives. As in Mountain Lake, the number of cooperatives in Hillsboro is impressive. A cooperative grain elevator was formed in 1918, a cooperative creamery in 1935, and a cooperative oil association in 1939.[26]

There must have been a strong undercurrent of cooperative philosophy in both communities. It is quite probable that General Conference Mennonites largely motivated cooperative activities in Mountain Lake because of the larger GC presence in the town. Wiebe suggests that the Mennonite Brethren leadership and participation were about equal with the General Conference in Hillsboro.

Reedley, California

A description of the Reedley, California community, which would provide a useful comparison with Mountain Lake and Hillsboro, was not possible. However, the occupational distribution of the Mennonite Brethren may be useful.

Table 8
MB Occupational Distribution, Reedley, California[27]

Business	1940	1960
Auto sales/wrecking/body shop/mechanics	4	18
Banking/insurance	3	4
Barbers	1	2
Blacksmiths	1	0
Beauty shops	1	0
Builders/carpenters	3	19
Doctors/chiropractors/dentists	0	3
Clerks	1	12
Cooks/housekeepers	0	2
Electricians	1	1
Farmers/ranchers	4	11
Laborers	3	13

Business	1940	1960
Laboratory technicians	9	4
Managers	0	4
Maintenance/janitorial	2	6
Meat markets	1	1
Nursing	1	3
Painters	3	2
Real estate	1	0
Repair/service	1	4
Retired	6	140
Sales	50	0
Service stations	1	1
Teachers	4	13
Trucking	1	1
Welding	0	2

Based on the Mountain Lake, Hillsboro and Reedley material presented above, it seems that by 1940, these communities had become increasingly involved in non-farming business, though depending on the support of agriculture. These enterprises began slowly before the turn of the century, but had been well established by the beginning of World War II. Foremost among these were flour milling,[28] dairy and creamery services, grain buying and selling, retailing of motor oils, heating oils, farm machinery sales, auto sales, lumber sales, sales of domestic supplies such as clothing and groceries, and a variety of services such as auto repairing, well drilling, plumbing and heating, shoe repair, cafes, and beauty shops (the latter clearly not traditionally Mennonite businesses).[29]

Although *Who's Who Among Mennonites*[30] does not statistically represent the entire population, some indications of the cumulative occupational/professional structure (at least for men) that existed in 1943 can be gained from Table 9.

Table 9
Occupations/Profession Distribution in *Who's Who Among the Mennonites*

Occupations	Total Mennonite	GC	MB
Accountants/bookkeepers	2	2	0
Artists	2	2	0
Barristers	4	3	0
Bankers	11	9	2

Occupation	Total Mennonite	General Conf.	Menn. Brethren
Chiropractors	3	3	0
Dentists	3	0	3
Farmers	6	6	0
Funeral directors	1	0	1
Grain buyers	1	1	0
Hatcheries	1	0	1
Ind. admin.	1	1	0
Insurance	5	4	1
Loan companies	1	1	0
Medicine	51	35	16
Millers	3	3	0
Manufacturing	2	1	1
Newspaper publishing	1	1	0
Academics	54	32	22
Totals	152	104	47

The astounding number of persons pursuing the medicine and academic categories provides some very interesting material for analysis.[31] Assuming the research methods did not favor the General Conference, it seems that the Mennonite Brethren are quite similar to their cousins except in the academic field.[32] Assuming conditions had not changed too drastically or rapidly from the 1940s, extrapolation backward from figures produced in 1975 may give us additional information of what the situation might have been like fifteen years earlier (See Table 10).

Table 10
Mennonite Occupational Distributions

Occupation	Warner[33]	Kauffman/ Harder 1975[34]	Kauffman/ Driedger[35] US MB 1989	Kauffman/ Driedger 1989[36]	Reedley 1945[37]	Reedley 1960
Professional and technical	12.10%	15.90%	17.8%	28.00%	15.00%	10.50%
Business owners and managers	7.40%	1.10%	5.5%	9.00%	8.00%	6.50%
Sales and clerical	8.10%	6.80%	7.2%	11.00%	7.00%	3.00%
Craftsmen and foremen	12.10%	4.90%	5.5%	5.00%	7.00%	12.00%
Machine operators	6.00%	4.80%	3.6%	4.00%	1.00%	0.00%
Laborers (farm and nonfarm)	12.80%	2.50%	1.7%	1.00%	2.00%	4.50%
Farm owners and managers	0.00%	10.90%	10.3%	7.00%	4.00%	1.00%

Occupation	Warner[33]	Kauffman/ Harder 1975[34]	Driedger[35] US MB 1989	Kauffman/ Kauffman/ Driedger 1989[36]	Reedley 1945[37]	Reedley 1960
Service workers	8.10%	3.00%	3.3%	4.00%	5.00%	7.00%
Housewives	0.00%	32.50%	29.7%	25.00%	0.00%	0.00%
Students	3.40%	13.80%	15.2%	6.00%	0.00%	0.00%
Retired	29.50%	0.00%	0.00%	0.00%	52.00%	52.00%
Miscellaneous	3.40%	0.00%	0.00%	0.00%	0.00%	0.00%

This table suggests that Mennonite Brethren in 1973 and 1989 were very similar to other Mennonite groups on occupational distributions. Without accurate statistics on church membership in all groups in either community, it is difficult to conclude definitively how the Mennonite Brethren compared on their economic, occupational and professional participation, with other Mennonite and non-Mennonites during the period 1940-1960.[38]

A comparison with other Mennonite groups on wealth and income would be most helpful, but little is available for this period. The Kauffman/Harder research of study of 1973 suggests that the MB income is less than the Mennonite Church (MC), while the Kauffman-Driedger research for 1989 shows that the Mennonite Brethren had the highest median income (39).

One other set of statistics on wealth, generated by Mennonite Central Committee, may be of some relevance. The following table reports on several categories of contributions.

Table 11
Comparative MCC Contributions[39]

Conference	Relief 1941-1950	Mennonite Aid 1945-1950	Membership 1950	Per capita contributions
Mennonite Church	$888,106	$313,362	$56,746[40]	$21.17
General Conference	$891,763	$252,311	$44,614	$25.64
Mennonite Brethren	$356,901	$169,424	$19,947	$26.38

According to this information, Mennonite Brethren per-capita giving was $26.38, as compared to $25.64 for the GCs, and $21.17 for the MCs. The conventional wisdom has been that Mennonite Brethren were not as committed to MCC material assistance as the other groups. Comparing the contributions to population, it is reasonable to suggest that Mennonite Brethren were as successful economically and as generous as the other groups.

ANALYSIS

The MB experience parallels very closely that of the other Russian Mennonite groups so that differentiating between groups is difficult. Even with less than adequate data, however, it is possible to make some observations or postulates that invite further analysis and study. The communities we have highlighted and other information do provide some "benchmarks" for theorizing about Mennonite Brethren economic life in the two-decade period.

External factors influencing Mennonite economic activity, 1940-1960.

1. The end of available new lands through the termination of the frontier and increasing population growth by 1940 created increased competition for agricultural land.

2. World War II exercised several demands, including military manpower and labor for war production, increasing the value of education and industrial employment in the larger towns and cities.

3. Economic opportunites in the west, especially in California, attracted many people and resulted in substantial migrations and mobility to the West Coast.

4. The increasing consolidation of family farms into larger agri-business began directing the excess populations toward larger towns, causing the smaller service villages to disappear or become bedroom communities.

5. The increasing opportunities and status offered through education became attractive to young people from the community.

Consequences for Mennonite communities.

1. Many young people forsook the family/farm matrix and moved into the professions and occupations, especially the service professions, to rationalize their leaving the "local orientation" for the "cosmopolitan".[41]

2. Many others left the farm to become laborers, service workers, and proprietors/owners of small businesses especially in the larger neighboring towns, and engaged in occupational forms determined by the "opportunity structure." [42]

3. Others became owners/managers of larger farms or

businesses as they were able to expand businesses based on the resources they inherited from their more successful family farm enterprises.

4. Still others were beginning to become entrepreneurs in the home towns. A few became owners or managers of businesses and companies, in part assisted by an advanced degree, personal drive and ability or family assistance.

In sum, Mennonites participated in the massive changes taking place in the United States. They benefitted from the general economic upturn, and were "caught up" with the prevailing individualistic economy by 1960. The exchange of the rural base of the Mennonite community and the family farm for the small town as center of the commmunity fabric seems to have taken place roughly during the period 1910-1920. The process was consolidated by the 1930s, but the Depression, the war and continuing migration disrupted the developing stability of the "town culture."

The years from 1940 to 1960 seem to have been the time of entrenchment, stability, progress and increasing prosperity for Mennonite communities. The Mennonite population capitalized on the opportunities presented by the economic prosperity resulting from the recovery from the depression, the stimulus of the war and opportunities provided by agricultural and related technological developments emerging nationally.[43]

Consequences for Religious Life.

The communal ethic emphasizing mutual aid and collective obligations and responsiblities seem to have given way to individualtistic interests between 1940 and 1960. In 1940 several of the more basic and substantive economic sectors begun as cooperatives, such as processing and sales of dairy, poultry and grain products, and some services, such as sales of oil and gasoline, were still operating.[44] By 1960, however, these cooperative organizations were gone, or were in the process of dissolution, either through privatization, or by being bought up by a larger organization beyond Mennonite control. No strictly locally owned cooperative existed at the end of the period for the three communities studied.

Larger social forces undoubtedly helped cause this trend, including individualism and religous fundamentalism, both of which were increasingly making themselves felt in Mennonite communties.[45] The demise of the cooperatives may thus best signify the "transition period" from communalism to individualism of Mennonitism in America.

The two decades may have been the high point in the transition from a "local" to a "cosmopolitan" sociological ethos. Robert K. Merton defines the "local" as a person who:

> confines his interests to [his] community, [which] is largely his world. Devoting little thought or energy to the Great Society, he is preoccupied with local problems to the virtual exclusion of the national and international scene. He is, strictly speaking, parochial.[46]

The "cosmopolitan" is one who:

> has some interest in [the community] and must of course maintain a minimum of relations within the community. . . . But he is also oriented   significantly to the world outside the community, and regards himself as   an integral part of that World. He resided in [the community] but lives in the Great Society. If the local type is parochial, the cosmopolitan is ecumenical[47].

This proposition cannot be fully derived from the evidence presented in this paper, but it also received substantive credence in other research I conducted in 1985-1986. Interviews with one hundred entrepreneurs presented unequivocal evidence that those who were in business before the war and until some years after the war, were "local" in their life-style and religious commitments. The entrepreneurs who emerged after about 1960 seemed to express the "cosmopolitan" value system and individualistic stance.[48]

Mennonite Brethren differ very little from the other Mennonite groups in specific terms. It seems, however, that several subtle characteristics can be identified. First, the Mennonite Brethren have proceeded further and earlier on the "cosmopolitanization" scale than the other groups. Mennonite Brethren became "cosmopolitan" academic scholars, medical professionals, musicians, and business executives in distant industries sooner and in greater numbers than the other Russian Mennonites.

Second, Mennonite Brethren have been more "enclavic" in their religious life in relation to other Mennonite groups; that is, other things being equal Mennonite Brethren associate with each other more in local religious and community activities. This naturally also is reflected in business affiliations, and hence they cooperate less with Mennonites of other groups in business affairs. This has resulted in a certain similarity in the type of occupations and enterprises in which Mennonite Brethren engage. This illustrates the sociological principle of sentiment/interaction"— i.e., similar sentiments among persons result in increased interaction between them and vice versa. In other words, the pietistic element in the Mennonite identity has tended to encourage Mennonite Brethren to turn toward fellow members rather than to others. The migration to California, and the tendencies to settle in enclaves as well as the concentration in certain economic activites (such as real estate) bears this out.[49]

The economic developments during two significant pivotal decades (1940-1960) contribute important material for understanding the development of the Mennonite Brethren. In many ways these developments mirror those of most other Mennonites of Russian origin, and other groups on the frontier of North America. However there are some differences, which need to be derived at least in part from their special "ideology."

I propose the causes for these hypothesized differences among Mennonite Brethren can be attributed to a unique blend of Anabaptism and Pietism. Their Anabaptist/Pietist blend contributed to more aggressive harmonizing of faith and personal striving considerably different from other groups. The Mennonite Brethren thus, I propose, would tend more to reflect Weber's famous "Protestant Ethic" thesis, in which he implied a compatability between capitalism and Calvinistic Christianity.[50]

IV.
Theological
Autobiography

Waldo Hiebert

When I think about my autobiography, about my personal life and development, I confidently say that nothing could have happened except by the grace of God. Autobiographies, I trust, are a testimonial rather than a record of activities.

I left for seminary in 1940. I was teaching high school in Oregon and doing summer graduate work at the University of Oregon. My mind had gone through a series of questions and doubts regarding the Christian life, but I figured that when I went to seminary these questions would be answered. Southwestern Baptist Seminary was a large Southern Baptist seminary. It is the largest in the country now, and even then had about six hundred to eight hundred students. Three hundred of us walked into class, the teacher would show up, he would lecture and then disappear. That was the way it went through the semester and at the end we had a true and false test. There was never an opportunity to dialogue and ask questions, unless you made an appointment with the teacher. I did make an appointment with my Greek teacher. I went to him and asked what it would take to become a Southern Baptist. The conversation went something like this:

He said, "you have to be converted."

"That I am."

"You have to be baptized."

"That I am."

"You have to be immersed."

"Well, I am."

"Yes, but by whom?"

"By my uncle in Oregon."

"Well that won't do, a Southern Baptist must baptize you to be part of the church."

That was too narrow for me. It hurt me no end. During my first year of seminary I found myself experiencing the greatest temptation in my life to give up faith and the church. I was rooming with four or five other seminarians who were young preachers. When they would return from their weekend experiences they would talk about how they had "lathered" the people. I didn't get a very good impression of what this seminary business was all about. I left with considerable consternation because I had not had the opportunity to ask difficult questions, except when I turned to authors described as "liberal": E. Stanley Jones, Harry Emerson Fosdick, and George Buttrick. Buttrick's writing on prayer absolutely turned my life around, simply because he asked the difficult questions and answered my inquiring mind. Jones had a profound influence on my life during college and university years. I remember one statement in his writings when I was having doubts about the miracles of Jesus. I had a debate partner who didn't believe in the miracles of Jesus, so I began to doubt. But E. Stanley Jones made a simple statement: "make up your mind who Jesus is and miracles are no longer a question." That settled that for me.

After the first year a small Mennonite Brethren church in Jansen, Nebraska called me to come for the summer because they didn't have a pastor. So I ministered on Sundays, and during the week I worked on the farm for them. In fall I went to Central Baptist Seminary in Kansas City, Kansas. This was a seminary of about 150 students, with an excellent faculty and lots of discussion in class. There were about fifteen to twenty students in class. I was there for two years. My twin brother Lando also came to that school. He had spent two years at Dallas Seminary while I had been at Fort Worth. So we caught up with each other and attended seminary together. The experience at Central led me to an interest in Christian Education as a major. I had been a high school teacher and enjoyed teaching very much. We had a teacher at Central by the name of Eric Hayden. He was a Yale graduate, very articulate, very open and very enthusiastic about religious education in the local church. I was enamored by the subject, majored in it and later taught it at Tabor College. I am forever grateful for his influence in my life.

After graduating from Central there was no place for me to go. I had no contact with my home church. There were no bulletins sent to me, I had no letters from them. In those two years in seminary the only MB contact I had was one visit by Dr. P. C. Hiebert. He came to the campus and made a visit. I recall that as a very warm experience.

On my desk was a contract from a Baptist college in Oklahoma, inviting me to come there and teach in my field. That was the only option I had. I really didn't want to go to the Baptists, but this was the one time in my life that I became inwardly angry with the Mennonite Brethren Church. They didn't care about me. I had no contact; there was nowhere to go; there was no one that was calling me for anything. I remember working through an inner anger and wondering whether it might be a good idea to go to the Baptists or another denomination. At that point it was not much of a deal for me. I would have gone to the Baptists except that ten days before graduation I had a phone call from Dr. P. E. Schellenberg at Tabor College. He asked me if I would come teach at Tabor. It didn't take me very long to decide because it was in my field of interest, and so I accepted the call. At Tabor we had wonderful years. One thing that I much enjoyed was teaching forensics, contemporary preaching and oratory.

Also at Tabor College was a librarian by the name of Rachel Wiebe. Rachel and I had met in high school and we had communicated occasionally when I would come through Hillsboro. She had taught at Zoar Academy in Inman, Kansas for a couple of years and then had come to the library at Tabor. We soon began a friendship and had what we thought was a secret courtship going. We didn't want people to know that we were doing this. She had a car and I didn't, so I would meet her at a certain dark street in Hillsboro. She would pick me up and we would drive out of town. However, it wasn't the secret that I thought it was. During this time it was my turn to make a chapel talk. I always appreciated the library in school, which to me has been a place not only of learning and research but of vision, prayer, inner searching and growth. In my talk I said that the heart of the college is the library. There was snickering in the audience and some students laughed throughout the talk though I was deadly serious. I wasn't talking about Rachel, I didn't even think about her. I was giving this serious talk to inspire them to go to the library. So I caught one of the students after chapel and said, "what in the world was so funny?" The student replied, "well, you were talking about Rachel, weren't you?" We were married in 1944.

Soon after our marriage Mennonite Central Committee asked if we would go to South America for two or three years to help reopen the high school in the Paraguayan Chaco that had been closed for a year because of Nazi influence there. Not knowing what was ahead of us we took a two-year leave from Tabor and went to Paraguay. At that time it took a week to travel from Asunción to the Chaco: first by river boat and then by train, then a night and a day on the buggy. This was 1945. When we came there we found a mixed welcome. There were those who embraced us as brother and sister and there were those who called us "the crazy Americans." Some asked, "How could the North Americans fight war with the communists against the Germans? The communists persecuted us. The Germans helped us to get into a new country. How crazy can you Americans be?" We went to the first meeting of the colony in Filadelfia. A large picture of Adolf Hitler was still on the wall. Some people on the streets were still greeting each other with "Heil Hitler." The situation in the colony was very tense. Once a North American worker informed the Paraguayan government that the colonists were being influenced by Nazism and that they were being asked to sign a pledge to defend the Third Reich. As soon as Germany won the war against Russia they would all move out of this wilderness of the Chaco back to their homes in South Russia. At one time 80 percent of the colonists signed such a paper. So one day the military trucks rolled into the colony. Government officials ordered three of the leaders onto the truck to be transported within twenty-four hours to another place in the country. When we arrived they had already put into place a new administration of people who had not signed the document to defend the Third Reich. These administrators were generous and kind, and sympathetic toward us. We started our school.

I remember waking up one morning to the sound of marching. I was so shaken that I went to Nicolai Siemens, who was editor of the *Mennoblatt* and stood staunchly against the Nazi position. I asked him, "What are we going to do here? How long is this going to continue?" It was difficult to sort out the literature in the library or the textbooks written from the German point of view. So he said, "Be a little patient. It will take time but we trust that our colony will be reunited." The Mennonite Brethren Church had split over the issues and there was much tensions and fear.

After the first year of teaching we were asked to do some interesting things. One was to lead a vacation Bible school in each of the eighteen villages. We led vacation Bible school in the morning and did evangelistic work in the evening. I told the brethren that I didn't consider myself an evangelist. They asked me to do it anyway because there hadn't been evangelistic meetings there in years. They had been too busy talking politics. So we undertook the task and God was very gracious. There was much melting and reconciliation. Many young people were converted then because they hadn't had an invitation to come to Christ for years. If there was anyone that wanted to talk about accepting

Christ we invited them back into the school house, where we would pray with them. The second year there witnessed an entirely different attitude and situation. We worked more harmoniously. Another teacher was added to the faculty and the school was growing.

When we were about to leave B. B. Janz arrived to help reconcile the situation in our Mennonite Brethren congregation. The leaders had pressed me for some time about undertaking some reconciliation efforts. As an MCC worker I felt it really wasn't my task. When Brother Janz came we made a trip by buggy through the villages. He gave his opening message and I gave my farewell message. Also at this time MCC sent its Vice-Chairman, H.A. Fast, to help in the reconciliation process. We had serious talks with him because we had endured much criticism. He asked, "Well, how far did Jesus go? How much criticism did he take?" That took our eyes away from ourselves and gave us a new focus. It was very helpful.

We developed lasting friendships in the Chaco that are still intact. This was one of the most enriching experiences of our lives. It was also one of the most difficult ones. We often found ourselves crying through the night because of the frustration that we endured.

The next chapter in our lives was the Hillsboro Mennonite Brethren Church. These ten years rebuilt my faith in the church. I was profoundly affected and influenced by that church. Marvin Hein reminded me once about what I had said to him when he became associate pastor there. As we looked into the auditorium and saw the people there I said to him, "You may not build this church, but they will build you." That's the way it happened to me. They built my faith, they restored my confidence in the church. The experience built in me a real desire and longing for pastoral ministry.

The janitor, a secretary and I were the only ones on the staff in this church of eight hundred members. After seven years I developed stomach trouble and went to the clinic. The doctor took me into his private office. He said, "Hiebert, you've got a choice. You either quit the ministry or get yourself some help" So I went to the council and they decided to get help. We found Marvin Hein pastoring a congregational church north of Hillsboro. He had graduated from seminary two years before that. He came to serve in the church and to teach at Tabor College.

In 1959 we received a call from the Seminary to teach Christian education. Initially, this was a difficult time. Particularly disturbing was the fact that there was little openness to discuss any opposing points of view. I once brought up the peace issue in a faculty meeting and was told that it had no relevance for the discussion. There was not very much dialogue.

In 1966 we went to Reedley to pastor for six years. Then we were called back to the Seminary. Let me say two things about Reedley. First, we tried to call out ministers from the congregation. We tried our best to find people who would be open to minister to one another. It came about in a critical time, a crisis time. At three o'clock in the morning in my first year a call came—the sister told me her husband had just died and asked me to come to the house. I called Henry Janzen, our part-time assistant. The church had five hundred families, served only by one-and-a-half pastors. Henry asked who had died. When I told him, he said he didn't know them. So we went to see these people. On the way home I told Henry, "This just can't happen again. Neither you nor I nor anyone else is aware when there is a sick person in our midst. We must do something." So we took the matter to the Board of Deacons. I attended their meeting and they called on me to give a talk. They hadn't warned me about that. I told them that I didn't have a talk, but I did have a question. I asked, "What's your job? What do you do?" They were all very quiet. They were rather embarrassed and did not answer the question, except to say that they served communion and helped the pastor. One of them finally said that the pastor usually gave them a list of the widows and they divided them among themselves for visitation. So we began to devise a plan. We doubled the size of the Board of Deacons from eighteen to about thirty-three and gave them each twelve to fifteen families to shepherd, to oversee, to visit, to counsel, to comfort. We called it their parish and we developed ten simple lessons that we later put into a little booklet. Henry and I taught a class during the Sunday school hour for them. They left their regular classes and attended this class for in-service training. Each Sunday we went over their questions and tried to give them guidance and encouragement. I noticed that the calls to the pastor's office became fewer and fewer. "Lay ministry" had begun! It was exciting to see men and women do shepherding work. It was especially encouraging to watch these servants grow in their faith and caring ministry. We were also able to organize small group work, which was spearheaded by Vernon Janzen, our associate pastor. At one time we had 150 people enrolled in small groups.

In 1972 we were asked to return to the seminary. My assignment was to serve as Dean of Students and teach pastoral subjects. My experience in those roles was most rewarding. I felt that I was in the field to which God had called me. I felt fulfilled by God's mercy. During this time I was asked by the faculty to create a course in spiritual formation. I taught this course for about ten years. Out of this experience came a ministry in leading "Personal Spiritual Retreats." The area of spirituality became very dear to me and led to a kind of personal renewal. My sabbatical semester at Fuller Theological Seminary was also devoted to the study of Christian spirituality.

The years at seminary have been most enriching and rewarding. I thank God and my colleagues for giving me the opportunity to share in God's ministry in this place.

V.
Church
and
Women

"She Hath Done What She Could": The Development of the Women's Missionary Services in the Mennonite Brethren Churches of the United States

Valerie Rempel

For the booklet commemorating the fiftieth anniversary of the Shafter (Calif.) Mennonite Brethren Church, Maxine Klassen submitted the following historical account for the Ladies Sewing Circle:

> During the early years of the Shafter Mennonite Brethren Church, there was one of our devoted mothers who saw a need for the young women and girls to become involved in the work of the local church. Her desire to serve the Lord and help these young people led her into forming a sewing group which met in the homes. They embroidered many beautiful articles, made quilts, and at the end of each year, together with home baked products and candy, they held an auction sale. This mother was Mrs. Helena Petker, and her vision and foresight took hold and this became an active organization in the local church. These sales provided a means of financing both home and foreign mission work. It also gave the young ladies an insight into the needs of the mission fields and the local church. Out of this early group came four missionaries, Rubena Schultz Pietsch, Helen Koehn Neufeld, Elizabeth Wall Dick, and Sarah Balzer Field."[1]

In one succinct paragraph, Klassen gives us one of the significant linkages in the Mennonite Brethren Church: that of women to the cause of missions.

Mention of women's organized mission activity dates back to some of the earliest North American Mennonite Brethren records. Conference minutes note donations from women's missionary societies as early as 1881—three years after the first unofficial conference meeting of North American Mennonite Brethren.[2] Women, both married and single, were also a significant missionary force in the developing mission fields funded by North American Mennonite Brethren.[3]

Though women are no longer instructed to keep silent during conference deliberations, as they were in an 1879 resolution of the Mennonite Brethren General Conference, their work has received little attention. The statistical reports presented at the Mennonite Brethren district conferences in the United States do not include data about women's organizations until 1949 in the Pacific District, 1956 in the Central District, and 1966 in the Southern District—although nearly every congregation, including home mission churches, had at least one mission or sewing circle. By contrast, conference statistical reports regularly included information on the number and membership of musical groups, youth organizations, Sunday school classes, Daily Vacation Bible Schools, and extension programs.

By the turn of the century, many of the earliest North American congregations were well-established and regularly contributed to mission causes. Early mission societies often included participation by both men and women in the activities of the day—women sewed while men met for Bible study and prayer.[4] Eventually, the societies became exclusively female. These early circles afforded an opportunity for fellowship and for inspiration. Together with mission sales, they provided support of both cash and goods to the fledgling mission projects of Mennonite Brethren, both local and foreign.

As Mennonite Brethren spread across the prairies and to the West, new congregations organized and settled into church life. A survey of congregational histories written for various anniversary celebrations reveals that mission societies or sewing circles were often among the early organizations of the local church, and grew out of the members' commitment to mission.[5]

As members and groups grew older, many congregations began new, or "junior" sewing circles. Often these groups attempted to meet the changing schedules and interests of younger women. For example, ten women in Buhler, Kansas, organized the Herwanna Chapter in 1937, and asked missionary Maria Pankratz to serve as a sponsor.[6] Among their projects was the support of an indigenous preacher and several orphans in India.[7] In Shafter, California, the *Nahverein* (Sewing Society) had disbanded in 1934, but in 1939 a "Bible Class and Sewing Hour" grew out of a Sunday School class taught by Anna Rempel. Besides relief sewing, the group canned fruit for the Civilian Public Service camps, and gave aid to people in need.[8] In Corn, Oklahoma, the junior sisters organized in 1945. This group chose to focus primarily on local mission projects, leaving the older group to continue serving foreign missions.[9] Among their ministries was a children's hour conducted before the message on the first, third and fifth Sundays.[10] In Reedley, California, the Christian Charity Workers organized with nineteen members on January 21, 1937 as a "junior sewing circle . . . formed especially for working girls and young mothers unable to attend day meetings."[11]

Many circles added sewing for relief to their list of foreign and home mission projects. The devastation of World War II and the work of the Mennonite Brethren Board of General Welfare and Public Relations with Mennonite Central Committee presented both a need and ways to meet that need. Tina Dahl, who helped in the administrative work, reported to the General Conference in 1943 that twenty-nine churches had "organized relief circles to sew garments for sale or for direct donations for Home Mission stations, for Red Cross or clothing sent abroad."[12]

The financial needs of home mission and other projects continued to receive support. For example, the Home for the Aged in Reedley, Calif., which was operated by the Pacific District Conference of Mennonite Brethren Churches, received donations from missionary societies for the furnishing of additional resident rooms.[13] The minutes of the Southern District Conference also record cash donations from individual circles for various home missions projects throughout the 1940s. At least one group contributed to the colonization and rehabilitation program for men who had served in the Civilian Public Service program during World War II.[14]

Sewing circles also provided funding for local church needs. In 1948 the editors of the fiftieth anniversary booklet prepared for the Harvey, North Dakota congregation noted that "when other departments of the church are in need of finances [they call] on this society."[15] They did so with good reason—between 1945 and 1948 the group contributed $1,076.88 to the church's general fund, $1,000 for a new parsonage, and $627.13 for "flowers, sick and funerals, cards, postage and merchandise."[16] In 1940 the women's groups at the Bethel Krimmer Mennonite Brethren Church[17] in Yale, South Dakota, offered to give up to $500 to improve acoustics in the church sanctuary. The next year they promised $250 for other church improvements. Local church historian Joseph A. Kleinsasser noted that in 1944, "the matter of giving some support to the boys in the Service was a concern of the men at the business meeting. They settled it by giving the Ladies Aid the responsibility."[18] In 1949, the Yale women contributed half the purchase price of the parsonage—$250.00.[19] Likewise, the women of Corn, Oklahoma assisted in the building and furnishing of the Corn Mennonite Brethren Church building after its destruction by fire in early 1949.[20] During the 1940s the "Willing Workers of God" in Dinuba, California, helped furnish the Zion Krimmer Mennonite Brethren church nursery and kitchen, and bought shrubbery for the church landscaping.[21]

Until 1948, no formal organization of the various women's groups existed on a district level. Each circle functioned independently. Most elected officers and kept records, and individual groups chose their own projects. They raised funds in various ways: circles catered meals, sold food at public auctions, held mission sales of goods such as handmade quilts and other items, or collected offerings. Women took an active role in relief efforts, and served as an additional funding source for special church projects. Although long important to local congregations and to various conference endeavors, they had no conference status or recognition. Starting in the late 1940s, however, that would change.

PACIFIC DISTRICT

In 1948 the Program Committee for the thirty-ninth Pacific District Conference asked Lydia Martens, a member of the Reedley Mennonite Brethren church, to survey the work of the various missionary societies and report to the Conference.[22] Toward the end of the convention held that fall in Bakersfield, California, Martens reported that each church in the Pacific District had organized at least one missionary society—a total of eighteen groups—with approximately 380 members.[23] She added that a recommendation to organize these groups together had come from several groups and closed with the following words,

> We know there is much to be done, and as Jesus' body would have missed its anointing but for Mary, so many things that are dear to the heart of our Lord will be left undone unless we women do it. Let us have "faith that worketh by love," that we may hear the Lord's words, "She hath done what she could."[24]

In response, conference moderator George H. Jantzen "encouraged the Missionary Society and asked them to go ahead and report next year at the District Conference."[25] Before the conference ended, and at the urging of women attending, Martens agreed to call an organizational meeting that then took place later that fall.[26]

Despite some opposition to the meeting, Martens, and those planning it, continued their efforts. They were unprepared for a letter that informed them that several groups would not be participating in the meeting. Lydia Martens recalled the issue as follows:

> It seemed that some were fearful that the women wanted to be on the Conference Program and gradually would take over. We made several long distance telephone calls trying to explain that this was not the case; we simply wanted to work together in a more effective way and encourage one another. We were informed that a letter had been written to our Pastor, Bro. J.B. Toews, that he would explain to us.[27]

Toews had received a letter reporting the resolution of the Shafter Church Council and asking that it be presented "to the sisters who are in charge of calling this meeting." The resolution read as follows: "We the Church Council of the Shafter Mennonite Brethren church, encourage our sisters to continue with the work but we do not wish them to organize with the intention to report to the Pacific District Conference."[28] The letter continued:

> We have also talked to our Sewing Circle. We have as a church no objection in their planning together and counselling together of how to carry on their work, but our Sewing Circle officers do not wish to be presented at the Conference in a report that is given by their organization as an official conference organization. They rather choose to work quietly under the direction of our local relief committee and Church Council who shall make it a point to report and carefully pray and support the worthy efforts of our Sewing Circle.[29]

Interestingly, the Shafter women had originally planned to attend the organizational meeting. The minutes of the Shafter Relief Workers indicate that they had moved their regularly scheduled Thursday meeting forward to Wednesday because of their plans to attend the meeting.[30]

Despite this incident plans proceeded, aided by the encouragement of Martens' pastor, J. B. Toews.[31] Toews spoke not only as pastor but with the support of several other conference leaders. In consultation with B. J. Braun (then a member of the Board of Reference and Counsel, and past Assistant Moderator for the Conference) and H. R. Wiens (newly elected to the Home Missions Department), the letter from the Shafter Council was held back. Toews subsequently wrote to Waldo Wiebe, pastor of the Shafter M.B. Church, informing him that they had not felt it appropriate to read the letter at the meeting "for as much as the Conference had passed a resolution recommending that this organization be effected."[32] Thus, with conference approval and pastoral encouragement, formal organization took place on November 14, 1948.[33]

The meeting took place at the Reedley Mennonite Brethren church with Lydia Martens presiding and J. B. Toews providing a devotional message. Representatives from various women's groups, plus a representative from Mennonite Central Committee presented reports, and the group elected officers.[34] An attachment to the minutes notes that "it was very encouraging to hear the reports of how many of [our] local Pastors are working with and encouraging the women to do all they can for the Missionary needs." It also expressed thanks for "the encouragement and support [given] to this committee by many of our Pastors."[35]

The new organization met annually together with the Pacific District Conference, and its meetings were primarily inspirational. Besides a "Gift Day" for the Home for the Aged in Reedley, there is little evidence of special project approval. The general budget remained small and dependent primarily on the offerings lifted at the annual business meetings.[36]

In 1950 the organization chose a name--"M.B. Missionary Service," although the organization was invariably called the *Women's* Missionary Service, or WMS.[37] By then, twenty-one circles had joined the Missionary Service. The statistical report submitted that year to the District Conference shows a total membership of 366, a cash income of $14,995.97, and an additional $11,906.49 valuation of goods in kind.[38] This represented a membership average of $73.50 per member. In comparison, the total receipts for the District Conference averaged $93.85 per member.[39]

During the mid-1950s the Women's Missionary Service made several significant decisions that shaped the Service for the future. In 1954, at the recommendation of the Executive Board, the WMS approved a provisional constitution, which stated that the purpose of the WMS was "to promote spiritual growth" and "to help the various needs of our church, District Conference and General Conference with our prayers, sewing, donations in kind and cash." Operating expenses were to be met by individual and group contributions, and offerings taken at the WMS meetings.[40] The constitution called for an eight-member Executive Committee. It listed its voting body as "the chairman of each sewing circle, the pastor's wife from each church, and one delegate for each ten members of the individual church sewing circles."[41] The chair of each circle and the pastor's wife from each church also served on an Executive Board.[42]   The minutes of the November 15, 1954 annual meeting reflect two other significant events. First was the approval of a motion to adopt a unified study plan in the circles. Second was approval of a request made by Mrs. Henry Kliewer , dietician at Pacific Bible Institute in Fresno, to fund the purchase of drapes for the dining hall.[43] The first event indicated a move toward a unified program among the circles. The second represented the first formal request recorded for special project funding from the WMS. Such requests would become a frequent occurence.

The first missionary rally sponsored by the WMS took place in Shafter on the morning and afternoon of March 17, 1955, much on the same lines as the annual meeting. It consisted of a brief business meeting and a program of inspirational music and missionary testimonies. Of particular importance, however, was the presentation and acceptance of a foreign mission project to build and maintain a maternity hospital on the mission field— "provided the churches are in favor." Each circle was instructed to "present the project to their local pastors and inform the Conference Chairman of their decision."[44]

When the Executive Committee met in April, 1955, they were apparently confident that the project would meet with the pastors' approval. The members agreed "that when the Maternity Hospital project is accepted the money will be collected according to membership, $3.00 per member plus Hospital Supplies."[45] Their faith was justified. At the annual meeting in 1955, Secretary-Treasurer Sophie Enns was able to report income of over $2,000— a figure that exceeded their goal.[46]

These decisions point to a growing sense of awareness among the WMS leadership about the strength of unified operation. Opposition to the Service had died and membership had grown, although caution was still clearly exercised in decision-making, as showed by the handling of the maternity hospital project. The

Executive Committee had already developed some stability by staggering the terms of office.[47] Now they had developed a regular program of missionary support through prayer and gifts. The Committee encouraged circles to be in contact with their assigned missionaries, and regularly made special missionary needs known to the circles.[48] They also encouraged them to exchange yearbooks modeled after the conference yearbook.[49]

At least one other significant decision took place during 1955. At the December 8 Executive Committee meeting, a motion was made and carried to appoint Marie Leppke and Mary Letkeman to a two-year term as WMS historians, a decision that suggests growing self-awareness of the significance of the WMS for women in the Pacific District.

In 1956 the Service was ready to take on additional projects. At the annual meeting in Dallas, Oregon the Service approved a recommendation by the Executive Board to fund a maternity hospital in Africa ($1,000 per year) and to accept "an educational project pertaining to groceries, clothing and baby furniture, at the Mennonite Brethren Biblical Seminary."[50]

By the end of the 1950s the WMS in the Pacific District had matured into a well-organized society, with a clear sense of direction and healthy finances. Foreign missions remained at the heart of the Service, although it also gave attention to local projects. A diminished need for sewing had been noted, and in its place, the Executive Board encouraged the circles to focus on prayer and Bible study.[51] The WMS increasingly funded a variety of missionary and special projects that required more in the way of finances than actual sewing. In 1959, over $7,000 of the $9,321.07 disbursed went to foreign projects and to missionaries. Relief work (sewing and the gathering of used clothing) continued to be channeled through Mennonite Central Committee.

SOUTHERN DISTRICT

In contrast to the Pacific District, the Southern District's organization was self-initiated and does not appear to have met with the resistance the Pacific District women experienced. Waldo Hiebert has attributed the desire to organize, in part, to a need for better control of Mennonite Brethren dollars.[52] Certainly the organization of the Pacific District women also played a part.

At the 1952 Southern District Conference in Hillsboro, Kansas, women from the local congregation hosted a meeting in which they exchanged information about their local circles and listened to reports from visiting missionaries. They also decided to meet again at the next conference. This meeting, however, failed to take place.[53]

During the fall of 1954 the General Conference met in Hillsboro, providing the women there another opportunity to encourage unification. They again hosted a meeting, but this time took even greater initiative, calling together several meetings for pastor's wives and officers of local circles.[54] They discussed problems as well as the possibility of a unified organization. Women visiting from the Pacific District shared the advantages of their own organization and a decision was made to call for a business meeting at the District convention scheduled for Fairview, Oklahoma, later that fall.[55]

At the Fairview meeting Marie Gerbrandt, chair of the Senior Circle at Hillsboro, spoke about the Pacific District's WMS and then "asked the ladies if they would like to organize in a similar manner."[56] They responded positively and elected her chair.[57] Twenty-nine circles appeared on the initial roster for 1954-1955.[58] Waldo Hiebert credits Gerbrandt for careful navigation through the political waters of the conference:

> Mrs. J. J. Gerbrandt, a born leader and an able women's worker with vision and insight, set about immediately to avoid, if possible, some of the rough spots the Pacific District women had encountered. One of their major struggles was to receive recognition and encouragement from the pastors of some of the churches. Mrs. Gerbrandt immediately called a meeting of the newly elected officers to compile a document for presentation on the floor of the district conference.[59]

The Committee reported to the delegates that there had been a "growing desire" to organize, that their purpose was "to promote a more uniform missionary program in our churches," that the organization would "serve as the channel through which the mission boards will be able to make their needs known to the individual circles." Finally, the committee assured the delegates that it would "not interfere in any way with the work of the local organizations."[60] They recommended the acceptance of the organization as an official conference entity, and also recommended that the WMS conduct its meetings during the annual district conventions. The delegates responded by referring the request for recognition to the Constitution Committee because of implications for the District constitution.[61]

In contrast to the Pacific District, the Southern District immediately sought projects for the newly formed organization. In January of 1955, the Executive Committee met with J. B. Toews and A. E. Janzen from the foreign missions office, and with members of the Evangelism Committee of the Southern District. They chose two projects, which they presented by letter to the membership.[62] A maternity hospital in Africa was presented as a foreign mission project. The committee requested that each circle donate $5.00 per month, and sew patterns for hospital gowns and baby shirts.[63] For a home missions project, the Committee proposed that the circles each pay $5.00 per month toward the rent for a meeting space for the new congregation in Denver, Colorado.[64]

Following the example of the Pacific District, the Southern District leaders immediately assigned missionaries to the various circles for their prayer support. For their name they chose "Women's Missionary Service of the Southern District Conference."[65] At the annual meeting held October 24, 1955, the membership established the delegation for business decisions as each circle chair, the pastors' wives and one delegate for each ten members of the various circles.[66] The members also accepted a recommendation to add a third area of service to their existing foreign and home missions projects. The Executive Committee recommended a budget of $3,000 to be divided equally between foreign missions, home missions, and Tabor College.[67] This represented a significant budget increase. The budget goal for the previous year had been $2,000, a sum they did not quite meet. It also signalled a commitment to place education on par with foreign and home missions. The actual projects chosen included hospital beds (foreign missions), furnishings for the home economics room at the El Faro, Texas mission (home missions), and furnishings for the Mennonite Brethren archives in the new Tabor College library.[68] They agreed that giving was to be based on membership, with smaller circles (less than twenty members) asked to contribute $100 and larger circles asked to donate $200.[69]

Although clearly a primary concern, the Executive Committee did not limit its vision to funding mission projects. Prayer chairperson Zola Janzen noted that during the 1955-1956 year, she wrote "forty-five letters to different circle chairmen and prayer chairmen concerning missionaries on their lists who might be in special need of prayer or other attention."[70] That same year the Committee raised the idea of a special page in *The Christian Leader*. It also explored the possibility of a women's meeting to be held at the triennial General Conference and raised the possibility of a regional missionary rally. A brief article in *The Christian Leader* mentions three rallies planned for Balko and Fairview, Oklahoma, and Buhler, Kansas.[71] Their success encouraged the membership to pass a motion in favor of continuing area rallies.

Although their budget was not large, the Southern District WMS defined its organization primarily as a support service and funding source for Mennonite Brethren missions. In a report submitted to the Southern District Conference meeting in Corn, Oklahoma, in 1956, Marie Gerbrandt stated that

> The purpose of this organization is to promote a more uniform missionary program in our churches. It serves as a channel through which the mission boards, and missionaries, can make their needs known. It is hoped that it shall also serve to harness some of the money that would otherwise flow into projects outside of our conference.[72]

The Executive Committee struggled with requests for financial aid that came from "the sidelines" and agreed that because their funds were budgeted, they could not take on additional projects.[73] They reiterated their commitment to working through the conference mission agencies. "If projects are important enough," they decided, "they must be cleared through the mission boards and then be suggested to us as possible projects for next year."[74] They also maintained a clear division between work done for Mennonite Brethren missions and that done for relief. In a letter to WMS secretary-treasurer Ferne Hiebert, dated January, 1958, WMS chairperson Helen Franz noted that

> in previous years the Relief and M.C.C. question has come up; the committee gave it serious consideration. We came to the conclusion not to reach out into another area but stay within the Mennonite Brethren conference, since we are all conference women.[75]

This is in considerable contrast to the Pacific District WMS, which from the beginning incorporated MCC relief work into their district organization.[76]

The focus on project funding, however, meant that circles had to have some sort of cash flow. Clothes sales, custom quilting, banquets and fellowship suppers, food service at auctions, monthly dues, mission sales, offerings, and wedding and banquet catering were fund-raising methods used by various circles.[77]

Throughout the 1950s, the Southern District WMS continued to divide their $3,000 budget three ways. They did the same for any funds raised above budget. The projects accepted by the membership tended to be practical. Given a choice, they opted for projects that benefited women. For example, when presented with a choice of small projects to be funded from the excess funds gathered in 1958, the members chose the purchase of a maternity delivery table for a hospital in Mexico over the funding of Bible school students or other hospital supplies. Likewise, they divided the home mission portion among fourteen "lady workers" in South Texas, and contributed to the purchase of a tile block floor for the Tabor College cafeteria.[78] In 1959 they donated $1,000 to the College for equipping the home economics department, and purchased folding chairs for the Newton (Kans.) and Topeka (Kans.) Sunday school programs.[79] Among the options on the 1959-1960 project ballot was a choice between renovations and chairs for the science lecture room at Tabor College and lounge furniture for the girls' dormitory. The women chose furniture.[80]

The circles also continued to do handwork. In the fall of 1959, Work Chairperson Mrs. J.D. Ens reported that twenty-eight circles provided approximately 818 pounds of material for foreign missions, 4,609 pounds for home missions, and 762 pounds for relief.[81]

The organization also extended a welcome to the Krimmer Mennonite Brethren (KMB) women living in the Southern District. Plans for merger between the Mennonite Brethren and the Krimmer Mennonite Brethren had been approved in 1958 and 1959, with formal merger taking place in November, 1960.[82] The committee had sent letters of invitation to KMB churches as early as 1958, encouraging their participation in the area mission rallies. In February of 1959, Elfreda Fast noted in a letter to Esther Ebel:

> I believe that the Springfield and Zoar [KMB] churches were invited last year. However, the invitation went to the pastor, I believe, and for some reason was not passed on to the women. I don't know the details, but would suggest that we find out who the leading women are in these two churches and then extend the invitation to them.[83]

Names of leading women were apparently found and letters went out to Mrs. Peter E. Heinrichs of the Springfield KMB church in

Canton, Kansas, and Mrs. Menno Prieb of the Zoar KMB church in Inman, Kansas. This time the pastors received carbon copies of the invitations.[84]

By the end of the 1950s the Southern District WMS included thirty-seven circles with a membership of over 770 women. The organization was clearly thriving.

CENTRAL DISTRICT

Although home to the oldest of the U.S. Mennonite Brethren mission societies and sales, those of the Carson and Mountain Lake, Minnesota churches, the Central District Women's Missionary Service was the last of the District Services to organize formally. Interest in a unified organization was evidenced by at least some Central District women who had contact with the Southern District WMS. At a 1959 Southern District WMS missionary rally in Joes, Colorado, a group from Paxton, Nebraska asked to join the Southern District's WMS because of the lack of a similar organization in their own district. Their request was granted.[85] That same year, Mrs. Marion Kliewer, Secretary of the Southern District WMS, forwarded information about the WMS to Mrs. Wayne Faul of Harvey, North Dakota.[86] However, it was at the request of the District Reference and Counsel Committee that formal organization took place.[87]

The District Conference had begun to include information about the various women's mission societies in its annual statistical reports in 1956. These figures are significant in comparison to total mission and relief giving for those same years. For example, the total Central District Conference giving to foreign missions (both Mennonite Brethren and other), home missions, relief and the endowment fund was $86,804.38 in 1956. That same year, thirteen sewing circles reported income of $10,599.49, most of which would have been channeled into foreign and home missions, relief, and local church projects.[88]

At the 1959 District Conference session, the General Conference Board of Foreign Missions presented to the Conference a "Statement of Our Fundamental Concept and Purpose of Missions." It delegated the responsibility for outfitting missionaries to the local constituency.[89] The "mother church" of the missionary, "through the channels of the respective district or provincial conference", or, if necessary, "by inviting other neighboring churches to participate" was responsible for providing the equipment needed by outgoing missionaries.[90] In addition, the statement said that

> the missionary societies of the respective church or district are requested to assume the responsibility for all the personal effects in the line of linen, clothing and personal household effects necessary for a normal maintenance of a household on the basis of average family standards.
>
> The constituency further provides for an outgoing missionary family the amount not to exceed $1200 in cash for the purpose of equipment which the missionary is responsible to provide as his own property.[91]

Missionaries home on furlough were to receive not more than $750 assistance for a family, and $500 for a "single sister" in preparation for return to the field.[92]

On October 10, 1960, during the Central District Conference at Mountain Lake, Minnesota, and at the recommendation of the District's Reference and Counsel Committee, Central District women met to formally organize a missionary service. Their report to the delegation stated that they had accepted the recommendations of the Reference and Counsel Committee and had established a temporary committee until they could set up a constitution.[93] Mrs. Waldo Dick, newly elected chairperson, also reported that

> our responsibilities will be mainly to work together as women's societies of the Central District Conference in outfitting our missionaries when they leave for the foreign field and other projects as they will arise.[94]

During the following year the newly formed organization met twice. They reported to the delegation at the District Conference held October, 1961, that during their first year they had outfited the outgoing missionaries from the district and had also established a newsletter, *The Challenger*, as a "means of contact between societies and committee giving the immediate needs of missionaries."[95] Their financial report indicated receipt of $2,141.46 from twenty-three churches, and disbursements to missionaries of $1,770.00.[96]

Although continuing to count membership, the District Conference statistics stopped reporting on the finances of the missionary circles after the WMS organized. The yearbook for 1960 reported mission society membership of 415 women among fourteen churches and income of $7,065.00 from twelve churches. Missionary society membership reported in 1961 was 622 among twenty churches. Given the reports of individual circle activity published in *The Challenger*, considerable income was still flowing from the societies through the churches.[97]

At their annual meeting on November 8, 1962, the WMS adopted a budget of $2,800 for the following year: $1,000 for foreign missions, $800 for home missions, $200 for relief, and $800 for Christian education.[98] Other recommendations included the continued outfitting of missionaries from the district, the assignment of missionaries to the various churches for prayer and support, and a decision to have the MCC relief project letter sent to each society.[99] Also during 1962, the Executive Committee drew up a constitution that they distributed to the various circles for approval.[100] According to the preamble, Central District women were organizing because they were "interested in the welfare of its [Central District] Mission Program, Relief Program, and Education Program," and to lend their "assistance in the promoting of its general interests."[101]

CONCLUSION

The united efforts of the Women's Missionary Services grew out of the work of the individual societies. The development of each organization reflected its times and the activities of its district. In 1948, the Pacific District women organized in the wake of World War II and the combined relief efforts mounted by the churches. Women wanted to unite and increase their efforts. In 1954, relief work had waned but the Mennonite Brethren home and foreign mission program remained strong. The Southern District women united as a funding source for foreign and home missions and education. The Central District WMS organized in 1960 at the request of the District leadership and shortly after the Board of Foreign Missions assigned outfitting to the home churches and district of the missionaries.

Each organization took a different form. The Pacific District women worked with a large executive board and coordinated efforts for relief, missions, the Home for the Aged, and schools located within the district. Large amounts of money flowed through their treasury. The Southern District women worked with a much smaller organization and kept their joint projects to a minimum, but they set up a unified study program eventually adopted by all three WMS organizations. The Central District women also worked with a small committee that fostered the work of home and foreign missions across a sparsely populated district, particularly through their newsletter, *The Challenger*. All assigned missionaries to individual groups for prayer and support.

Mission personnel and pastors regularly exhorted WMS members to serve, but often questioned women's desire to be a part of decision-making bodies. Their sermons and devotionals delivered at the various annual meetings are often very telling, and need be studied as a part of the larger question of women's full participation in the life of the church.[102] Often these messages simply reflect an era, and should be read in that context. However, the messages that women were responsible for suffering and sacrifice, that they were to "stand in the gap" and "lead the cause of Christ," need to be evaluated for their impact on the lives and service of Mennonite Brethren women.

The story of women's missionary societies is an important part of Mennonite Brethren church history. It provides a witness to the commitment of Mennonite Brethren women to the work of the church. They did what they could with the resources available. They did what they could given the restrictions placed on women for service in the church. Their story needs to be incorporated into the historical record and memory of Mennonite Brethren.

Canadian Mennonite Women's Societies: More Than Meets the Eye

Gloria Neufeld Redekop

When Mennonites immigrated to Canada, Mennonite women's societies, or *Vereine*,[1] were organized in Canada along with the establishment of churches. A precedent already had been set in Gnadenfeld, Russia, during a renewal movement in the mid-1840s that contributed to the formation of the Mennonite Brethren (MB) Church in 1860. Within this context, under the preaching of Lutheran evangelist Eduard Wüst, a frequent speaker at Mennonite mission festivals, women's societies evidently first emerged. According to Jacob Bekker, "It was agreed to organize a Women's Society during the winter months to enable the women to meet once a week in the afternoons to knit and sew for missions."[2]

How the church often viewed these societies is evident in a story told of a Mennonite leader's daughter in 1895. As secretary to her father, she inquired whether the words *Frauen Missions Verein*[3] should be capitalized. He answered, "No, such a society is only ordinary." The daughter replied, "Not right, father, if the words were *Männer Missions Verein*,[4] then I would have to write in large letters."[5] Known by some as "coffee klatsches," a common perception was that women's *Vereine* were primarily gossip centers. But women such as Maria Derksen, president of the Ebenezer *Verein* in Steinbach, Manitoba from 1936-1948, defended the women's society against accusations such as these. In her 1944 report she wrote, "Sometimes the Ladies Aids are ridiculed and sarcastically spoken of as being mere 'coffee-klatsches' but that is not true of our congregation. Neither is that remark deserving of any Ladies Aid."[6]

In the late 1940s, a poem telling the story of how the women's society of the George Street Mennonite church in Kitchener, Ontario raised the funds to replace the church roof, also illustrates this common perception of Mennonite women's groups:

> Once a few men were standing outside the church door
> As if they knew everything, and were thankful for it too.
> They talked about this and that, about women's societies

It's not all good that they said, "Yes," one interrupted,
"Why do they sew so much; it's just to pass the time
They only gossip and turn their heads from their bodies."
"Yes," said a second man, "They let everything else go;
They neglect household duties."
The third one said quietly, "We need money badly.
Where in all the world will we get it?
We need this and that in our church.
We're sitting deep in debt, what can we do?"
Then they all agreed to approach the *Verein*.
It wasn't the first time they had done this.
And when they asked the women's society if they would help,
An auction was held and see how the money rolled in.[7]

When women in Mennonite women's societies found out I
planned to document their contribution within the Mennonite
church, several expressed the need for such a history. For instance,
a member of the Arelee (Sask.) MB Women's Missionary
Fellowship wrote, "recognition of women's contributions to
church and community is long overdue."[8] Indeed, an examination
of historical studies in the field of Mennonites in Canada reveals
only a few references to Mennonite women's societies.[9] This lack is
not unique to the Mennonite community. Pauline Bradbrook, who
wrote an account of Anglican women's societies in Newfoundland,
refered to the same phenomenon: "It is commonly said that the
church would not have survived over the years without the support
of women. While most people would agree with this observation,
there has been little documentation of precisely what their
contribution has been or what it has meant to the church."[10]

That Mennonite women have been left out of history is due to
a number of factors. Two issues are most critical. First, until
recently, women's history has been missing from traditional
historical studies, which focuses on aspects of historical events and
institutions in which women did not participate. Second, even
when the field of women's history began to develop in the 1970s,
the emphasis was on the history of feminist thought and feminist
organizations. Especially lacking in this new history was the history
of non-feminist religious women's organizations. But recently,
Canadian historians such as Ruth Compton Brouwer maintain
there is a growing realization that this story needs to be told as well:

> There has been a certain tendency to "approve of" women's
> religious zeal only when and as it has seemed to serve as a way-
> station on the road to feminist consciousness. Personal
> spirituality and transcendent concerns have largely been

overlooked, along with forms of religious activism that did not necessarily bear fruit in a larger sphere for women.[11]

It is exactly this aspect of "personal spirituality and transcendent concerns"[12] that characterized Mennonite women's societies.

GROWTH OF MENNONITE WOMEN'S SOCIETIES, 1940-1960

In Canada, the 1950s witnessed tremendous growth within women's organizations. In the United Church, for example, attendance in women's societies almost doubled between 1942 and 1955.[13] A similar phenomenon occurred among Mennonite women's societies. In CMC and MB churches established between 1874 and 1952, available sources suggest that there were four times as many new groups organized during the twelve-year period of 1947 to 1959 as were organized during the next twenty-seven years, 1960 to 1987.[14]

While we need to be cautious in suggesting a direct correlation, it may be significant that the flowering of Mennonite women's societies occurred concurrently with both the emphasis on women's role as homemaker and the reinforcement of women's subordinate role within the church. In the 1950s both society and church promoted the "happy homemaker" image for women.[15] Besides this emphasis on the role of Mennonite women as homemakers and mothers, there seemed to be increased restriction for Mennonite women within the church. One indication of this trend was the rescindment of ordination for women. Before 1957, the MB Church ordained both married and single MB female missionaries for mission work; the ordination procedure was the same for both men and women. But in 1957, after three years of study, the General Conference of Mennonite Brethren Churches accepted a resolution changing the former method of ordination of women to commissioning:

> In view of the fact that we as an MB Church, on the basis of clearly conceived scriptural convictions, do not admit sisters to the public gospel preaching ministry on par with brethren, we as a Conference designate the fact of setting aside sisters to missionary work "a commissioning" rather than "an ordination."[16]

It is difficult to determine exactly what the change from ordination to commissioning meant to Mennonite women, but it might be significant that Mennonite women's societies flourished during this time. If the movement was in the direction of further restrictions for women within the church, they still could serve God within the context of their societies, which became their primary outlet for service.

THE SERVICE ORIENTATION OF
MENNONITE WOMEN'S SOCIETIES

Service remained the primary reason for establishing Mennonite women's societies through the 1940s and 1950s. Canadian church historian John Webster Grant notes that "among Protestants, women were the first to organize for the furtherance of the missionary cause and in Canada they have always been the chief instigators of enthusiasm for missions."[17] Church women's societies generally responded quickly to expressed needs. Earl Merrick, a historian of Baptist women's organizations, admits that "men have never given women credit for the speed at which they can move when something captures their enthusiasm."[18] Mennonite Brethren women's societies were no exception. According to J. B. Toews, Executive Secretary of the Mennonite Brethren Board of Foreign Missions from 1959 to 1963, if the Board of Foreign Missions had an urgent financial need he found it more effective to contact leaders of women's societies than church pastors because then he knew the request would get immediate action.[19]

Mennonite women's societies contributed large sums of money in the support of foreign missions, home missions, and the local church. Mennonite Brethren women's societies generally became aware of potential mission projects through the Board of Foreign Missions. The societies were "a channel through which the Board of Foreign Missions and missionaries could make their needs known."[20] There also were times when women's societies contributed remarkable amounts of money to the local church, as exemplified in the report of MB women's groups of Clearbrook, British Columbia:

> It began as a tiny grain in 1934 or 35, with twelve sisters in the home of one of the pioneers. They gathered for fellowship and prayer and were busy with their hands. It is said that money for the material for the first sanctuary built in 1940, which amounted to $700.00 was raised by the Ladies Fellowship. This was done through a Mission Sale in the Poplar Hall.[21]

As in other Protestant traditions, the annual mission sale became a common way for Mennonite women across Canada to sell articles they had sewn and knit during the year.[22] Mennonite women also used other creative methods as well to raise money for projects. A group in Saskatchewan wrote:

> when money was needed for a certain project, an apron was passed around to each member. Then each one would sew a patch onto the apron with a donation underneath it. When it had made its round, the apron was relieved of its patches and the money was sent away.[23]

This central focus on service by Mennonite women's societies is illustrated by the names they chose for their groups. The following tables show the distribution of names of Mennonite Women's Societies organized in immigrant churches between 1940 and 1960.[24]

Table 1
Percentage Distribution of Names of CMC Women's Societies 1940-1960[25]

CATEGORY	NAMES	NUMBER	%
Missions	Sunshine Mission Circle, Loving Deeds Mission Circle, Women's Missionary Society (4x), Mission Helpers (2x), Goodwill Mission Circle, Women in Mission, Mission Circle (4x), Mission Workers, Marissa Mission Group, Mission Helpers, *Missionsverein*	18	18.6%
Sewing	Sunbeam Sewing Circle, Junior Sewing Circle, Busy Fingers Sewing Circle, *Nähverein* (2x), Girl's Sewing Club, Sewing Circle (2x)	8	8.3%
Aid/Help/Service	Young Women's Charity Club, Willing Hands Ladies Aid, Women's Christian Endeavour, Servettes, Willing Workers, Helping Hands (4x), Willing Hands, Goodwill Society (2x), Willing Helpers (3x), *Wohltätigkeitsverein*, Women's Auxiliary, Ladies Aid (13x), Home and Abroad Ladies Aid, *Verein Helfende Hände*, Ladies Auxiliary, Busy Bees Circle, Merry Co-Workers Club	35	36.1%

CATEGORY	NAMES	NUMBER	%
Biblical Woman's Name & Aid	Magdalene Ladies Aid	1	1.0%
Biblical Woman's (Name)	Dorcas Circle, Tabitha Circle, Maria Martha Women's Society, *Tabea Verein,* (3x), *Maria Martha Verein*	7	7.2%
Fellowship	Harmony Hearts, Homemakers Fellowship, Fellowship Group, Friendship Circle, Ladies Fellowship (2x), Women's Christian Fellowship	7	7.2%
Other	Young Women's, Guiding Mothers, Morija Circle, *Verein* (13x), *Frauenverein* (2x), *Abendglocken Verein, Schnetke Conference, Sonnenstrahl Verein*[26]	21	21.6%[27]
TOTAL		97	100%

Table 2
Percentage Distribution of Names
of MB Women's Societies: 1940-1960[28]

CATEGORY	NAMES	NUMBER	%
Missions	Junior Ladies Missionary Prayer Group, Ladies Missionary Prayer Group, Missionary Prayer Group, Sunbeam Mission Band, The Mission Group (2x), Ladies Mission Circle, *Missionverein* (3x), Women's Missionary Service, Young Ladies Mission Group, *Missionskränzchen*	13	38.2%
Sewing	Ladies Sewing Circle, Sunshine Sewing Circle	2	5.9%
Aid/Help/Service	Women's Ministries, Willing Helpers (2x) , Work and Prayer Group, Ladies Aid, (3x), Christian Service Club	8	23.5%
Biblical Woman's (Name)	Dorcas Ladies Group, Mary Martha Group, Mary Martha *Verein, Tabea Verein*	4	11.8%
Biblical Name and Fellowship	Mary Martha Fellowship	1	3.0%
Fellowship	Ladies Fellowship, Ladies Christian Fellowship, *Schwesternbund*	3	8.8%
Other	Pleasant Hour, Sunshine Club, *Frauenverein*[29]	3	8.8%
TOTAL		34	100%

As shown in Tables 1 and 2, names denoting missions, sewing, aid, help, and service (including names of biblical women who served) comprised 71.2 percent of CMC women's society names and 82.4 percent of MB women's society names. During this era, only 7.2 percent of CMC societies and 11.8 percent of MB societies identified themselves as fellowship groups. This number increased substantially after 1970.

Clearly, Mennonite women's societies' primary focus was service, especially in the support of missions. But what motivated them? Why were they so eager to serve the church in this way?

THE BIBLICAL MOTIVATION OF
MENNONITE WOMEN'S SOCIETIES

Mennonite women received their motivation for society work from their faith experience. The story of the Women's Auxiliary of the First Mennonite Church in Saskatoon serves as an example: The Women's Auxiliary was established on January 13, 1958 with sixteen women in attendance. It adopted as its motto, "Serve him with a perfect heart and willing mind." (I Chr. 28:9). It was customary for Mennonite women's societies to choose biblical texts as mottos, and the choice of these mottos reveals their biblical motivation for service.

Mottos chosen between 1940 and 1960 were predominantly oriented toward service. The most common was "And let us not be weary in well doing: for in due season we shall reap, if we faint not. As we have therefore opportunity, let us do good unto all men, especially unto them who are of the household of faith" (Galatians 6:9-10).[30] Examples of other mottos chosen during this time include:

By love serve one another (Gal. 5:13).

She stretcheth out her hand to the poor; yea, she reacheth forth her hands to the needy (Pro. 31:20).

For we are laborers together with God: ye are God's husbandry, ye are God's building (I Cor. 3:9).

And whatsoever ye do, do it heartily, as to the Lord and not unto men (Col. 3:23).

And whatsoever ye do in word or deed, do all in the name of the Lord Jesus, giving thanks to God and the Father by him (Col. 3:17).

Therefore, my beloved brethren, be ye steadfast, unmoveable, always abounding in the work of the Lord, forasmuch as ye know that your labor is not in vain in the Lord (I Cor. 15:58).

Let your light so shine before men, that they may see your good works, and glorify your Father which is in heaven (Matt. 5:16).

Serve the Lord with gladness: come before his presence with singing (Ps. 100:2).

Inasmuch as ye have done it unto one of the least of these my brethren, ye have done it unto me (Matt. 25:40b).

But be ye doers of the word, and not hearers only (James 1:22a).

Now then we are ambassadors for Christ, as though God did beseech you by us: we pray you in Christ's stead, be ye reconciled to God (II Cor. 5:20).

The frequent reference in their mottos to service—"serve," "do," "deed," "well-doing," and "good works"—indicates women's identification of their work with obedience to the biblical text. From it they took their mandate for service. Some of these verses even appear as commands: "serve one another," "serve the Lord," and "be ye doers." Mennonite women seemed to believe that through their society work they were "laborers together with God" (I Cor. 3:9), and "ambassadors for Christ" (II Cor. 5:20). This opportunity for obedience to their perception of the Christian calling was one factor that made their involvement within societies meaningful.

THE MEANING OF WOMEN'S SOCIETIES
FOR MENNONITE WOMEN

Excluded from many workings of the institutional church, Mennonite women, within the context of their own societies, were able to contribute to the mission of the church. Their need to do so is illustrated in this 1944 *Verein* report of the Ebenezer Church in Steinbach, Manitoba:

Even though the women work separately from the rest of the congregation, we still feel that we are very much a part of the whole. . . . The women do their part and the men, theirs. . . .

> The congregation had the responsibility to pay its debt. We
> women felt the responsibility as much as the men, and we
> decided to help. How could we help? Through the work we do
> in the Aid.[31]

Besides offering them the opportunity to serve God,
Mennonite women's societies provided a context within which
they could receive friendship and personal support. The South
Western Ontario Women in Mission even considered this part of
the definition of the word *Verein:*

> Literally translated the word *Verein* means a union, society, or
> club. However, to the women in the *Vereine*, the word has
> come to mean much more. As we know it, it is a group that
> works together for a common goal, yes, but it is also a group
> whose members give each other friendship and support as
> they experience the various stages of their lives and the joys
> and struggles they bring.[32]

In the early 1940s Maria Duerksen of the Ebenezer *Verein* in
Steinbach, Manitoba, wrote about the value of the *Verein* in this
way:

> It is not only an organization to do good work and support
> missions, but for the woman the Ladies Aid has great personal
> value. Once or twice a month she frees herself from her
> household tasks and gets together with her sisters. She leaves
> her troubles at home, shares with her fellow sisters and then
> arrives back home refreshed.[33]

However, the opportunity to serve God and fellowship with each
other were not the only benefits of Mennonite women's societies
to Mennonite women. Just as significant was the spiritual
nourishment they received through worship rituals.

The spiritual component of *Verein* meetings was an important
aspect for Mennonite women. The groups sometimes mentioned
this as one of their purposes. In 1959 the Altona (Man.)
Homemakers Fellowship stated that "the objective of the group
was to promote the spiritual enrichment of the women and to
assist in the work of the church."[34] Women's groups of the
Leamington (Ont.) MB Church reported that "meetings always had
a strong spiritual emphasis with different sisters taking part in
scripture reading, devotionals and prayers and singing our favorite
hymns."[35] *Verein* worship commonly began with Bible reading,
prayer, and singing. Sometimes there was a Bible study or
devotional. They discussed business matters and took an offering.

For a portion of the meeting, women often worked on their handwork while one member read from a devotional book or the Bible. Meetings generally closed with prayer and eating together.[36]

It is understandable that the components of their worship bore a striking resemblance to the weekly Sunday worship in Mennonite churches. What Mennonite women knew about worship they had learned from the church, where services included prayer, scripture reading, singing, an offering, and at least one sermon. But while men commonly led the Sunday morning services, Mennonite women could participate in every aspect of their *Verein* worship. Although records show that in the early years men often opened and closed women's meetings with Bible reading and prayer, the women's society became a context in which, for the most part, women could decide how their own spiritual needs would be met. They could study the Bible for themselves, decide which songs they would sing, and choose which religious books they would read. In 1986, Canadian Mennonite historians Frank Epp and Marlene Epp argued that "the women's organization traditionally was, and in some ways still is, the primary vehicle for channelling women's creativity and leadership skills."[37] As such, we could ask whether Mennonite women, perhaps inadvertently, were participating in a kind of parallel church. This possibility is suggested in a recent publication on the ministry of MB women in the church, in which Katie Funk Wiebe wrote:

> These women's groups were transplanted to America from Russia and here underwent various transformations, sometimes functioning as an auxiliary to the church and later on sometimes almost as a church in themselves, operating almost parallel to the congregation with its own budget, aggressive program, membership list, and annual meetings and retreats.[38]

Women's societies became a context where Mennonite women, motivated by the biblical text, could serve God through the support of missions, fellowship with the sisterhood, receive spiritual nourishment, and fully participate in every aspect of their worship ritual. While restricted in their roles in the larger church institution, they made up for it in their own *Verein* meetings, in which, de facto, they formed their own *ekklesia*, in many ways parallel to the local Mennonite church. Truly in the story of Mennonite women's societies from 1940 to 1960, there is more than meets the eye.

Rempel, Redekop and Reflections About Women's Organizations Among the Brethren

Katie Funk Wiebe

W hen my late husband, Walter Wiebe, was working on the 1960 centennial celebration book, *A Century of Grace and Witness*, I told him that there had to be an article on women's contributions. I feared the whole celebration would come and go and women's contributions would be left out. His response was "Who will do it?" I said that I would.

I got addresses of leaders of Mennonite Brethren women's organizations from the Board of Foreign Missions, the only conference board to acknowledge the gifts and contributions of women at the time, and wrote to them. I asked for a response to a questionnaire that dealt with the history of women's work in their area and present goals and trends. I base my comments on these responses. They concern mostly Canadian women because I was living in Canada during this period.

WHAT HAS BEEN THE FOCUS OF THE WOMEN'S COMING TOGETHER?

Women's volunteer work in church and society has been part of the North American scene since the late 1800s. In the Mennonite Brethren world, the word "club" was a bad word, with connotations of spiritual deadness, rather than of service. It was important for MB women not to call what they attended "a club." Yet they wanted to get together.

Women began gathering as early as 1898 in Corn, Oklahoma; 1913 in Herbert, Saskatchewan, and 1930 in Ontario and Alberta. Mrs. C. W. Vogt of Corn, Oklahoma, wrote that in the very early years, the women met only every other week at members' homes because of scarcity of money. They traveled either by horse and buggy or wagon, some coming on foot if not too far distant. It was the host farmer's duty to put up and feed the visitors' horses for the day. The men used this day for visiting and fellowship, frequently gathering in an adjoining room for Bible reading and prayer while the women quilted and sewed.

As Gloria Redekop suggested, names or organizations are important and give us some idea of the purpose of their gathering. The generic name for these groups was *Nähverein*, or sewing circle. They later became "ladies aid," "society" or "auxiliary," and still later, "women's auxiliary." Understandably, women chose biblical names or names derived from biblical concepts because of their goals, both spoken and implicit.

WHAT WAS THE POINT OF THEIR MEETING TOGETHER?

First, they did so to serve the Lord by using the special skills of homemakers. One article about Mennonite women's organizations spoke of them as "handmaids to the Lord." The women who took part in women's organizations in the Mennonite Brethren church in the period 1940-1960 had experienced the Depression and World War II. In Canada, many of them were first and second-generation immigrants. They had learned the skills of making do. They functioned comfortably as an "aid" or "auxiliary." This was their biblical and theological orientation. Most of them were politically unsophisticated.

They worked in this handmaid capacity by holding *Missionsausruf* (mission sales) of handcrafts. The proceeds went to missions. This sale was a big event for the entire congregation. It often began with a missions festival during the day and concluded in the afternoon and evening with the sale. The sale itself was sure to include much high-spirited bidding to push up the price. Women modestly prided themselves on making the set of pillowcases or other item that brought the most money. The bidding was open so that everyone knew what the other person was willing to pay.

Another early service project was sewing for nationals "so they would be clothed." Naked natives were an affront to American morality. The next step in the process was sewing outfits for missionaries and their families. If there were children, the women made dresses and shirts in three sizes, sometimes from the same bolt of cloth. This would allow for up to seven years' growth, the average length of a term of service. The women also raised money for special mission projects, for Mennonite Central Committee, for local church needs (particularly for the kitchen), and for other church-related institutions such as schools and the needy in the area.

Second, they gathered to study, to pray and to fellowship. To pray for missionaries was highly important, and many circles had a time of specific prayer for them and their work. In early years, sometimes one woman read while the others sewed to prevent gossiping, one older friend told me.

We undercut the importance of fellowship if we attribute only philanthropic goals to the women. Fellowship was often more important than service for many women before 1960. Men's activities in the church have always been self-justifying. Women have had to justify their coming together by identifying with the highest moral and social good instead of their own needs as women. Many of them were farm women who might not see other women except briefly on Sundays. They often brought young children to meetings.

This fellowship aspect of the meetings is highlighted by a lengthy report of a twenty-five year celebration of the Kitchener (Ont.) women's organization in 1955. It contains forty-five testimonies, some quite lengthy, of what it meant to them to attend the *Frauenverein*. "I am happy that I feel so close to the other sisters," is the general tenor of the testimonies. It was a place where every woman addressed the other woman with the familiar "*du*."

These stated goals had two serendipities. First, they united the women into a close-knit group. Second, they unconsciously trained women as leaders in leading devotions, organization, Bible study and public speaking. Elections, however, were uncomfortable affairs because no spiritual woman could openly admit to wanting leadership.

Both Redekop's and Rempel's chapters allude to certain trends during this period. First, they describe the organization into districts. It is not clear whether the directives for this organizing came from examples set by other denominational women's groups or from direct encouragement from the Board of Foreign Missions. I think it was the latter. During this period they had little contact with other denominational groups.

Women in some areas experienced opposition to district organizations, as Rempel points out. They were seen as a mustering of power, not suitable to Mennonite Brethren women.

After World War II, Mennonite Brethren experienced a tremendous surge in missions activity. New fields opened up and new missionaries were assigned to them. They needed to be outfitted, but the economy and culture into which these missionaries went was changing rapidly. It became apparent that it sometimes was cheaper to purchase missionary clothing overseas than in America. Sewing for missionary outfits was no longer necessary. Some women experienced great consternation as they sensed elimination of the very basis of their coming together.

Mission sales had also lost their popularity under the increasing criticism of merchandising in the house of the Lord. Women needed a function in the church. The women's movement had not yet reached the grassroots of our congregations. This transition represented a crisis in the thinking of some women. I recall this as a period of deep soul-searching and agonizing. What task could women do?

The mission board tried to guide this transition from sewing missionary outfits to fundraising for their outfits with great care. As Rempel has suggested, the board delegated responsibility of outfitting missionaries to their local constituency, which essentially meant the women.

General Secretary J. B. Toews, speaking in Ontario in the fall of 1960, encouraged the women by recognizing their important role in the work of the kingdom of God. Though Eve was the cause of the fall, she received the first promise of redemption. Mary was the first to see the risen Christ. Women were the first to help meet Christ's needs. Women were the first to be called *Mitarbeiter* (coworkers). He commended their realistic, practical nature, but noted that change had taken place. New vistas lay ahead.

In the very early years, women's groups communicated directly with the missionary to ascertain needs. That served well during that period, but not now when the board was sending out about two hundred missionaries. Toews suggested that groups were organizing by districts to establish better contact with missionaries through the mission board and the executives of the women's groups. Consequently, local groups would receive more mission information. He made it clear that the district organizations were not conferences in themselves, but a function of the church. Each group would have designated missionaries, for whom they would provide a house, furniture and other items while on furlough, and other needs while overseas. Women's groups also should supply funds for special projects in the missions budget and outside it.

Women again had a task! They dug right into these new assignments with the highest-priority task now being to raise money rather than to sew. I think the board knew a goose that laid golden eggs when it saw one.

This shift, however, was not the only change women's organizations were dealing with. Some women were employed outside the home and could not attend day meetings. They agitated for a different type of meeting. Older women were still asking: "What shall we do if we can't sew?" For them quilting and making articles for sale was an enjoyable task; listening to women speakers was a new and sometimes uncomfortable experience. They experienced other tensions as names changed from the all-purpose "sewing circle" to "ladies' aid" or "women's circles," which allowed for a greater variety of functions.

I have some notes my husband Walter made for a talk on unity and mutual understanding to the women's organizations in Hepburn, Saskatchewan. His notes suggest there was disagreement about changing the name *Nähverein* to Ladies Auxiliary. He expressed hope this would not be the beginning of a long history of schism, and asked how obstacles could become opportunities. He suggested a joint mission sale sponsored by the two groups. "Satan would like nothing better than to divide the ladies. If he can divide the ladies, he has divided the church."

I also have in my files notes for the first public presentation I ever gave. I spoke to a meeting of all the women of the Kitchener MB Church as they discussed dividing the popular *Gabenverein*, consisting of about ninety members, into two groups. For some women this change was life-threatening. I tried to emphasize that in Christ women are sisters, not rivals. There is no place for rivalry in the intimacy of the mission circle.

WHAT WERE THE TRENDS IN WOMEN'S ORGANIZATION DURING THIS PERIOD?

1. Women became fund-raisers for missions. They learned to develop budgets and work together to achieve their goals. Women still did not have much of their own discretionary income to donate, but instead harnessed the traditional women's skills to make money (e.g., custom quilting or catering meals).

2. The popular mission sales were disbanded.

3. The content of meetings shifted from sewing to study. In the 1970s and 1980s they began to have speakers or entertainment—such as fashion shows, flower-arranging, or bridal shows—as a means of bringing in the unchurched instead of missionary programs. Some groups shifted their time of gathering to the evenings to accommodate women working outside the home.

4. Meetings moved out of homes into the church basement to accommodate the size of the groups and the needs of women employed outside the home who did not have time to prepare homes and refreshments. Most churches by this time had adequate kitchen facilities.

5. During the 1950s and 1960s Mennonite Brethren women first began to hold rallies and retreats. At first the women gave missionary reports and the men preached at these rallies. As one woman wrote me, "We still prefer men preachers!"

Women's organizations are still changing: Some women attend community Bible studies instead of traditional women's groups. Some congregations now have boards of women's ministries and professional women's groups. The influence of the women's movement is becoming more prominent as women function in pastoral roles and participate in conference structures. This makes attending parallel women's activities at conferences less of an option.

The relationship of women's organizations to the mission board will continue to change as the mission board becomes one of several groups competing for women's interest, time, talent and money. Many rallies and retreats no longer have mission themes. In many congregations, women are still the main overseas mission supporters, but I see a slight movement toward becoming more involved with peace and social justice concerns. This seems more true in Canada than in the United States. It will take time before Mennonite Brethren women organize nationally and internationally. For their dedicated work and significant contributions in past years, the women in the trenches of our congregations deserve our strong affirmation and high praise.

VI.
Theological
Autobiography

J. B. Toews

In the fall of 1940 my wife Nettie, young son John and I moved from Portland, Oregon to Freeman, South Dakota. It was the beginning of the two decades that we are examining and that would be very eventful decades for our personal pilgrimage. But the story cannot begin there.

My childhood and youth date back to Russia, where I completed my grade school, high school and four years of university. My childhood was a deep immersion in the faith of our fathers. The instruction in high school and in grade school demanded extensive religious education. The first hour of every day was Bible instruction. By age twelve I could have passed the Seminary Bible Content Exam with flying colors. But that calm era underwent dramatic change. After high school followed four years of university at the time when communism took over the educational program. The little Mennonite school, an agricultural college in Gnadenfeld, was accredited and integrated into the University of Kiev. Instead of daily religious instruction there was daily political propaganda and the persuasion of materialism. I could not but be influenced by that four years of indoctrination. Then I dared suddenly to ask a serious question regarding the origin of life. That caused me difficulty. I had embarrassed our political instructor by asking such a question. I went underground and succeeded in getting across the border. After I landed in Holland, I contacted the Mennonite Relief Committee. They provided opportunity for me to continue studies at the University of Amsterdam. There I was deeply immersed in the question of agnosticism. I was at sea, searching for answers. It was providential that subsequently in England I shared a room with Dr. Benjamin Unruh, who was at the time in charge of the Mennonite emigration from Europe. He was an intellectual and discussed with me at length issues of faith. He recommended to me Frederick Kendall's book, *Jesus*. Kendall analyzed the secret and mystery of Jesus, but also gave rational reasons for the belief that he was the incarnation of God. Kendall's book helped me to consider again the reality of the revelation in Jesus.

My background of high school and grade school, the religious training there and the deep, deep commitment of my father and mother also influenced me. My father was a very deeply committed Anabaptist person. The literature of Menno Simons was well known to me. I had read all of it when I was a high school student and I returned to it occasionally while at the university.

That is how in 1928 I came to Coaldale, Alberta, our new home in Canada. My spiritual pilgrimage there was one of accommodation. I could not ask questions, though I had many of them. After two years I had the urge for further training. I had to learn English. Dr. Henry W. Lohrenz, the president of Tabor College, came to our home during this time. Knowing some of my background, he invited me to Tabor. The time at Tabor, 1930 to 1932, was for me partly a disappointment, because there was no clear direction. I have no question about the faith of H. W. Lohrenz. He was deeply devoted and I would say he was a genuine Anabaptist. But how does one then explain the Bible conferences where all the speakers were fundamentalists? At that time there also were controversies about the inspiration of the Scriptures.

A second cause for disappointment was that they did not realize that I already had been at the university for more than five years. When I came to Tabor College, they would not give me any credit. They said that I first had to have a certificate from the high school, the academy. You will find at Tabor College a picture of the academy graduates and there I am, because I had not had American history or civics. That was why they could not give me credit.

There were two experiences at Tabor, however, that were very important. In H. W. Lohrenz's theology course we read Edgar Mullins, *The Christian Religion and Its Doctrinal Expressions*. That book helped me for the first time to form a consistent, theological position.

The second, and more important, experience was that I met Nettie Unruh, my life's companion. She came from a wealthy South Dakota farm family. As our relationship matured her father warned her not to marry a minister because they moved around a lot and were always poor. I had not yet made a commitment to enter the ministry. While at Tabor I had to choose between an offer from the Shell Oil Company to go back to Europe as an executive, or to commit myself to working within the church. I had grown up in a minister's household and knew very well what it meant to be poor. It was a very long and severe struggle. Finally it was Nettie who said, "John, it's all right to be poor." When she said that, that evening we committed ourselves to each other, and with the words, "it's all right to be poor," headed into the ministry. We turned down the offer from Shell Oil of $320 per month plus commission, and instead went to Hepburn (Sask.) Bible School. There we received $26.40 per month and lived in a shed during our first year of marriage. The years in Hepburn were happy times, but they predate 1940.

My seminary education at the Northern Baptist Seminary in Portland, Oregon also predates 1940 but they very much impacted what I did in the subsequent decades. When I went there, I was not fully committed to the Mennonite Brethren Church. But when faculty members heard that I came from a Mennonite background they were very much interested in me. There were two men who had a marvelous influence on me: Dr. W. W. Milligan and Dr. Colin Kline. They reminded me that the Anabaptists were the foundation for the Baptist movement. They also told me to remain where I was, with the Mennonite Brethren. It was in a Baptist seminary, with the help of Dr. Milligan and Dr. Kline, that I committed myself to the Mennonite Brethren Church. I again had to make a choice between remaining with the Baptists for a much larger salary or return to work with the Mennonites.

In the fall of 1940 we moved to Freeman, South Dakota to begin teaching at Freeman Junior College. Freeman was Nettie's home community so we moved there partly to be next to her family. The move, however, turned out to be fortuitous for my future ministry. Freeman College, though owned and operated by the General Conference Mennonite Church, was truly an inter-Mennonite institution. The communities of Freeman and nearby Marion and Bridgewater had a cluster of churches representing various ethnic and conference affiliations. Besides several General Conference churches there were also Krimmer Mennonite Brethren, Evangelical Mennonite Brethren, Hutterite and Mennonite Brethren. The students from these churches represented an evangelical stew. Faculty members also represented several Mennonite varieties. Despite their own uniqueness of character, these church traditions functioned well together.

The Freeman sojourn, though short, broadened my experience with the various Mennonite groups. For a few months I served as an interim pastor in the Salem Mennonite Church (General Conference Mennonite) and taught their catechism class to baptismal candidates. The pulpit committee, seeking a permanent replacement for Dr. Peter R. Schroeder, their pastor for many years, even invited me to consider becoming the permanent pastor.

In the summer of 1941 I left Nettie and the boys with her mother on the farm and went to Southwestern Baptist Theological Seminary in Fort Worth, Texas, to begin studies toward a doctorate in theology. It seemed possible that by spending summer there I could complete the residency requirements and the dissertation could also be written while living elsewhere.

In 1941 and early 1942 invitations came to us from the Buhler (Kans.) Mennonite Brethren church and from Tabor College. We choose the Buhler pastorate and will always cherish the three years we spent there. Entering the very life of a congregation there, and subsequently in Reedley, California, were some of my most satisfactory experiences.

While in Buhler, I continued to work toward my doctorate in theology at Southwestern Baptist Theological Seminary. As I was nearing completion of the studies, my dear uncle B. B. Janz visited me and said, "now you have gone too far." At that time no one active in the Mennonite Brethren church had a doctorate in theology. Uncle B. B. was convinced that my future ministry would be jeopardized if I continued. He said it with such persuasion that I did not complete the last three months of my doctoral course work or the dissertation.

In 1945 I became president of Mennonite Brethren Bible College in Winnipeg. There I received further confirmation of my commitment to the Anabaptist view of faith. Abraham H. Unruh, the first President and a continuing faculty member, was firmly committed to the Mennonite theological tradition and mentored the rest of the faculty.

The college board was dominated by Canadian Conference leaders who had shown great vision in bringing the new institution into being even before the constituency was ready. However, they quickly demonstrated a desire for strict control and some isolationist tendencies that I knew would make our journey together difficult. At the first board meeting in the fall of 1945, they already made clear to me that they had a rather fixed understanding of how the college should be run. I found several features of their understanding distasteful.

For one, they indicated a desire to be sharply separate from other Mennonite groups. There was no interest in entering into discussion with the General Conference Mennonites who were also moving to establish a college. I was also concerned about an apparent desire to remain culturally isolated. German, I was told, should be the language of the college, with a minimum of instruction in English.

With all the affirmation and encouragement that came from constituents as they saw the rapid development of the college, I could not reconcile myself to the narrow vision of the board to whom I was responsible. I was not interested in fighting these cultural battles and therefore resigned after three years.

From Winnipeg we went, in 1948, to the Reedley (Calif.) Mennonite Brethren Church. I sought to bring the church into line with my biblical perception of a church. It was a tremendous struggle, but also a tremendous reward. That was a time of struggle regarding Arminianism and Calvinism. We had a large group of Pentecostals in the church at that time. My childhood biblical training and a historical perspective helped me in this context.

During that time I also moved into conference work. In the Board of Reference and Counsel we struggled with the transition regarding pastoral leadership. There were also the very difficult conversations concerning eternal security and the relationships of faith and culture.

In late 1953 we left the Reedley congregation and moved to an administrative position with the Board of Foreign Missions. That move was prompted, in part, by a visit in 1952 to our mission field in what was then known as Belgian Congo, later Zaire. Traveling from village to village with veteran missionary Aaron A. Janzen and reflecting on the spiritual condition of the people made a deep impression on me.

The insights gained from the trip required time to process. The post-war period had created unlimited opportunities for the expansion of missions abroad. Two centuries of colonialism had come to an end and all of the colonies were crying for independence. The dedication of Mennonite Brethren missionaries, the conference and the Mission Board were deeply sincere but it seemed clear to me that the entire orientation of the program would have to be changed because of the new political realities. I sensed that our mission personnel as well as our constituency were not prepared for the changes that were coming. The Board's need for additional administrative leadership to make this transition weighed heavily on me following the Africa trip.

When I arrived in Hillsboro to take up the mission work, I consumed every available book to help me find my way: Roland Allen, Leslie Newbingen, John R. Mott, Steven Neil. I searched for direction in foreign mission programs for the next ten years. We were still operating on the idea of a mission station as the center of operational outreach. The Mission Council, consisting of all bona fide missionaries on the field, took full responsibility for the program of evangelism and institutional services (including schools and hospitals). Missionaries were given a permanent place as "fathers and mothers in Christ" in the indigenous church. They would remain part of the indigenous congregation for life.

With several members of the mission board, in particular George W. Peters and Henry H. Janzen, we sought to move toward a new way of doing missions. That new direction was articulated in a document that I wrote, entitled "Partnership in Obedience." We presented it to the 1957 General Conference convention in Yarrow, British Columbia, where after extended discussion, it was accepted. The document projected the role of the missionary to conform to the New Testament expansion of the gospel. Like Paul, the missionary proclaims the good news and serves as the planter of the church. The mission is only the enabling agency to help plant the church and then provide assistance in teaching and nurture with the local church becoming responsible for its own expansion within its respective culture.

After ten rich but exhausting years we concluded the mission work in 1963 and then went to the Mennonite Brethren Biblical Seminary in Fresno. I was asked in 1955 to accept the position of the Seminary president. I declined then, because the Board had first selected the faculty, and then asked me to come take the presidency. It was then an evangelical seminary, whereas today it is a Mennonite Brethren/Anabaptist seminary. That transition, which was subsequently important for the theological direction of the conference, occupied much of the 1960s. But that story is also beyond the confines of the two decades that are central to this short theological autobiography.

When I summarize not only the 1940-1960 period but also my entire life pilgrimage, it is a marvel of God's grace. I have experienced the transition from a deep pietistic Anabaptist orientation in childhood and youth to the influence of atheism, rationalism and agnosticism. Then came the long struggle when I did not have a direction, but received help from Baptists to find my way. Since then there has been no theological wavering.

Those struggles, while personal in some ways, also have been the struggles of the Mennonite Brethren church. Just as I marvel at God's mercies to me as an individual, so I marvel at God's mercies to us as a denomination. I can trust God for the personal future and for the Mennonite Brethren Church. As a movement we may periodically hit bottom, but if there is sufficient inward vitality it can be born again. New birth requires death. May God help us to always be open to both death and new birth.

VII.
Church
and
Cultural
Transitions

North American Mennonite Brethren at Mid Century: Ecclesiological Developments

Richard Kyle

B y the middle of the twentieth century most aspects of North American Mennonite Brethren life and culture had undergone significant changes. These developments naturally influenced the Mennonite Brethren church and its various institutions. Consequently, the years from 1940 to 1960 were a time of transition, witnessing many new ecclesiological developments.

Broadly interpreted, the subject of ecclesiology touches upon many areas of Mennonite Brethren life and culture. Three are of primary importance here: the shift from a fundamentalist outlook to an increased Anabaptist awareness; ministerial changes, especially the transition to a single salaried pastor; and alterations in the conference structure, including the "constitutional crisis" of 1954 and the merger with the Krimmer Mennonite Brethren in 1960. While these developments affected the Canadian Conference, their greater impact in the 1940s and 1950s was on the United States Conference.

These ecclesiological changes, however, did not take place in a vacuum. They occurred in the larger context of the acculturation of the Mennonite Brethren. The Mennonite Brethren definitely represent a separationist type of Christianity. Though separation has meant different things throughout Mennonite Brethren history, until about the middle of the twentieth century, the Anabaptist doctrine of the two kingdoms and cultural isolation have been the major components in Mennonite Brethren separation from the world.[1] On the matter of separation, Mennonite Brethren theology has been relatively static. It has taught nonconformity to the world, separation, and a rigorous ethic since its Anabaptist origins and it teaches such now.[2] However, the idea and practice of separation from the world has acquired different meanings and interpretations as historical circumstances have changed.

Space only permits generalizations, but the history of the Mennonite Brethren in North America is one of progressive acceptance of cultural traits from the wider society on one hand, and a largely unsuccessful resistance to this acculturation on the other. Many factors contribute to this development, but the positive image of United States and Canada and the change from German to English must rank high.[3] Generally, it seems that a tendency toward isolationism and ethical legalism held sway in Mennonite Brethren circles until the mid-twentieth century in the United States and perhaps a decade longer in Canada. Therefore, when industrialization, urbanization, secularization, materialism, and the use of English became part of the Mennonite Brethren way of life, the old separationist cultural standards began to crumble. The Mennonite Brethren, for the most part, have not successfully replaced their earlier cultural separation with an equally rigorous biblical separation.[4]

The assimilation of the Mennonite Brethren into American and Canadian culture had been going on for most of the twentieth century. Nevertheless, as Paul Toews suggests, "the cumulative impact of the North American experience was obvious by the 1940s and 1950s."[5] What Orlando Harms says about the Southern District at the end of the 1950s was true for most Mennonite Brethren in the United States and somewhat later for their Canadian counterparts. They were "almost completely acculturated to the society around them. They spoke the same language, they dressed like everyone else, they and their children heard and saw the same radio and television programs which largely shaped their interests in the same direction."[6] This acculturation affected many aspects of Mennonite Brethren church life. The question of a fundamentalist or Anabaptist orientation and the change to a professional ministry were particularly shaped by currents in North American culture.

THEOLOGICAL INFLUENCES

Since their origins in 1860, the Mennonite Brethren have encountered many non-Anabaptist and Mennonite theological influences.[7] In Russia the Pietists, Baptists and Darbyites helped shape Mennonite Brethren religious beliefs in various degrees. Upon their arrival in North America, the Mennonite Brethren encountered Baptists, Seventh-day Adventists, Lutherans, Swedenborgians and other Mennonites, plus a wide array of religious movements including millennialists, prohibitionists, universalists and revivalists.[8]

As the twentieth century progressed, the list comprised many other groups including dispensationalists, fundamentalists, perfectionists, charismatics and evangelicals. The greatest general outside influence on the Mennonite Brethren experience in North America, particularly in the United States, came from the Baptists, dispensationalists, fundamentalists, and contemporary evangelicals.

A variety of religious and cultural forces have shaped Mennonite Brethren beliefs and practices. In this sense, the years from 1940 to 1960 do not represent a striking departure from the usual Mennonite Brethren pattern. However, the two decades from 1940 to 1960 represent something of a transition. For most of these years, Mennonite Brethren theology came under the sway of fundamentalism and one of its variants, dispensationalism. The groundwork was being laid, however, for a revival of the Anabaptist-Mennonite identity, which became prominent during the 1960s. As the year 1960 approached, indications of more interest in Anabaptist-Mennonite history and theology could be detected.

Mennonite Brethren have been susceptible to outside theological currents because they have a non-creedal orientation and lack a strong doctrinal identification. In Russia their semi-isolation in ethnic enclaves softened the influence of non-Mennonite theological systems. In North America the Mennonite Brethren did not live in ethnic colonies. Yet, for a while they succeeded in maintaining a degree of cultural identity.[9] As a result, the Mennonite Brethren never developed a clear theological focus. Thus, as their cultural cohesiveness broke down they were attracted to fundamentalist and dispensational doctrines that bore an affinity to their own beliefs.

Dispensationalism made its appearance in Mennonite Brethren churches in both Russia and North America at approximately the same time—the first decade of the twentieth century.[10] These ideas, however, had their greatest impact in the United States. Dispensationalism is a theological system that envisions redemptive history in terms of seven distinct dispensations, during which people are tested in respect to obedience to the disclosed will of God.[11] In particular, this system brought to the Mennonite Brethren Church a system of rigid biblical interpretation and a premillennial-pretribulational eschatology.

Fundamentalism has many definitions, some broad and some restrictive. According to George Marsden, fundamentalism in American religion best can be defined "as militantly antimodernist evangelical Protestantism." Though fundamentalism's roots go back much earlier, the term was not coined until 1920. It soon came "to describe all types of American Protestants who were willing to wage ecclesiastical and theological war against modernism" in religion and the cultural changes that modernists welcomed.[12]

The decades of the 1920s, 1930s, and 1940s saw fundamentalist and dispensational ideas make their way into the Mennonite Brethren Church via several avenues. The primary vehicle for dispensationalism to filter into the evangelical churches of North America was the *Scofield Reference Bible*. Nearly every Mennonite Brethren minister owned and used this version in varying degrees. Some even came close to giving Scofield's notes a status equal with Scripture. The writings of other dispensationalists found their way into Mennonite Brethren circles. Most popular were those of Lewis S. Chafer, and Arno C. Gaebelein. In Canada, the publications of Erich Sauer, a teacher at Wiedenest Bible School in Germany, were widely read after World War II.[13]

Other means for disseminating fundamentalist/dispensational doctrine into Mennonite Brethren communities were radio broadcasts, Bible conferences and especially the influence of Bible institutes.[14] Of great importance, the Bible institutes attracted many Mennonite Brethren young people, giving them their leadership training and understanding of Scripture. Consequently, these Bible institutes—especially Biola in Los Angeles, Moody in Chicago, and Northwestern in Minneapolis—powerfully influenced the spiritual development of the Mennonite Brethren Church.[15]

At Biola numerous future Mennonite Brethren leaders received their training from the noted fundamentalist, Reuben A. Torrey. In other more direct ways Torrey influenced Mennonite Brethren spiritual life. For several years, he was the speaker at the Tabor College Bible Conference and frequently conducted Bible conferences in Mennonite Brethren churches. His book, *What the Bible Teaches*, provided a doctrinal direction for some Mennonite Brethren for decades.[16]

Several Mennonite Brethren also studied at Northwestern Bible Institute, then under the leadership of William Bell Riley, a well-known fundamentalist. Moreover, Mennonite Brethren read the writings of a Northwestern faculty member, Norman O. Harrison, from the 1930s to 1950s.[17] Moody Bible Institute also influenced Mennonite Brethren spiritual life. Dwight L. Moody's devotional books provided preaching material for many Mennonite Brethren lay ministers. James M. Gray, the president of the institute after Moody, wrote *Synthetic Bible Studies*, which became a text in Mennonite Brethren Bible schools.[18] The periodical *Moody Monthly* also found its way into Mennonite Brethren households. Another significant influence came from John R. Rice, a fiery fundamentalist preacher and prolific author. His Christian weekly, *The Sword of the Lord*, which promoted fundamentalism and attacked modernism, penetrated Mennonite Brethren homes.

Fundamentalist and dispensational teachings were readily and indiscriminately accepted in Mennonite Brethren ranks for several reasons. The firm position of fundamentalism against modernism and for the essentials of the Christian faith matched the position staunchly held by many Mennonite Brethren.[19] On a national level the Mennonite Brethren had little choice but fundamentalism or liberalism. Liberalism, with its rejection of the historic Christian faith was not an option.[20] Therefore, the Mennonite Brethren bought into fundamentalist/dispensational teachings because of its positive attitude toward the authority of Scripture and salvation by grace.[21] Furthermore, fundamentalism attracted many Mennonite Brethren because it reinforced certain characteristics already present in the fellowship, namely, authoritarianism, separation and legalism in ethics.[22]

The decades of the 1940s and 1950s, especially the earlier years of this period, demonstrate the dominant role that fundamentalism and dispensationalism played in Mennonite Brethren Church life. One example is the conference's readiness to affiliate with conservative Protestant organizations such as the Evangelical Foreign Missions Association. The Mennonite Brethren joined this organization at its inception in 1943 and in subsequent years even held key leadership roles.[23]

In 1943 conservative Evangelical Christians in the United States formed the National Association of Evangelicals (NAE) as an alternative to the more liberal Federal Council of Churches (renamed the National Council of Churches). In 1945 the Mennonite Brethren became the first Mennonite body to join this organization. While the initial impulse among Mennonite Brethren for joining the NAE came from the Board of Foreign Missions, one of the three reasons given for joining this organization was "to support morally the stand against modernism."[24] In the years following, the Mennonite Brethren affirmed this initial decision in several ways. In 1954 the General Conference voted subsidies to reduce the NAE debt. In 1968 the United States Conference voted to become an official member of the NAE.[25]

During the 1940s and 1950s, several articles in *The Christian Leader* expressed support for the Mennonite Brethren affiliation with the NAE. Citing the combative fundamentalist, Carl McIntire, Elmo Warkentin linked the Federal Council of Churches with a Communist conspiracy. He criticized Federal Council leaders such as E. Stanley Jones, George A. Butterick and Harry Emerson Fosdick for their support of Russia and socialism, and their rejection of the deity of Christ. Conversely, he praised the NAE for its promotion of evangelical truth and resistance to modernism.[26]

Other *Christian Leader* articles expressed a similar perspective, hinting at Communist connections in the World Council of Churches and endorsing the NAE for its support of the historic Christian faith.[27] The Mennonite Brethren objections to liberal organizations and support for fundamentalism, evangelicalism, and the NAE must be seen in a context. Not only did the Mennonite Brethren side with the NAE in its resistance to modernism but they identified with fundamentalism's crusade against Communism. As German immigrants from Russia, the Mennonite Brethren had reasons to dislike Communism and were easily caught up in the tensions of the Cold War years.

In several other ways, the Mennonite Brethren became identified with fundamentalism and dispensationalism. During the 1930s and early 1940s, Tabor College displayed a fundamentalist orientation. For years the annual Bible Conference featured many nationally known fundamentalist/evangelical speakers including Reuben A. Torrey, Jasper A. Huffman, William Evans, Kenneth Kantzer and Leonard Lewis. In addition, A. E. Janzen, Tabor's third president (1935-1942), was a staunch premillennialist. Outspoken dispensationalists on the faculty during this era include William Bestvater and P. R. Lange.[28]

The fundamentalist orientation of Tabor College and its constituency could be seen in the suspicions directed toward its fourth president, P. E. Schellenberg, who served in that role from 1942 to 1951. Questions about Schellenberg arose because he had a Ph.D. in psychology from a secular institution and because he had more Anabaptist leanings. People questioned whether an individual who was not a minister could give spiritual direction to the college.[29] In a 1947 article entitled, "How to Detect the First Signs of Modernism," Arthur Willems expressed concern that modernism could possibly creep into Tabor College. According to Willems the first signs of modernism can be detected in educational institutions because "Satan makes the school his special object of attack."[30]

During the 1940s and 1950s the Mennonite Brethren Church became a willing partner with the fundamentalists in their crusade against modernism and Communism. An interest in such an agenda can be illustrated by the articles published in *The Christian Leader* and *The Voice*. Some examples include "Mennonitism and Modernism," "What is Modernism and How Can It Be Detected?," "The Marks of a Modernist," "Some Recent Literature on the Recent 'Fundamentalist Controversy,'" and the previously mentioned article, "How to Detect the First Signs of Modernism."[31]

In some of these articles, the Mennonite Brethren clearly identify themselves as fundamentalists. For example, in "Mennonitism and Modernism" Walfried Dirks of North End Mennonite Brethren Church in Winnipeg referred to the Mennonite Brethren "as Mennonites and fundamentalists."[32]

In other ways, the Mennonite Brethren adopted the fundamentalist/dispensational agenda. A series of articles in *The Christian Leader* entitled "Evangelism and 'The New Version'" assessed the validity of the "Revised Standard Version" of the Bible.[33] Other articles strongly endorsed the premillennial/ pretribulational position on eschatology and suggested that post-millennialism is a mark of modernism and socialism.[34]

According to Wesley Prieb, approximately 90 percent of the Mennonite Brethren in the early 1940s identified themselves, in varying degrees, as fundamentalists. This figure, however, must be modified by several factors. Many Mennonite Brethren who would have called themselves fundamentalists still upheld the peace position. Also, in 1940 the term fundamentalism did not have the negative connotation that it has today. Moreover, at this time Anabaptism had not yet been clearly defined and a moderate evangelicalism, somewhere between fundamentalism and liberalism, was just emerging.[35] Therefore, the Mennonite Brethren found it easy to slip into the fundamentalist camp.

By the mid-1960s a revival of interest in Mennonite history and theology was underway in Mennonite Brethren circles. This Anabaptist renewal occurred primarily after 1960 and is not a subject for this paper. Nevertheless, the roots of this renewal could be found in the decades of the 1940s and 1950s.

The Anabaptist identity began to take shape with the publication in 1944 of Harold S. Bender's influential work, "The Anabaptist Vision."[36] While this now-classic article had little immediate impact in Mennonite Brethren circles, it laid the ground work throughout American Mennonitism for a recovery of the Anabaptist heritage. Its influence has been immense.

World War II and the draft forced many Mennonite Brethren to examine their historical and theological roots. The reality of a world torn by war made the Mennonite peace position and concept of service more relevant. Young men had to choose between the regular military service, Civilian Public Service (CPS), or non-combatant service. According to Wesley Prieb, the young men who entered CPS encountered other Mennonite traditions and ideas. This process helped to develop an interest in Mennonite history and values, a step that preceded the more institutional movement toward Anabaptism that would come later.[37]

Tabor College in the early 1940s has been described as a "Dallas [Theological Seminary] controlled school." President A. E. Janzen's "entire (theological) system was wrapped around the premillennial view" of eschatology. Gradually, however, a shift began to take place. Janzen himself upheld the peace position and was active in promoting Mennonite Central Committee relief programs. During the war years, The Peace Club was active and vigorous discussions in this regard took place. Two presidents, P. E. Schellenberg (1942-1951) and Frank C. Peters (1954-1956) had Anabaptist leanings and promoted the peace position and relief efforts.[38]

Vernon Wiebe says that many Mennonite Brethren in the 1940s were "one issue people—the social gospel versus fundamentalism." During the decade few Mennonite Brethren would "dare to challenge premillennialism." But even by the late 1940s some Mennonite Brethren began to realize "that fundamentalism depended too much on human knowledge."[39] The human mind could not know everything. The scope of human history did not necessarily fit the neat and tidy dispensational scheme of things.

During the 1950s Mennonite Brethren publications began to

focus more on the historic Anabaptist-Mennonite distinctives. At the forefront of this endeavor was John A. Toews. He lamented the identity crises that the Mennonite Brethren were experiencing and believed that the answer to this problem was a return to Anabaptist roots and a close relationship with other Mennonite groups.[40] Twenty years before the 1975 publication of his major work, *A History of the Mennonite Brethren Church*, his articles articulated a clear Anabaptist-Mennonite perspective of history.[41]

In the late 1950s other voices spoke out for the Anabaptist renewal. Articles in *The Christian Leader* and *The Voice* by Frank C. Peters, Cornelius Wall, Orlando Harms, and Clarence Bauman promoted the Mennonite peace position.[42] Included in several articles by Henry H. Dick was a focus on the conference's Anabaptist roots and several Anabaptist principles such as nonconformity and discipleship.[43] While G. W. Peters was not known for his strong Anabaptist stance, he did write several articles that alerted the constituency to its historic Anabaptist-Mennonite roots.[44]

The Canadian Mennonite Brethren had fewer problems in restoring their Anabaptist-Mennonite heritage, largely because they had not departed from such roots to the extent that their counterparts in the United States had. Substantial numbers of Mennonite Brethren did not come to Canada until the 1920s. By then the tensions in Russia with other Mennonites associated with the succession of 1860 had largely healed. Also, the difficulties associated with the Russian Revolution encouraged Mennonites of all stripes to close ranks. Thus, the Canadian Mennonite Brethren maintained closer ties with other Mennonite groups than had their counterparts in the United States.[45]

Several other factors facilitated the Anabaptist renewal in Canada. Of considerable importance, the Canadian Mennonite Brethren did not feel the influence of fundamentalism and dispensationalism to the extent that their counterparts in the United States did.[46] Consequently, the repercussions of the fundamentalist-modernist fight were less in Canada. Also, such dispensational doctrines as premillennialism had less force in Canada.

Second, the cultural-political situation in Canada lent itself to a stronger Mennonite identity. The Canadian Mennonite Brethren had less exposure to the forces of acculturation than have the United States Mennonite Brethren. They maintained the German language barrier several decades longer. The Canadian national setting has nurtured the existence of an ethno-religious pluralism, thus permitting groups such as the Mennonite Brethren to maintain their cultural identity. The Canadian Mennonite Brethren did not have to choose between being Canadians and Mennonites. The World War I experience made it difficult for Mennonites in the United States to be simultaneously good Americans, Germans, and Mennonites.[47]

Paul Toews claims that "a reclamation of Mennonite history and identity did take place among the U. S. Mennonite Brethren." He points to two institutions, Pacific College (originally Pacific Bible Institute) and the Mennonite Brethren Biblical Seminary as the sources for this renewal. From the opening of Pacific Bible Institute in 1944 and the seminary in 1955, these institutions were dominated by fundamentalist-dispensationalist influences. Part of the rationale for starting Pacific was that Tabor, which already had experienced some Anabaptist stirrings, was perceived as "too liberal."[48]

However, this situation would change by the early and mid 1960s. In 1960 Arthur J. Wiebe became president of Pacific Bible Institute. Not only did he turn this institution into a liberal arts college, but he facilitated a Mennonite revival by recruiting faculty members with a strong Anabaptist perspective. The process of changing the Mennonite Brethren Biblical Seminary from a "miniature Dallas Theological Seminary" to an Anabaptist institution began in 1964 when J. B. Toews assumed the presidency. Again, the heart of this process was his hiring a faculty and administration committed to the Anabaptist vision.[49]

How successful this Anabaptist-Mennonite renaissance has been in the United States remains open to question. On one hand, fundamentalist and dispensational views no longer hold sway at any of the major Mennonite Brethren institutions. In most Mennonite Brethren schools today the term fundamentalist is one of disrepute. The seminary, with a largely Canadian faculty, still maintains a strong Anabaptist stance. Moreover, most Mennonite Brethren today probably have a better awareness of their history and beliefs. On the other hand, moderate evangelicalism has made its inroads in both the Mennonite Brethren educational institutions and churches. The Anabaptist revival has come at a time of extensive ideological and cultural pluralism and does not seem to have had an extensive impact on the churches.

LEADERSHIP PATTERNS

The patterns of leadership in the Mennonite Brethren churches in the United States underwent significant changes during the years from 1940 to the early 1950s. The churches in Canada experienced similar transitions two decades later, from about 1961 to 1971. The major change was the move from a multiple lay ministry to the single-pastor professional ministry. A second related shift was from the ordained deacon to the elected deacon. Another resulting transition concerned a subtle shift in interpreting Scripture—from an exegetical community to the seminary and Board of Reference and Counsel.

These transitions must be seen as but an aspect of the acculturation that the Mennonite Brethren experienced in North America. Especially important was the language change, urbanization, a rising level of education, and increased contacts with non-Mennonite religious groups. The heightening of Mennonite distinctives that took place in Mennonite Brethren ranks during the middle years of the twentieth century might be seen as a return to historic Anabaptism. The changes in respect to the ministry and the interpretation of Scripture, however, cannot be regarded as such. They run counter to Anabaptist principles.

The details of these transitions, especially the shift to the single pastor, are difficult to document. In keeping with the congregational polity of the Mennonite Brethren, it was a matter for the local church, not the General Conference. By 1951 the resolutions of the General Conference took for granted the existence of salaried pastors. Beyond specifications on how to select and discipline a pastor, little was said about the matter on the conference level.[50] Historian John A. Toews has also noted the lack of church records regarding this issue.[51] In research for his history of the Southern District, Orlando Harms suggested that even the minutes of individual churches say little about the matter. The change to the single pastor system "just happened."[52] Beneath this official silence, however, there were often struggles, pitting those favoring the transition to the single pastor model against those who wished to retain the lay multi-pastoral system.

The early Anabaptists maintained the doctrines of the priesthood of believers and the congregational church polity. They did not consider the "ministry of the Word" to be a function of a special ecclesiastical profession. Instead, they regarded as ministers those individuals who had been called by the church to this office, even if they lacked special training. Moreover, these ministers and teachers were not the head of the congregation; they had authority only to preach the Word and administer discipline. The church had only one head—Jesus Christ.[53]

Among the leaders of the MB secession in 1860, that is, the eighteen "founding fathers," none were ordained ministers or deacons. This renewal movement emphasized the priesthood of the believer and sought the active participation of all members of the congregation. What emerged was a congregational polity with an unsalaried, multiple lay ministry. The pulpit work was a shared ministry, with most of the preachers being drawn from the teaching profession, though few of them before World War I had any formal theological training.[54]

In North America the Mennonite Brethren preserved the unsalaried multiple lay ministry. Both the congregational and denominational leaders came from within the local congregation. Training took place primarily within the local congregation, which indoctrinated future leaders with scriptural principles.[55] The call to the ministry came because the congregation recognized the gifts of a particular individual, who more often than not came from the farming and teaching vocations. Several individuals within each congregation shared in the ministry of the Word.[56]

But this would all change. By the late 1930s a process began that would transform the leadership pattern in the United States to the single salaried pastor. The church in Buhler, Kansas had a salaried pastor by 1930. By 1936 the Hillsboro (Kansas) Mennonite Brethren Church had introduced the pastoral system. From 1936 to 1943 at least five Mennonite Brethren churches in the Midwest adopted the single pastoral system. Between 1940 and 1945 at least seven congregations in the Pacific District did so. By the early 1950s nearly all Mennonite Brethren churches in the United States had shifted from the multiple lay ministry to the single pastoral system.[57]

This change came about largely for pragmatic reasons. According to John A. Toews, the issue of the single pastoral system received little discussion in principle "within the context of New Testament teaching . . . or the Anabaptist-Mennonite heritage." The arguments within individual Mennonite Brethren Churches for or against this system were primarily practical in nature.[58]

The general acceptance of American culture since 1874

hastened such an alteration. More specifically, the transition from German to English in worship services and the general rise of the educational level among church members accelerated the change to the pastoral system. According to Frank Epp, the Mennonites in the United States assumed, to a greater degree than those in Russia and Canada, that the linguistic and cultural forms of Mennonitism could be changed without great danger to the content of their religion.[59] Therefore by 1935, which James Juhnke has called the "critical year" of language change, most families in the United States with growing children had ceased the habitual use of German. Most churches had made the transition from German to English by 1950.[60]

Because of the language change, a higher level of education, and the influence of outside religious groups, the Mennonite Brethren began to desire well trained preachers who could communicate in English. Such a demand encouraged ministers to study outside the fellowship, where they brought back new ideas about church polity. When they received such theological training, especially at the seminary level, they often did not accept positions as part time unsalaried lay pastors. Such men usually wanted salaried pastorates. If the Mennonite Brethren did not provide such a position, the Baptists would.[61]

Other pragmatic considerations played a role in the pastoral change. Some people wanted "better preaching," although there is some question whether the salaried pastors were a significant improvement. Others believed that the pastoral system would be a "more effective ministry." Still other people believed that better trained pastors who spoke English could best retain the young people in the church. Also, in the urban centers a full time pastor could better meet the churches' counseling and visitation needs.[62]

While most Mennonite Brethren in the United States supported the new system, voices spoke out against the change— some with considerable bitterness. The intensity of these objections varied from congregation to congregation, but they usually centered on practical matters rather than theological issues. The subjects of the pastor's salary, vacation, and professionalism often came to the forefront. Some objected to paying a pastor, others accepted the principle of a salaried pastor but questioned the amount of the remuneration. Especially objectionable was when a potential pastor made the matter of salary an issue.[63]

In the 1940s and 1950s, the thought of a pastor taking a vacation provoked some church members. A poem submitted to *The Christian Leader* in 1943 may have caught such a spirit. A small portion of the poem read:

> Would the farmer leave his cattle
> Or the shepherd leave his sheep?
> Who would give them care or shelter,
> Or provide them food to eat?
> So it strikes me very sing'lar,
> When a man of holy hands
> Thinks he needs to have a vacation
> And forsake his tender lambs,
>
> Did St. Paul get such a notion?
> Did a Wesley or a Knox?
> Did they in the heat of summer,
> Turn from their own needy flocks?
> Did they shut up their meeting
> Just to go and lounge about?[64]

The fact that ten years later *The Christian Leader* ran an article supporting a pastor's need for a vacation suggests that the issue had not entirely gone away.[65]

Three other tendencies emerged. While accepting the principle of a salaried pastor, church members rejected the idea that the pastor should approach his job as if it were another profession. Also, the pastor was not to do his job alone. There may have been a single pastor but the laity were still quite active, providing some semblance of a shared ministry.[66] Third, Mennonite Brethren had high expectations for their pastors. Articles in *The Christian Leader* elaborating on the job of a minister present a demanding if not impossible job description.[67] One is left with the impression that if the Mennonite Brethren were going to pay their pastors, they were determined to get their money's worth.

The transition to the single pastoral system came about two decades later in Canada and is thus not a subject for this study, except as its background relates to the 1940s and 1950s. Before 1960, only about 25 percent of the Canadian Mennonite Brethren enjoyed a full-time pastor. Nevertheless, the idea of the salaried pastor was well rooted by 1960. The same forces that propelled the United States Mennonite Brethren along this path—urbanization, the language change, increased contacts with outside religious groups, and an improved level of education—facilitated the rise of the pastoral system in Canada. After 1961 the change came swiftly.[68]

However, in Canada the transition to the pastoral system was not as complete as in the United States. The large scale immigration of Mennonite Brethren from Russia to Canada in the 1920s has had a dramatic affect on Mennonite Brethren church life. The late arrival meant that the language change came later in Canada. This fact helped reduce the acculturation of the Canadian Mennonite Brethren, including their desire for a full time, salaried pastor who would preach in English.[69] Moreover, among the *Russländer* (as the 1920s immigrants were called) were many who had been church leaders in Russia. These gifted individuals provided leadership in the Canadian churches, strengthening the concept of the lay ministry for years to come. Furthermore, the Canadian Mennonite Brethren placed considerable emphasis on Bible school training, a factor that also produced an abundance of lay leaders for the church.[70]

As in the United States, the Mennonite Brethren in Canada turned to the salaried pastorate for practical reasons: better preaching, more efficient ministry, and a better community outreach. Nevertheless, some individuals believed that the multiple system was more biblical and that the lay preachers were less prone to seek popular approval. Because of these arguments and the factors delaying the transition, the Canadian Mennonite Brethren were more reluctant to accept the new pastoral system.[71]

Paralleling the change in the pastoral system was the transition from ordained deacons to ones elected for a set term. In Russia and during the earlier years in North America, the congregation elected and ordained deacons for life. But several questions arose: why was the deacon ordained for life when other church officers were not? In the New Testament, was a person selected to the office for a specific service and time duration, or for life?[72] These and other questions prompted the Mennonite Brethren to examine the role and function of the deacon. By the 1970s very few churches in the United States and only about half in Canada ordained deacons for life. Instead, most deacons were elected for a term of several years.[73]

Wesley Prieb has suggested that this change was linked to the transition to the new pastoral pattern. The ordained deacon was the "cornerstone of lay leadership" in the Mennonite Brethren churches. Ordained for life, the deacon "represented continuity in lay leadership, more power to the congregation," stability, and support for the pastor. On the other hand, the elected deacon did not bring the same level of commitment or the same quality of leadership. Like the salaried pastor, they were something of a "revolving door."[74]

Despite the shift to the single pastoral system, the Mennonite Brethren have retained more lay involvement in the church than have many religious denominations. The Kauffman and Harder study of the early 1970s showed that slightly more than 50 percent of the Mennonite Brethren still participated in some form of the shared ministry (e.g., Sunday school teacher, committee member, deacon).[75]

Nevertheless, the years around the middle of the twentieth century witnessed a shift of authority in the Mennonite Brethren Church. Decisions on faith and lifestyle in the Mennonite Brethren fellowship, in theory at least, had rested on a community process, in which the interpretation of Scripture emerged out of a wide consensus. With the coming of the pastoral system, decisions on the theological matters began to be made by the professionally trained leaders, with the seminary and Board of Reference and Counsel wielding considerable influence. By the later twentieth century, the Mennonite Brethren had moved from an exegetical community with the center of power in the congregation to a religious denomination run more on the corporate model.[76]

STRUCTURAL CHANGES

The period 1940-1960 witnessed two changes in the structure of the Mennonite Brethren Church of North America. First was the 1954 reorganization of the North American Conference structure. Then in 1960 the intermittent relationship between the Mennonite Brethren and the Krimmer Mennonite Brethren finally culminated in a merger of the two groups.

The Mennonite Brethren, from the very beginning, have shown a remarkable propensity for conference organization and conference work. By 1872, only twelve years after their origin, the Mennonite Brethren had founded a conference in Russia. This development came eleven years before the much older Mennonite churches in Russia organized an official conference in 1883.[77]

Five years after the first migration to North America, the first duly - constituted Mennonite Brethren Conference met in 1879.

John A. Toews has described the growth of the General Conference in North America in four stages. Regarding conference structure, the years from 1879 to 1909 were generally characterized by centralization. Conference work during this period was naturally limited, consisting primarily of the beginning activities in missions, education, and publications. In the next phase, 1909-1924, the conference divided itself into several districts (Southern, Central, Northern, Pacific) and until 1954 the fellowship functioned in a more decentralized manner. Under this arrangement, conference responsibilities were divided between the General Conference and districts.[78]

The third phase, 1924-1954, saw a significant redistribution of Mennonite Brethren membership. By 1924 Hillsboro, Kansas was the "New Jerusalem" of the Mennonite Brethren world, the undisputed center of General Conference activity. Located in Hillsboro were Tabor College, the only Mennonite Brethren institution of higher learning, and the conference publishing house. Moreover, the largest concentration of Mennonite Brethren in North America could be found in the Southern District, the district in which Hillsboro was located.[79] But this would change during the next thirty years. Because of the influx of *Russländer* beginning in the 1920s, the Northern District (later the Canadian Conference) grew dramatically. By 1951 its membership surpassed that of the other three district conferences together. The Depression had a scattering affect on the Mennonite Brethren within the United States, encouraging many of them to move to the West Coast. As a result, by 1953 the membership of the Pacific District surpassed that of the Southern District.[80]

These new demographic realities caused a reorganization in the General Conference. The demographic shift had not been reflected in the conference representation, policy, and organization. Thus, tensions developed between Mennonite Brethren in Canada and the United States and between the Pacific and Southern Districts in the United States.[81] Mennonite Brethren in Canada and the Pacific District insisted on a conference structure more in harmony with the new population distribution.

These tensions centered particularly around the operation of Mennonite Brethren institutions and agencies. Educational efforts began to be polarized. Mennonite Brethren in Canada and the Pacific District felt the need for institutions of theological training in their areas. Thus, in 1944 two new Mennonite Brethren institutions of higher learning opened—the Mennonite Brethren Bible College in Winnipeg and Pacific Bible Institute in Fresno.[82]

Other developments caused the Canadians to want a separate conference. The preservation of German for two decades longer in Canada reinforced the polarization between the United States and Canadian conferences. Canadians complained about the lack of news coverage on subjects of interest to them in *Zionsbote* and *The Christian Leader*. Therefore, they established their own publishing house in Winnipeg and in 1962 began the *Mennonite Brethren Herald* as the official publication of the Canadian Mennonite Brethren Conference. Furthermore, in 1946 the Ontario Conference of Mennonite Brethren joined the Northern District (Canadian Conference). This further strengthened the Canadian Mennonite Brethren in respect to size, education, evangelicalism and home missions.[83]

The questions caused by the numerical growth of the Canadian Mennonite Brethren and the operation of conference agencies and publications culminated in the "constitutional crisis" of 1954. At the meeting of the General Conference in Hillsboro in 1954, the idea of "area conferences" emerged. By 1953 the Canadians had already made certain activities area conference responsibilities: higher education, youth work, home missions and church schools (including Sunday schools). They would cooperate with the General Conference only in foreign missions, relief, the Committee of Reference and Counsel and the Board of Trustees. At this meeting the General Conference structure was reorganized to include two area conferences: the United States and Canada. Each of these national conferences contained subdivisions—districts in the United States and provincial conferences in Canada, which still enjoy a measure of independence.[84]

The second structural change concerned the 1960 merger of the Mennonite Brethren and Krimmer Mennonite Brethren conferences. The Krimmer Mennonite Brethren Church began in the Crimea area of Russia in 1869. Jacob A. Wiebe (1836-1921) was its founder and early leader. This new church stressed conversion, baptism by immersion, church discipline, nonconformity, nonresistance, refusal of the oath, and footwashing. The Krimmer Mennonite Brethren left the Crimea in 1874 for America. They were the first church body to leave Russia in the 1870s for America, establishing their center in the village of Gnadenau, near Hillsboro. The group expanded into other areas of western North America, with the two main centers being Kansas and South Dakota.[85]

The lengthy courtship of the Mennonite Brethren and the Krimmer Mennonite Brethren was an occasional process that dated back to Russia. In the United States overtures toward merger continued for over eighty years with several obstacles arising to prevent a denominational union. One hindrance was the mode of baptism: the Krimmer Mennonite Brethren practiced forward immersion rather than backward as performed by the Mennonite Brethren. The Krimmer Mennonite Brethren were also reluctant to merge with the Mennonite Brethren because of the later group's position on the millennium and their contacts with the Baptists. Also, the Krimmer Mennonite Brethren did not want to be swallowed up and became a small part of a larger group.[86]

As time went on the two groups nevertheless developed a close inter-church fellowship and cooperative working relationships in several areas. By the time of World War II, their differences had nearly disappeared. The Gnadenau Church led the movement toward merger. Yet the difficulty of merging the Krimmer Mennonite Brethren mission program, which operated under several mission boards, and the unified program of the Mennonite Brethren Conference still presented an obstacle. In 1949 the Mennonite Brethren reactivated negotiations and pursued the possibility of a merger. In 1952 and 1953 the Krimmer Brethren responded negatively to these overtures, voting not to merge.[87]

However, in 1954 the Gnadenau Church withdrew from the Krimmer Mennonite Brethren and joined the Mennonite Brethren Conference. The loss of the founding Krimmer Mennonite Brethren congregation in North America prompted more unified action by the Krimmer Mennonite Brethren Conference. Other Krimmer Mennonite Brethren churches joined the move to unite with the Mennonite Brethren. In 1957 the Krimmer Mennonite Brethren Conference voted by a two-thirds majority to merge with the General Conference of Mennonite Brethren Churches. The Mennonite Brethren approved the plan toward union in 1958 and 1959, and the official merger took place in 1960 at Reedley, California.[88]

CONCLUSION

This chapter has addressed three ecclesiological developments in the Mennonite Brethren church: the fundamentalist-Anabaptist issue, the transitions in church leadership, and the changes in the conference structure. These developments were significant and in varying degrees left their permanent imprint on Mennonite Brethren church life. Yet, Mennonite Brethren differ in their acceptance of these changes, often viewing them as a mixed bag.

As noted earlier, the attempt to bring about an Anabaptist-Mennonite revival has met only partial success. The Anabaptist-Mennonite renaissance has come at a time of weakening denominational distinctives and loyalties throughout the United States. Many Mennonite Brethren feel quite at home in the theological hodgepodge that makes up modern evangelicalism. Sharp theological distinctives are not at home in a day when ideological pluralism reigns supreme. Thus Mennonite Brethren, particularly in the United States, will probably continue to live with a muddled theological identity.

The shift to the pastoral system was an inevitable aspect of acculturation. Despite recent attempts to resurrect aspects of the multiple lay ministry, the salaried pastoral system is here to stay. In the larger churches, the multiple staff is replacing the single pastor, but it is still a professional ministry. In a day of urbanization when both spouses work, there is little time to labor in the vineyard of the church. Instead, we hire surrogates—the professional minister.

The restructuring of the denomination in 1954 was also inevitable. It reflected trends that have continued—namely a shift of power in Mennonite Brethren ranks from the United States to Canada and within the United States from the Midwest to the West Coast. Hillsboro, once the "Mecca" of the Mennonite Brethren world, now has a much reduced role in conference affairs. These trends will continue, with the United States Conference becoming even more of a junior partner in the General Conference of Mennonite Brethren Churches.

Making a Home in the City: Mennonite Brethren Urbanization in California

Kevin Enns-Rempel

The Mennonites who migrated from Russia to North American beginning in the 1870s were a decidedly rural people. Most had lived for decades in agricultural colonies in South Russia, where they had little contact with major cities. Even before coming to Russia, these Mennonites had a long tradition of rural existence in Prussia or the Netherlands. Some of them—or at least their ancestors—had lived in major European cities such as Danzig or Amsterdam. By the 1870s, however, such past urban experiences had little relevance for most Russian Mennonites on their way to America.

Their choices of destinations in North America confirmed the rural preferences of these Mennonites. Like most German-speaking immigrants, Mennonites from Russia moved to rural farming communities in the Midwest. The Mennonite migration of the 1870s and 1880s resulted in no urban settlements at all.

For Mennonite Brethren (MB), the inclination toward rural settlement also reflected conference policy. At the 1883 MB General Conference in Henderson, Nebraska, delegates passed a resolution on living in cities. They agreed that while members could not be forbidden to move to the city, they should be warned of the dangers accompanying such a decision. Evidently the secretary assumed that everyone knew what those dangers were, since he chose not to enumerate them in the conference minutes.[1]

Over the following half century most Mennonite Brethren followed the guidelines of 1883. Those warnings notwithstanding, however, increasing numbers of Mennonite Brethren did move to the city in the next several decades. The first period of large-scale Mennonite Brethren urbanization in North America took place from 1940 to 1960. In 1941 only about 10 percent of North American Mennonite Brethren lived or worshipped in or near cities of fifty thousand or more residents.[2] By 1960 23.7 percent of them did so.[3] The following table summarizes the urbanization trends for the twenty-year period, 1941-1960.

Urbanization of North American Mennonite Brethren: 1941-1960

	1941		1960	
	# of urban members	% of urban members	# of urban members	% of urban members
California	423	14.8%	1924	37.4%
Manitoba	824	36.3%	1780	46.2%
Ontario	178	22.1%	990	45.6%
Br. Columbia	188	16.6%	620	13.9%
Saskatchewan	136	4.9%	408	17.9%
Oregon	53	15.4%	179	.0%
Kansas	---	---	172	7.0%
Alberta	---	---	135	11.3%
Colorado	---	---	113	51.4%
Oklahoma	---	---	80	3.8%
Minnesota	---	---	34	7.1%
Washington	---	---	27	14.1%
Nebraska	---	---	11	3.6%
Total U.S.	476	4.7%	2334	17.8%
Total Canada	1326	16.8%	4070	29.2%
Total N.A.	1802	10.0%	6404	23.7%

This chapter will focus only on the process of MB urbanization in California. While California is not the only example of large-scale urbanization among Mennonite Brethren at mid-century, it is one of the best examples. In 1960 California was home to more urban-dwelling MB Church members than any other state or province in North America. The state also represents the location of one of the earliest urban MB settlements in North America, established at the turn of the century. During this period a few Mennonite Brethren families relocated from the Midwest to southern California, where they formed the first MB community in that state. Today California remains the most heavily urbanized MB center in the United States, and, with Vancouver, Winnipeg and southern Ontario, is one of the four major urban MB centers in North America.

EARLY SETTLEMENT IN LOS ANGELES

The first Mennonite Brethren known to have settled in the Los Angeles Basin were Johann and Justina Ratzlaff, who moved from

Henderson, Nebraska to Glendora in the spring of 1895. While Glendora was a small town in the 1890s, it was located only about twenty miles east of Los Angeles, one of the fastest growing cities in the country. With a population of 11,000 in 1880, Los Angeles had grown to 50,000 by 1889 and over 170,000 by 1900. Glendora, like all nearby communities, was affected by such growth.

It seems that loneliness would have been the least of the Ratzlaffs worries in such a place. Yet their earliest letters from Glendora, printed in the *Zionsbote,* suggest that they were indeed lonely. In June of 1895 Johann Ratzlaff noted that he and his wife were "physically well but spiritually lacking. We miss our fellow believers here. We must pray and believe that some will come here."[4] The Ratzlaffs would pray and hope for several years before other church members joined them. By 1902 Peter and Maria Wall, also from Henderson, Nebraska, had moved to nearby Azusa. Shortly after their arrival, the Walls reported meeting with other Mennonite Brethren, suggesting that they and the Ratzlaffs were not the only ones in the area.[5] A funeral for the Ratzlaff's two-year old son in Azusa during the summer of 1903 drew forty of "unserer Deutschen" ("our Germans"), a common term then used by Mennonite Brethren to describe fellow church members in non-German contexts such as this.[6]

Rather than settling in a compact area, Mennonite Brethren migrants to southern California scattered across the region. The Walls reported visiting their children in Los Angeles in the spring of 1903, with whom they travelled twenty-five miles southeast to Anaheim. There they attended the dedication of a German Baptist Church led by Johann Berg, a former Mennonite Brethren from Marion County, Kansas. While in Anaheim the Walls also visited with a Mr. Huebert, who had come to visit his children, and the Peter Bergs, who lived there.[7] They reported in September of that year that Mennonite Brethren were scattered over a forty-mile area, and that they were trying to visit as many of them as possible.[8] In April of 1904 the Walls traveled to Long Beach, about fifteen miles south of Los Angeles, where Peter conducted evangelistic meetings.[9]

On August 14, 1904, Mennonite Brethren in the Los Angeles area gathered for a business meeting at the home of Peter and Maria Wall. At this meeting they agreed to conduct quarterly meetings beginning the first Sunday of September.[10] One can make the case that this decision represents the first organized Mennonite

Brethren congregation in California, ten months before the group at Reedley formally organized itself.

The quarterly meetings were thrown temporarily off track when Peter Wall, who seems to have been the leader of the group, died on September 3. After a brief delay, the group gathered in a Long Beach school house for its first meeting on October 9, 1904.[11] Six months later, itinerant evangelist Johann Harms travelled from Hillsboro, Kansas to conduct meetings at Long Beach and baptized ten persons there into the Mennonite Brethren Church. The candidates for baptism came from various towns, including Pasadena, Los Angeles and Anaheim. Thirty-four members attended the baptismal service.[12]

Mennonite Brethren in the Los Angeles area continued to meet on a more or less quarterly basis for the next few years. The congregation suffered a serious blow in 1907, when several families moved to Escondido, a small town north of San Diego. Franz C. Penner of Long Beach, one of the first to move, noted that because the Mennonite Brethren were so scattered throughout the Los Angeles area, some preferred to move to a more compact settlement.[13] While Los Angeles Mennonite Brethren continued to meet together in the following years, the group seemed to lack the same level of energy and organization that existed during the years 1904-1906. The Los Angeles congregation, which appeared in lists of MB churches printed in the General Conference annual reports of 1905 and 1906, vanished from those lists beginning in 1907.[14]

Prospects for a Mennonite Brethren church in Los Angeles brightened again in the 1920s, particularly with the arrival of young adults coming to study at the Bible Institute of Los Angeles (Biola). The Los Angeles Mennonite Brethren Church organized itself with forty-two charter members on June 22, 1924, almost twenty years after the first quarterly meeting of Mennonite Brethren in Los Angeles.[15]

EARLY CITY MISSION WORK IN CALIFORNIA

For a few Mennonite Brethren the city was a place to settle; for others it was a place in which to evangelize. Rather than meeting the needs of MB members living in the city, these city mission programs reached out primarily to people of lower socio-economic backgrounds with no church affiliation.[16] The programs often directed their efforts at children, who generally were more receptive to the message and who the missionaries hoped would influence their parents for the Gospel.

The Mennonite Brethren Conference adopted its first city mission program in 1909 in Minneapolis; another mission was established in Winnipeg in 1913. Discussions regarding such a project in California first took place at the 1913 Pacific District Conference. There, Bernhard J. Friesen, pastor of the Bakersfield Mennonite Brethren Church, expressed the opinion that the time had come for Mennonite Brethren on the West Coast to make a start in this area. Friesen cited the need for such a program in Bakersfield, a city of fifteen thousand with a church population of only fifteen hundred. In Bakersfield, said Friesen, "Suffering, godlessness and sin may be found on every street."[17] The Conference discussed Friesen's comments at length, but decided that it was too small in number and weak in finances to begin such a project. It did, however, appoint a committee to examine the issue further.[18]

Unwilling to wait for the conference, Friesen undertook the work as a local project of the Bakersfield Mennonite Brethren Church. At the 1914 sessions of the Pacific District Conference in November, Friesen reported that they had acquired a house in which to conduct a Sunday school program. The members of the Bakersfield Mennonite Brethren Church provided the mission staff. Evidently impressed with the Bakersfield congregation's initiative, the conference agreed to contribute $300 to the project.[19]

The Bakersfield city mission drew considerable support from the Mennonite Brethren Church established there in the spring of 1910. While Bakersfield hardly represented urbanization on the same scale as Los Angeles, it was a sizable city by the standards of the time. Several members of the Bakersfield church worked in the city, including its first paid minister, B.J. Friesen, who held a second job in the office of a local utility company.[20] The decision of the Bakersfield church to establish a city mission there suggests that they perceived themselves to be living in an urban area.

Reports from the Bakersfield city mission appear in the minutes of the Pacific District Conference for the next few years, but by 1920 had for the most part disappeared. The eventual fate of the city mission program is unclear, since no formal announcement of its closure seems to have appeared in print. For whatever reasons, it was unable to sustain its initial momentum.

Within a few years the Los Angeles congregation had also begun city mission projects. Only a few months after the organization of that congregation, it established a Sunday school program in nearby Lynwood under the direction of Jacob D. Hofer. After only about one year, however, the Los Angeles church turned the Lynwood project over to a Baptist congregation.[21]

Considerably more successful was the city mission project that became known as the City Terrace Mennonite Brethren Church. Organized in the fall of 1926 by A.W. and Margaret Friesen, the mission originally targeted the Jewish and Catholic population of east Los Angeles. It focused particularly on Sunday schools and after school clubs for the children of the neighborhood. By 1929 the Friesens reported a Sunday school enrollment of 110 and a staff of twelve to fifteen workers.[22]

Throughout the 1930s the Pacific District repeatedly discussed whether it should accept greater financial responsibility for the City Terrace mission. In 1940 the district took a major step in that direction by agreeing to purchase property and fund construction of a building at Whiteside and Herbert Streets, which was completed in 1942.

Early reports from City Terrace emphasize the work there among Jewish people. By the mid-1940s, however, this section of Los Angeles had undergone significant demographic shifts. An increasingly diverse ethnic population complicated the mission's program. In his 1945 report to the Pacific District Conference, A.W. Friesen noted that "it is difficult to harmonize the many nationalities that attend."[23] The following year he reported that "more and more colored people are moving into the district," and that "this has caused quite a problem—many of the white people object and keep their children at home."[24] In 1947 the mission found a temporary solution by conducting separate Sunday school and vacation Bible schools for the white and "colored" children.[25] In 1954 pastor Wesley Gunther noted that the City Terrace community consisted of three distinct ethnic groups: a Jewish neighborhood, in which the church had worked with little success; a variety of working-class white ethnic groups, with whom the mission had its greatest success in the past; and a dominant Hispanic population, with whom Gunther suggested "our greatest opportunities lie in the future."[26] His assessment of the future was largely correct, since in subsequent years the City Terrace church's work became increasingly Hispanic.

THE 1940S AND THE RISE OF MB URBANIZATION

Despite these efforts at settlement and mission work in Los Angeles and Bakersfield, the Mennonite Brethren Church in California was still overwhelmingly rural by 1940. Less than 15 percent of the members in California lived in or near significant urban areas. A large percentage of that number, furthermore—particularly those near Bakersfield—would have lived in ways appearing quite rural by most present-day standards. The creation of MB congregations in San Jose (1940) and Fresno (1942), however, marked the beginning of more rapid and systematic urbanization among California Mennonite Brethren.

The origin of the San Jose congregation dates from the 1920s, shortly after the creation of the Los Angeles Mennonite Brethren Church. In 1925 B. D. Schultz reported in the *Zionsbote* that twenty Mennonite Brethren were living in the San Jose area. Since they had no minister, they attended other churches in the area. Schultz expressed hope, however, that a Mennonite Brethren congregation could soon be established.[27] A little over one year later Jacob J. Unruh reported that he and his wife met on Sunday afternoons with three other MB families, and that they had discussed the possibility of regular Sunday evening worship services.[28]

Many Mennonite Brethren who moved to San Jose during the 1920s and 1930s took employment at local fruit canneries. Jacob J. Unruh reported that he had done so in 1927, and there had "experienced a taste of slavery." Besides the difficult and unpleasant work, Unruh complained of "all the godless people who work there." He noted that "it requires much grace not to be dragged along by them. . . . It has been a great struggle for me, but the Lord has given me the victory."[29] Unruh's comments suggest something of the ambivalence that many Mennonite Brethren experienced in the heterogeneous cultural and moral environments of urban settings.

Job opportunities in the canneries during the depression-ridden 1930s brought increasing numbers of Mennonite Brethren to San Jose. Many stayed only for the summer, but by the late 1930s more decided to make their homes in San Jose. This growing permanent MB population led to renewed interest in starting a congregation there. In March 1940 a group met with C. N. Hiebert from Hillsboro, Kansas, in the home of Abe and Anna Gerbrandt. Hiebert led the service in the German language. This reportedly was a source of great encouragement for the group, which out of necessity had been attending various English speaking churches in San Jose. Bolstered by Hiebert's visit, the group began meeting every other Sunday afternoon, and after about two months began weekly Sunday morning services. In September Dick Gerbrandt accepted the call to be their first minister. Prior to his arrival in San Jose, Gerbrandt had served as a minister in the Sawyer, North Dakota MB congregation. The San Jose congregation held an organizational service on October 13, 1940, with twenty charter members.[30]

A similar, though accelerated, process took place in Fresno. Hope for employment during the depression brought several rural MB individuals and families there beginning in the late 1930s. Most seem to have taken jobs in sales, construction or machine work. The group met socially for the first time in 1938, and within several months began meeting for mid-week worship services in a series of rented facilities. By 1941 the group had started a Sunday school program and rented a building on a long-term basis. The little group suffered a setback that year when their lay leader, John F. Krause, was transferred out of Fresno by his employer, the Standard Oil Company. Rural Mennonite churches seldom encountered situations of involuntary relocation like this. In January of 1942 the Fresno Mennonite Brethren Church organized with forty-seven charter members.

The time between the first identifiable MB settlement in San Jose and the organization of a congregation there was fifteen years. In Fresno the process took only a little more than five years. The more rapid MB urbanization in Fresno probably can best be explained by location: San Jose was isolated from other MB communities, while Fresno was situated near large Mennonite communities in Reedley and Dinuba. Mennonite Brethren moving to Fresno could take advantage of urban opportunities while participating for a time in nearby established rural MB communities. Most Mennonite Brethren in Fresno drove each Sunday to church services in Reedley during the first few years before they were able to establish their own congregation.

The large Reedley congregation served not only as a magnet for Mennonite Brethren from other areas moving to Fresno, it also functioned as a source of members for the growing MB community there. Persons in Reedley seeking work outside a small town environment would have tended to seek such opportunities first in nearby Fresno before looking further afield. Of the original forty-seven charter members at Fresno, more transferred their memberships from Reedley than any other location.[31] No such community existed to feed Mennonite Brethren into San Jose.

Despite their different situations, the congregations in both San Jose and Fresno grew rapidly in the ensuing years. San Jose surpassed one hundred members by 1943, exceeded two hundred by 1948 and reached three hundred in 1956. Fresno's growth was even more rapid. In less than two years it had one hundred members. By 1949 it had two hundred, and in 1955 it surpassed four hundred members. The creation in Fresno of Pacific Bible Institute (1944) and Mennonite Brethren Biblical Seminary (1955) undoubtedly drew even larger numbers of Mennonite Brethren to that city than would otherwise have been the case.

The accelerated pace of urbanization of California Mennonite Brethren beginning in the 1940s occurred in part because of larger economic trends. Production demands accompanying the Second World War caused a major transformation of California's economy. Orders for all manner of products soared in the early 1940s, bringing the depression to a dramatic close. Thousands of new residents moved to California cities, or relocated from rural to urban California, many seeking employment in defense-related industries.[32] The Mennonite Brethren who came in increasing numbers to California's cities in the 1940s were part of this larger phenomenon. While no statistics are available indicating how many Mennonite Brethren entered jobs directly related to defense production during the 1940s, it seems more than coincidental that MB membership in urban areas would shoot up simultaneously with the demands of the defense economy. Even those Mennonite Brethren who chose not to enter defense industry-related jobs would have found improved job opportunities in urban areas due to the general economic stimulation of the wartime economy.

San Jose and Fresno were not the only two urban centers to draw new Mennonite Brethren migration; the Los Angeles congregation did so as well. Organized in 1924 with about fifty members, it doubled its membership by the end of that decade but then dropped to about seventy-five members during the depression. The onset of the Second World War, however, coincided with an increase in the congregation's membership: from 73 members in 1941 to 119 in 1942, eventually climbing to 137 members by the end of the war. While these are not large numbers, the increase is significant when compared to the stagnant and even declining growth rate of the previous decade.

DISTRICT HOME MISSION INVOLVEMENT
IN MB URBANIZATION

Through the 1940s the Pacific District Conference of Mennonite Brethren Churches took a largely passive role in the urbanization process. Individual MB families in urban areas sought one another out, began meeting informally, and eventually reached a point at which they wished to organize a regular congregation. Not until that point did the conference, through the Board of Home Missions, generally become involved with the new group. Nor did the conference take much initiative in establishing city mission programs. The missions in Bakersfield, Lynwood and East Los Angeles all arose from local initiative; only after several years did the conference provide major support for Bakersfield and City Terrace.

Beginning in the 1950s, as the pace of urbanization quickened, the Pacific District Conference became a more active participant in developing urban congregations and mission projects. When its churches were still overwhelmingly rural, the conference could afford to take a casual attitude toward the few members who ventured to the cities. As that number increased the conference was forced to take them more seriously or risk losing a significant portion of its membership. Rather than waiting for almost fully organized congregations to approach it for assistance, the Board of Home Missions began to enter the process at a much earlier stage, offering help and encouragement almost from the outset.

The earliest example of this changing attitude is evident in Board of Home Missions discussions regarding the establishment of new congregations in Sacramento and Santa Cruz during 1951 and 1952. In the spring of 1951 Board members met with four MB families in Sacramento about becoming the nucleus of a new congregation. The following year it agreed to "accept the challenge of the Sacramento field with definite plans to establish a church there."[33] However, not until 1964 was a Mennonite Brethren congregation organized in Sacramento. That the Board would become involved with such a small core group so early in the process marks a radical departure from its earlier policies toward developing urban congregations.

The same situation can be seen in Santa Cruz. Aware that a

small group of MB families were living in that city, the Board asked Allen Fast, pastor of the Ebenfeld MB Church near Hillsboro, Kansas, to hold four weeks of meetings in Santa Cruz. By the time of the Pacific District Conference in November, Fast could report a core group of seven families and optimistically announced that a new Mennonite Brethren Church had been born.[34] Within a few months, however, dissension arose within the group, some of them preferring to establish an independent congregation rather than one in the MB conference. By May 1953 the Board of Home Missions had abandoned the Santa Cruz project.[35]

The Home Missions approach in Sacramento and Santa Cruz carried with it the potential for failure, or at least delayed success. Under the old methodology, the Board waited until an urban congregation had proven itself ready for membership in the conference, and therefore was reasonably assured of surviving for the foreseeable future. Now that the Board had begun entering the process earlier, no such assurances existed.

> Early difficulties notwithstanding, the Board of Home Missions had committed itself to a program of urban church planting. This new commitment was evident in Board Secretary Dan Goertzen's report to the 1953 Pacific District Conference:
> The hope of Home Mission lies in the establishing of new indigenous churches in our rapidly expanding suburban areas. The natural barriers of language and culture have to a large extent disappeared for this generation. . . . New neighborhoods are being built up and established in nearly every large city, and in these districts many of our own Mennonite Brethren young couples find themselves. These areas offer the greatest opportunity for Home Mission to this generation.[36]

The Board of Home Missions implemented this vision by establishing three urban congregations during the 1950s: in Fresno, Pacoima (later Arleta) and Santa Clara. The congregations in Fresno and Santa Clara resulted from outreach and growth within existing urban congregations; Pacoima/Arleta represented MB urbanization in a new area near Los Angeles.

By the early 1950s MB population in Fresno had grown to such a point that discussions took place regarding a second congregation there. A formal request to that effect was made to the Fresno Mennonite Brethren Church (now the Bethany MB Church) in fall of 1953, and by the spring of 1954 the Board of

Home Missions took initiative for this project. Large numbers of MB families had moved to the southeast part of the city, resulting in the decision to locate the new congregation in the area.[37] In 1955 land was set aside next to the proposed campus of Pacific Bible Institute and Mennonite Brethren Biblical Seminary and in 1957 the Butler Avenue Mennonite Brethren Church was organized there.

A similar process took place in Santa Clara. The San Jose Mennonite Brethren Church organized a Sunday school project in the El Camino district of that city, which by 1956 had an enrollment of one hundred. A large upper middle class population with no church in the area convinced Board of Home Mission members that El Camino was a prime location for a new congregation.[38] The Board offered to pay for the lot and one-quarter of the initial building costs for a new church in Santa Clara.[39] This kind of cost sharing between the conference and the local congregation became the regular practice for subsequent Home Missions funding projects. The Pacific District Conference accepted the El Camino church at its 1956 sessions.

Butler Avenue and El Camino represented outreach by local urban congregations; the Board of Home Missions carried primary responsibility for beginning the work in the San Fernando Valley north of Los Angeles. In November of 1955 Dan Goertzen reported to the Pacific District Conference on an appeal from four or five young couples living in the Burbank area, and noted that more MB families were likely to move to the area in the coming years. Goertzen encouraged the conference to consider their request, stating that "we cannot disappoint them. . . . A work is needed to conserve those who will go there in the years to come."[40]

The San Fernando group met for the first time in December of 1955, with an attendance of about twenty. In June of 1956 the group began meeting for regular worship in the town of Pacoima and at that time adopted the name Valley Mennonite Brethren Church. All of the original participants were young Mennonite Brethren families, most of who had come to the area for education or work. Also included were several young Mennonite Brethren men fulfilling government alternative service assignments. In June 1956 Arthur Wiebe visited the fledgling congregation and submitted a report to the Board of Home Missions. He noted that the "youth and enthusiasm of the group . . . argues well for the future of this work." However, such a group also lacked long term stability, since those in the area for school or government service would likely not remain beyond that time. Wiebe also noted that the congregation had a high ratio of men to women, largely because of the number of young single men in the area fulfilling alternative service requirements. He expressed concern that this unbalance threatened the survival of the congregation, since these single men might find it necessary to visit other churches in which there were more single women in their age group.[41]

Accepted by the Pacific District Conference in 1956, the Valley Mennonite Brethren Church moved to nearby Arleta in the early 1960s and adopted the name Community Bible Church. It never achieved a high level of numerical strength and stability, and at its peak in the early 1980s, had fewer than sixty members. The congregation closed in 1987 and the Board of Home Missions appropriated the facility for a new Hispanic congregation.

The concern for conserving existing church members dominated most discussions of urban church planting projects through the 1950s. This is evident in the concern for MB young people living in the San Fernando Valley, but also in the origins of the Butler Avenue and El Camino congregations. Both of the latter were established in part to meet the needs of MB families living some distance from the existing congregation in their city. While mission projects such as West Park and Sunset Gardens near Fresno in the early 1950s reached out mainly to non-Mennonite Brethren persons, the Board did not use that approach when establishing other congregations. It perceived urban church planting primarily as a conservative action to keep existing members in the conference and only secondarily for bringing in new members.

Shifting demographics brought about the birth of some urban MB congregations; it caused the demise of others. In 1957 the Los Angeles Mennonite Brethren Church closed after twenty-three years. The church was located in south central Los Angeles, an area that underwent significant population changes during the 1950s. As increasing numbers of minority groups came into the area, most middle-class whites retreated to outlying suburban areas. Included in this "white flight" were many members of the Los Angeles Mennonite Brethren Church. Without a local membership base, the congregation found it increasingly difficult to continue in its existing location. Rather than move, however, the congregation voted to disband and requested that the Board of Home Missions explore establishing a new church in the Downey/Lakewood area southeast of Los Angeles. The Board made numerous investigations into such a project, but no congregation was ever established in that area.[42]

Despite its aggressive efforts to start urban churches in the 1950s, it does not appear that the Board of Home Missions had a significant impact on the urbanization of California Mennonite Brethren. In areas such as Fresno, San Jose/Santa Clara and Bakersfield, where large numbers of MB families settled, stable congregations developed by 1960. In areas such as Santa Cruz, Arleta or Los Angeles, no amount of Home Mission support could create or sustain a congregation in which a strong MB core group did not exist.

CONCLUSION

In 1883 the Mennonite Brethren Church actively discouraged its members from moving to the city; less than seventy-five years later the city had become very much a part of the church's life. The years from 1940 to 1960 witnessed a remarkable transformation in MB Church demographics. By 1960 approximately nineteen hundred members, or 37.4 percent of all MB members in California attended congregations in cities larger than fifty thousand residents. This figure far exceeded the North American MB average of about 24 percent. Though the urbanization of California's Mennonite Brethren began several decades before 1940, the decades of the 1940s and 1950s mark the real beginning of the church's urban transformation. No longer an exclusively rural people, Mennonite Brethren in California were making a home in the city.

From "Getting the Words Out" to "Enjoying the Music": Musical Transitions Among Canadian Mennonite Brethren[*]

Doreen Klassen

The move from singing German gospel songs to English hymns among mid-century Canadian Mennonite Brethren was only one of several musical transitions. That more than a language shift was involved is evident from the range of musical arenas in which change occurred. Youthful church choirs of the 1940s gave way to older robed choristers in the 1960s, self-trained conductors and instrumentalists bowed out to formally trained musicians, pump organs were replaced by electronic models, and communication media such as radio were adopted for musical outreach ministries. In fact, in this era, change occurred in every facet of MB music-making.

Musical transitions accompanied other changes within the church, and like them, were subjected to societal trends and influences. Post-war affluence, rising consumerism, increasing urbanization, improved travel options and new communication media offered Mennonite Brethren, like other Canadians, many new options. At times these factors seemed to take precedence over theological moorings in determining the direction of change within the church. On this basis, some scholars have concluded that post-war Mennonite musical practices moved from "piety to sophistication."[1]

Mid-century music-making, and MB belief and praxis in general, were not, however, contextualized only within the larger society. They also were entwined with Evangelicalism,[2] at times even in its more fundamentalist manifestations like dispensationalism.[3] In fact, MB historian John A. Toews argues that fundamentalism eroded MB theology through its "restricting influence on the gospel message as portrayed in the New Testament."[4] He credits fundamentalist Bible School teachers and periodic literature with having "weakened the historic evangelical Anabaptist foundations of Mennonite Brethren faith and practice" through being "strangely silent" about "the demands of Christian discipleship."[5] The fundamentalist gospel songs which many MB congregations sang in the earlier part of this century contributed to this weakening and prepared the way for an easy identification with Evangelicalism. Because singing and preaching worked in tandem in this movement, Mennonite Brethren, with their strong tradition of congregational song, could be persuaded enmasse to avoid "sophistication" and instead move to greater piety.

Having abandoned, a century earlier, a close identification with an Anabaptist counter-culture model, Canadian Mennonite Brethren were particularly susceptible to affiliation with evangelical groups. By the mid-twentieth century, Mennonite Brethren failure to articulate a counter-culture stance had led to a hegemony or compliance with Evangelicalism. MB willingness to forgo a definitive stance concerning nonresistance allowed affiliation with the National Association of Evangelicals at its inception in 1944 and demonstrated MB vulnerability to theological traditions complying with the state.[6] This resulted increasingly in a shift from an "insider/outsider" status to a "participant" status with respect to the larger society, "from feeling estranged from or dominant over the culture to taking one's place with others in joint responsibility for the culture."[7] I contend it was this liaison with Evangelicalism which mediated musical transitions among mid-century Canadian Mennonite Brethren.[8]

But MB identification with Evangelicalism had its own internal variants. Canadian Evangelicalism, in particular, did not present a united front. Instead, as Canadian church historian John G. Stackhouse, Jr. argues, the movement bifurcated into what he calls "churchish" and "sectarian" streams. The first he characterizes as "actively engag[ing] contemporary culture and scholarship, including biblical and theological studies."[9] The second he regards as engaged in a more literal, fundamentalist religiosity.

The MB alliance with Evangelicalism not only facilitated changes in music-making. Tensions in the process of musical transitions frequently symbolized these two opposing stances on how the church engages in dialogue with its surrounding society. This is evident in several mid-century musical transitions: the displacement of the church choir from the musical center to the periphery of church community music-making; the move from lay musicianship to formal musical training; the transition from local church to conference level music evangelism via radio; the exchange of gospel songbooks for denominational hymnbooks; the changing attitudes toward and uses of instrumental music; and the changing focus and function of music within the national MB conference structure.

FROM MUSICAL CENTER TO PERIPHERY

By the 1960s Mennonites could no longer comment critically, as Saskatoon church organist Walter Thiessen once did, about mainline churches in which "all these old people were in the choir [while] we had all this youth."[10] Instead, Mennonite Brethren were attempting to maintain a balance of young and old in their own choirs. Their struggle often paralleled that of mainline Protestant churches coming to grips with a rapidly modernizing society. Yet, most MB churches had entered the 1940s with vibrant church choirs, often in addition to large youth choirs engaged in musical outreach ministries.

Musical activity in most Canadian Mennonite Brethren churches of the early 1940s exemplified a reasonable degree of continuity with the preceding decade. Congregations, influenced by fundamentalism, continued to sing gospel songs, usually from the *Evangeliums-Lieder*. Church choirs still used German collections like *Zionslieder* and *Liederperlen*, but had also adopted the bilingual *Ausgewaehlte Lieder*,[11] all of them gospel song collections published in North America.

Musical training for the average church member in the early 1940s was often centered around the church. This was particularly true in rural areas where youth regarded choir practice as spiritually and socially enriching and choir conductors conducted it as an outreach ministry.[12] Singers and instrumentalists were often self-taught,[13] although the occasional aspiring rural musician travelled to urban centers like Winnipeg, Regina, or Lethbridge for private music instruction. In Mennonite centers, public school teachers with a commitment to promoting choral music also helped to train youth. Most young people, however, received their musical training through the church choir.

The choir, it was assumed, existed to "assist the minister, draw people otherwise not attracted to church, and get youth involved in ministry."[14] In fact, said former MB Church leader J. Benjamin Janz of Vauxhall, Alberta, the choir

> builds the church. And since mostly younger people are in the
> choirs . . . they get well practiced in singing part harmony.
> They become the church congregation later, so it carries over.
> The choir is sort of a school for the congregation . . . so then
> the congregation can sing well in parts.[15]

Musical continuity between choir and congregation was not only
assumed but assured.

The mixed choir of the 1940s was regarded as the church choir,
while men's and "ladies'" choirs, as women's choirs were called in
that era, were considered to be "special" choirs.[16] Membership in
the church choir was generally restricted to baptized believers,[17]
but youth choirs were accessible to all regardless of religious
commitment because they were viewed as the crux of youth
work.[18]

Musical emphasis in choir singing, as in Russia, continued to
focus on textual clarity, itself regarded as the quintessential
communication aspect of sacred music. Conductors felt one "had
to get the words out so that the congregation could understand
them."[19] This emphasis gave continuity to a tradition already in
effect at an 1894 *Sängerfest* (song festival) at Rueckenau in the
Ukraine. There Wilhelm Neufeld, a minister and choir director in
the Gnadenfeld Church, encouraged Mennonite Brethren singers

> to cultivate beauty and purity of tone without neglecting
> clarity of pronunciation and expression . . . The text was the
> main thing and the melody was of secondary importance, for
> the melody was only the means to an end.[20]

As in Russia, Canadian Mennonite Brethren regarded clear
communication of the text—or the message—of the song, as the
primary purpose of choral music. Some conductors emphasized
rhythm and others dynamics,[21] but these elements still remained in
the service of the text.

As choir conductors chose more complex musical idioms and
began using piano accompaniment, cipher notation became
impractical and gave way to staff notation.[22] Influenced by
instruction at denominational Bible schools, this change had
already begun in the late 1930s.[23] Choir conductors of the 1940s
recall endless hours of copying uncopyrighted materials and
translating cipher to staff notation for choir members who said,
"We can't read the numbers."[24] By 1947, only one of the forty-five
Canadian MB choirs surveyed still used exclusively cipher
notation.[25] Of the others, thirty-three used staff notation, while
eleven relied on a combination of staff and cipher notation.

Choir work afforded women one of their first opportunities for public ministry. As conductors, women were often relegated to directing women's, children's and girls' choirs or making music "with just little Sunday School groups."[26] Justina Wiebe of Winkler, Manitoba, who had already begun a girls choir in the late 1940s, recalled a request by the Mary Martha Fellowship to begin a women's choir because the women wanted "to do something else besides just sit[ting] and knit[ting] and embroider[ing]."[27] In a report on MB music in Vancouver in the 1950s, church correspondent Susie Warkentin commented that "because so many women [were] working as domestics in the city [the church] found it necessary to also found a women's choir."[28] The fifty women singers were led by a conductor identified only by her husband's name: Sister/Mrs. Ed Barkman.

Other women gained access to public ministry through serving as pianists. Increasingly complex choir repertoire demanded instrumental accompaniment and many of these women had received the formal training enabling them to meet these demands. As accompanists, they were commended for "playing quietly,"[29] while men were lauded for trumpeting "special numbers" at occasions like song festivals.[30] Because women were seen to be in support roles, their presence in music ministry posed no perceived threat to established gender roles. Yet, as women participated in the blurring of gender roles that the "all hands on deck" attitude of Evangelicalism permitted—if not endorsed[31]—their involvement signalled a move to greater equality in opportunities for public ministry, particularly in the Sunday morning worship service.[32]

Both men and women, however, participated in changes with respect to solo singing. In the 1940s, modesty often prohibited the singing of solos by a single individual, but the desire for musical variety permitted selected individuals to join in the singing of solo portions of choral anthems.[33] Two decades later, conductors freely assigned solo roles to individuals but still shared these opportunities among those considered qualified to sing them, rather than adopting the paid soloist model of the surrounding liturgical churches. This growing freedom to express individualism was reflective of changes in society and in other evangelical churches.

By the late 1950s, numerous other musical changes had occurred. Church choir practices were competing with sports schedules[34] and aging choristers in choir robes were singing English anthems.

The experience of the Scott Street Mennonite Brethren Church in St. Catherines, Ontario, exemplifies this change. Church minutes reveal that concerns in the 1940s centered around appointing choir directors and pianists, accommodating language changes and participation in inter-Mennonite music events.[35] By 1954, the issues had shifted. Now the agenda included accommodating an aging congregation with hearing difficulties through carefully engineered church sanctuary acoustics, purchasing an electronic organ and acquiring choir robes. Choir robes were finally purchased in 1964 from funds raised by a choir program, but then the question became, "should the song leader wear a choir robe?"[36] Unlike many other MB churches, Scott Street MB continued to send singing groups to the blind, aged and sick and to supply a male voice choir for a church-run radio program even into the 1960s.[37]

By the 1960s, many youth had abandoned church choir repertoire for folk music styles accompanied by guitar. In fact, many youth no longer looked to the church either for musical models or as a social center. This certainly contrasts with the experience of Helmut Janzen, who as a young man in Sardis, British Columbia, claimed that "even in his unconverted state" it was the conducting of visiting choral directors who inspired him to become a church musician.[38]

Yet increasingly at Scott Street, as in other MB churches, concerns moved from drawing youth into the musical ministry of the church to being led in worship by choristers clad in matching choir robes. And so the visualization of respectability took precedence over communal participation.

FROM LAY MUSICIANSHIP TO FORMAL TRAINING

Changes in local church choir music-making were, however, tied into changes happening at the national denominational level. Throughout Canada, local MB choir activities of the 1940s were complemented by regional song festivals and conductor's workshops.[39] "The need for more systematic instruction in choral directing"[40] was addressed in 1942 by the appointment of a *Reisedirigent* (travelling clinician) at a meeting of twelve Manitoba MB choir directors.[41] Although these workshops were instituted to assist in the training of musicians for local church ministry, they paved the way for significant musical change in MB congregations.

It was not the 1944 founding of the Mennonite Brethren Bible College (MBBC) and its program in sacred music, as some would suspect, but a new brand of *Dirigentenkurse* (conductors' workshops) that created a disjuncture in the MB musical continuum in the mid 1940s. Led by urban Mennonite choral conductors with formal training from institutions like the Bible Institute of Los Angeles (Biola) and Moody Bible Institute these workshops often introduced new concepts. Ben Horch, a workshop leader and graduate of Biola, describes his innovations as including:

> conducting with two hands (one *'Taktablagen'* [maintaining the beat] and the other expression), Music Theory I (basic notation) and Music Theory II (mini-courses in harmony, counterpoint, musical form, the simple composition of hymns).[42]

Lay musicians often cite the introduction of the classical repertoire as the most radical offering of these trained choral conductors. In this regard they mention cantatas and oratorios like "Christ and his Soldiers," Stainer's "Crucifixion" and Handel's "Messiah." For the choir accustomed to singing little more than hymns and non-classical anthems, these works offered an exciting challenge.

But the innovations went beyond the musical complexity of the repertoire. They extended to the dynamic, expressive character that the formally trained song festival conductors brought to their musical leadership. It was the charisma which conductors like Horch brought to *Kernlied*[43] [traditional MB gospel song] and oratorio performance alike that captured the imaginations of young people and provided inspiration for them to engage in further musical training.

For John Regehr, whose youth was spent in Herbert, Saskatchewan, the impetus for further study came from watching Horch conduct. He recalls that

> we were sitting in the balcony in the Herbert Church and the downstairs was loaded with music . . . it was not a terribly wide church . . . one of those old ones. And Ben Horch was using the whole width of it—in the front—running to the piano with his hair all over the place, and his arms—like he needed the whole front—just as excited as he could be. And that for us, for me, was just a beautiful experience. There was excitement. Like

music can be exciting stuff. So that was my first impact of Ben Horch. So when we came to Winnipeg, "Oh Ben Horch is here!" Oh, like that was it. And then coming to College here, actually having him as a teacher was a highlight. Uncle Ben, we called him.[44]

Regehr's excitement rested not only in the theatrical aspect of Horch's conducting, but rather in the realization that there was "freedom [to] do more than keep time."[45] It was this vision that motivated young people from Ontario to British Columbia to move to Winnipeg for musical studies at MBBC.

When Horch organized MBBC's Sacred Music program in 1944, he modelled it on the *Sängerfest, Dirigentenkurse*, and the musical outreach of the local church. The *Sängerfest* provided the choir models. The mass choir became the oratorio choir, and the church choir, the A Capella choir.[46] The one-week *Dirigentenkurse* workshops were extended and expanded into a four-year college music curriculum. Lastly, Horch, who as a young Lutheran had been drawn into Winnipeg's North-End MB Church through Rev. Erdman Nikkel's church orchestra, also established a Mennonite Symphony Orchestra. This orchestra, he assumed, would draw in young people to accompany oratorio choir performances at the college.[47]

Horch's vision for this curriculum was that it would develop the compositional skills of church musicians. "The sacred music course, from its inception, was to be a school for young Mennonite composers first and the training of others in performance in a role subordinate to that of the courses in composition."[48] It would tie together advanced education with the needs of the local church by encouraging youth to create music rooted in their own musical and theological heritage. The program recognized the musical sophistication young people had gained through the public school, private study and music festival, yet channelled these abilities for use in and for the local church.[49]

Had the composition program continued, it would have addressed a perpetual problem for choir leaders: obtaining suitable choir repertoire. By 1947 MB church choirs were using some forty different songbooks,[50] yet they engaged in an on-going search for suitable, new music. The rare choir conductor who tried composing for his own choir introduced his compositions cautiously. As J. Benjamin Janz, one of Horch's students, recalls, secretly you sneak one of those compositions, the song, into the choir, but don't tell them. And if they like it, then you were successful. . . . If they would have found out that this material was home-made, perhaps they wouldn't have liked it.[51]

Most choir conductors, however, remember long hours of copying and hectographing choir music to deal with the need for repertoire. Annual MB conference reports, also indicate a perpetual concern with trying to obtain and distribute choir repertoire.[52] By 1947, choirs were already using 24 percent English repertoire, but the 76 percent using German repertoire[53] often had difficulty finding appropriate music due to the unavailability of German materials during and even after World War II.[54] Publishing German songs from Switzerland in the *Konferenz-Jugendblatt der Mennoniten Bruedergemeinde in Canada* after 1947[55] was one attempt by the conference Music Committee to deal with this situation.

The failure of MBBC administrators to understand Horch's vision resulted in the curtailment of the composition program. This left the Sacred Music Program with only its performance component. It was beholden to traditions outside of the church and open to the suspicion that its goal was to serve its own performance ideals. These were perceived to be at dissonance with those of the church. That the roster of award-winners at Winnipeg's annual music festival during the 1950s and early 1960s included many MBBC-trained singers confirmed for some critics that successful performance in secular venues had replaced preparation for church ministry. What these critics failed to grasp was the "spiritual depths felt" by instructors like Victor Martens, who recalled "weeping through Bach's 'Jesu, meine Freude,' because the text was such a moving rendition of Romans 12."[56] Instead, they demanded Martens apologize to the conference for leading the A Capella Choir in "unspiritual" music. This may be one of the most poignant musical clashes among Canadian Mennonite Brethren between those of "churchish" and "sectarian" evangelical persuasion. Those committed to exploring, questioning and deepening their faith musically were taken to task by those committed to replicating dogmatism and willing to brand alternative stances as "secular."

Many of the first graduates of MBBC's music program in the 1940s faced similar criticisms. Like Henry P. Neufeld, they found their way to Mennonite Brethren high schools and Bible schools because they had been given "a foundation [they] could continue with the young people."[57] They organized string groups at institutions like Coaldale High School in Alberta[58] and performed Handel's "Messiah" in cities like Lethbridge, Alberta, but received "quite a bit of criticism."[59] The problem, the critics claimed, was that the older generation no longer shared a common repertoire with their young people. Earlier, as retired English teacher David D. Duerksen recalled, old and young had "more songs in common that would be the homeland of the heart for both," but now it was "different between the generations."[60] Churches that, in the wake of growing awareness of developmental stages in learning, had taught their Sunday school children "special" children's songs[61] now balked at having teenagers and young adults seek a repertoire suited to their musical interests and abilities. Yet increasingly, musical activity reflected the fragmentation engendered in the age-graded learning units into which the fundamentalist Sunday school movement had divided the church.

The essence of the disjuncture was not that of formal versus informal training. Nor was it necessarily that of hymnic versus choral repertoire. Instead, tension arose because of differing valuations of text and tune. For "churchish" evangelicals, text and tune were of equal value. Hymnologist Esther Horch claimed, "We are influenced by the melodies, not just the words." Her husband Ben affirmed this, saying, "The music says as much as the words."[62] For "sectarian" evangelicals, however, the text was of paramount importance, so they easily applied labels like "secular" and "modern" to differing perspectives. The musical changes Horch and his successors had introduced to incite spiritual vitality were thus dismissed by the "sectarians" as a move from 'piety to sophistication.'

Consequently, young people who had been given the vision for the expressive performance of music that placed musical sound on par with its accompanying text, but who had not been challenged to express this knowledge in the composition of choral works based on their own tradition, now had to look outside their tradition for musical models. These sources of inspiration, though often part of the sacred classics, were found beyond the bounds of the local church congregation, and well beyond the musical and theological horizons of those who, in the late 1950s were being mesmerized by glamorous musical renditions of "Just as I am" in tent revival meetings with American Mennonite evangelists like George Brunk.[63]

RADIO: FROM CHURCH CONGREGATION
TO RADIO AUDIENCE

The mid-century blossoming of religious radio programming among Mennonite Brethren paralleled the rise of private AM radio broadcasting during the late 1940s and early 1950s in the larger Canadian society.[64] Both post-war affluence and interest in religion[65] generated funds for ministries like that of religious radio broadcasting. Wartime reliance on radio news had attuned people to regard radio not only as an entertainment medium, but also as a source of valuable, life-saving information.[66]

Not only the perception of radio as a source of critical information but also the existence of religious broadcasts persuaded Mennonite Brethren to consider using radio as a ministry tool in the 1940s. Through listening to "popular gospel programs"[67] they began to question the warnings of fundamentalists who called radio an instrument of "demoralization" leading to "distraction" from, and "inconstancy" in, the faith.[68] Instead, programs like the "Old Fashioned Revival Hour" gave many Mennonite Brethren a vision for using this relatively new medium for outreach. Consequently, leaders like Herman Voth, British Columbia's MB Youth Director in 1950, welcomed radio because they could use it "to bring the joyful news of salvation to the lost world."[69]

When conference-level discussions concerning radio ministry began in 1940-41, they centered on youth involvement. Henry S. Rempel, missionary to Saskatoon claimed, "We have such a mass of lovely young people . . . and Br. H. S. Voth has said, 'Give the young people work, or they will create work.'"[70] Giving the young people work in the church, generally meant involving them in choir, and particularly in outreach ministries such as radio.[71] Many MB radio programs of the late 1940s and early 1950s were, in fact, initiated as outreach ministries by local youth—often by a youthful male quartet in conjunction with a minister—who sensed "the need for a sound gospel broadcast, locally produced."[72]

A male quartet, often with a name like "Gospel Bells Male Quartette,"[73] served as the primary musical performance group for these radio broadcasts, while nameless "ladies trios" "add[ed] to the variety of the program."[74] The focus on male quartets was partially modelled on the practice of American evangelists visiting Canada. According to Ben Horch, "the evangelist would speak in

English to identify with the young people, and they would sometimes bring along their own . . . male quartets."[75] Male quartet singing similarly reflected the trend in prairie Bible schools, where they were considered to be "the IN thing"[76] for youth to imitate in Sunday evening services.

The concept of variety was central to many of these radio programs, though there was also an "attempt . . . to tie the songs together with suitable poems and readings."[77] Pioneered in the heyday of secular radio drama, these religious radio programs were, however, modeled on the communal literary evening and the *Jugendverein*, a bilingual Sunday evening church service organized by youth essentially for youth but presented under the watchful eye of the elders. This emphasis on variety distinguished both the radio program and the *Jugendverein* from the Sunday morning worship service with its almost liturgical insistence on a given number of congregational songs, choir songs and sermon(s). The variety program format, it was assumed, would more likely capture the attention of a society ever increasing its pace of life.

Increasing awareness of cultural and religious differentiation from their surrounding society kept Mennonites cognizant of barriers to inter-ethnic communication of the gospel. They were keenly aware that their German language church services were inaccessible to their English-speaking neighbors, but phrased their discomfort in terms of those who "wouldn't feel welcome in our churches" because "they don't know German." English-language radio programs often predated the move to English-language worship services by some ten years. Radio, therefore, offered a helpful alternative to church-centered outreach and yet an acceptable means of presenting the gospel to the surrounding society.[78]

The first Canadian MB radio broadcast, begun in October 1940 by Rev. Henry S. Rempel, had certain distinctions from its successors. In keeping with the Canadian War Measures Act, which prohibited broadcasting in enemy languages such as German, the program was broadcast in English. Rempel's program was unique in that it was presented by an English-speaking congregation drawn primarily from American MB immigrants from Mountain Lake, Minnesota. The program fostered growth in a fledgling church in the Caswell Hill District of Saskatoon as listeners were drawn to Christian commitment and to the church.[79] Initially their program was "devotional in style, for the purpose of bringing church services into the homes of those who were unable to attend church regularly."[80] A name change from "Morning Devotions" to "Gospel Tidings" signalled a change in focus as intensifying war efforts made Mennonites more aware of their theological distinction from their neighbors.   Using the language of its listening audience, this congregation could employ radio as a "church-centered [outreach] strategy," in keeping with its concept of lay involvement in evangelism.[81]

Listener response to MB radio broadcasts was generally affirmative, although in the absence of effective evaluative processes, results could often only be surmised. One broadcaster in Saskatchewan concluded, "Outlying settlements like Lac La Ronge would know [the impact of the broadcast]. That family who gathered around a small radio in a northern country store would also know, for it was that morning that a new life began."[82]

Local religious radio broadcasts added "Canadian content" to Canadian radio in the post-war era when Canada was trying to forge its own identity over against the United States.[83] Religious broadcasts may not, however, have been perceived by station managers as having enough drawing power to maintain a loyal radio audience within the attraction of an emerging television broadcasting era of the 1950s.[84] Similarly, religious radio programs, with their other-worldly focus, did little to encourage the level of commercial consumption necessary in the "transition from a wartime to a peacetime economy."[85] As a result, radio features like "Hymns at Eventide" with speaker Frank C. Peters were discontinued because they were religious in nature and "the manager didn't want too many religious programs."[86]

By the late 1950s, the flowering of local MB radio programs had withered somewhat,[87] often because young people involved in the ministry had moved away for further study. In lieu of locally produced radio broadcasts, the Gospel Light Hour, begun by several MBBC students in 1946, was adopted by the Manitoba Mennonite Brethren Conference in 1954. By the late 1960s, the program had become part of the evangelism effort at the Canadian Conference level. Musical outreach, which two decades earlier had been a way of involving local youth in local church ministry, became the domain of a select few at the conference level. While this option eventually made MB radio programs available to a larger listening audience, in many congregations it now substituted for church-centered musical outreach and local youth involvement in that task. By the 1960s, MB young people, unlike their Anabaptist forbears, had ceased singing their way into the hearts of the people.[88]

FROM *EVANGELIUMS-LIEDER*
TO DENOMINATIONAL HYMNBOOKS

Both in Russia and in Canada, Mennonites of other denominational backgrounds joined the MB church "because the MBs sang a lot more than [they] did."[89] It was often the singing of the choir which drew these people into the church, yet, congregational singing was at the heart of MB music making. And it was in the area of congregational song that opposing theological stances were most evident.

The gospel songs of the *Evangeliums-Lieder* still served mid-century MB congregations. Yet there was a long-standing realization that a more denominationally oriented songbook was needed. Already at the 1914 Northern District Conference—as the Canadian MB Conference was called at that time—there had been comments that having no standardized hymnbook was a problem. The suggestion at that time was to have church choirs introduce the historic *Kernlieder* from *Glaubensstimme*[90] in order to improve congregational singing. It was assumed "if the choir use[d] it, the congregation [would] gladly sing from it."[91]

It was not, however, until 1944 that the conference took action. At the Northern District Conference that year, the music committee expressed the need for revision of *Evangeliums-Lieder*, or alternately, for producing a book with more chorales for use in the choir.[92] Their recommendation was not accepted, but the conference did commission publication of the *Gesangbuch der Mennoniten Bruedergemeinde* the following year.[93] That hymnal was published in 1952. The committee's rationale for this book centered around several needs: for music celebrating special occasions in the life of the church and home, for a book of denominational background in the place of borrowed hymnals, and, lastly, for recapturing a lost musical heritage.[94]

The vision for this book, as articulated by Ben Horch, was "to serve the inward life of [the] people and to challenge [them] to reach for ever increasing spiritual maturity, a quality that evangelical song ha[d] not served to the same degree."[95] Of particular concern was the need to move away from teachings like eternal security and dispensationalism, central to many fundamentalist gospel songs, yet antithetical to the Anabaptist-Mennonite tradition.[96] Language was not yet an issue. Instead, the concern lay with providing a musical and theological fare beyond the confines of the gospel idiom in the then popular *Evangeliums-Lieder*.

In terms of content, the *Gesangbuch* balanced gospel songs with *Kernlieder* and chorales, bringing together various strands of the MB musical and theological heritage. Musical integrity and continuity were ensured by notating songs in "a rhythmic and harmonic idiom that Mennonites looked upon as indigenous,"[97] or, as committee member Ben Horch argued, "how we as a people have sung and learned to love them."[98]

The *Gesangbuch* committee used various means to foster interest in the book. At annual Canadian MB conferences they encouraged choirs to help introduce the new hymnbook[99] and local music committees to plan a Sunday evening congregational rehearsal of new songs.[100] Horch further facilitated access to *Gesangbuch Kernlieder* by recording them with the MBBC A Capella Choir.[101]

Response to the songbook, however, varied. Some, like former MBBC music professor Peter Klassen, welcomed it because it contained "a new and necessary emphasis on the Christian Life, which . . . was sadly lacking in [the] *Evangeliums-Lieder*."[102] Others were critical, arguing that the *Gesangbuch* was "too stuffy."

> They had too many of the *Kernlieder*, chorale types . . . for us in a closed community like Yarrow . . . Especially the young people did not enjoy it. When the book came out—and it was used a lot—we as young people used to sneak out Sunday nights and go to the Alliance Church in Chilliwack because the music spoke to us and was something that we understood.[103]

The new songbook did not communicate well with those entrenched in Evangelicalism.

Opinions on the book were divided but by 1955 it was already in its fourth edition. Its wide distribution, however, owed as much to its acceptance by churches of other Mennonite denominations as by Mennonite Brethren themselves.

The introduction of an English translation of the *Gesangbuch* in 1960 was, according to the conference Hymnbook Committee, a recognition of the bilingual reality of mid-century Canadian MB church life.[104] Furthermore, it was an attempt to offer continuity to a European past within a North American present. An English language parallel, they argued, would

> first,—afford the best opportunity for adopting into another language the spiritual heritage of congregational song epitomized for our forefathers by the term "Kernlieder" and second,—assure the present time as most favorable for the retention of just such a bi-lingual position indefinitely and third,—preserve the unifying concept of a "one hymnbook" congregation regardless of changing language problems.[105]

Ratified in 1955 and published in 1960, *The Hymn Book* found limited acceptance. Whereas the bilingual *Ausgewaehlte Lieder* had facilitated the language transition for the church choir, *The Hymn Book* failed to find a welcome home within the congregation. The failure can be attributed to several factors. First, it was affected by the earlier resistance to the *Gesangbuch* and its *Kernlieder* tradition. Second, Horch thought that "about 50 or 60 of the translations lacked poetic merit in varying degrees."[106] Third, Canadian Mennonite Brethren had the option of using the *Mennonite Brethren Church Hymnal* published by American Mennonite Brethren in 1953. This hymnal reflected more of the English hymn tradition to which Canadian Mennonite Brethren were attuned. Even a congregation like Scott Street MB, which had decided in 1947 to wait with English hymnody until "it [was] necessary,"[107] already purchased this English hymnal in 1953,[108] several years before it began unilingual English church services in 1957.[109]

The inclusion of repertoire for the church year or specialized ministries was an issue for some. For others it was the need for children's songs,[110] although the conference had already recommended purchasing English songbooks for Sunday school in 1944.[111] For the most part, however, it was the desire for an English repertoire that appealed to second- and third-generation immigrants willing to shake off what they perceived as the restricting influence of mother-tongue language and old world concepts. Additionally, it was a move from "the Depression milieu, where we were poor and needed a lot of grace" to an era where Mennonites could afford a "worship emphasis."[112] Although this era occurred a decade or two later among Mennonite Brethren than within the larger North American church,[113] it was characterized as a "period of respectability" in which worship was regarded "as an aesthetic experience" and "enriching our worship" seemed equivalent to "the experience of beauty."[114]

For Ben Horch, this move to 'enriching our worship' was exemplified more fully a decade later in the 1971 publication of the *Worship Hymnal*. He saw this hymnal as "now rooting a succeeding generation of MB's *into* the hymnody of Presbyterianism, Methodism, Congregationalism," that is, into a formalization of worship—as its name implies—and "away from our traditional congregational song roots since 1860."[115] And in this respect it was a move to a repertoire regarded as having more sophistication, though the arguments were often phrased in the language of piety. Yet, for seers like Horch, this move exemplified "the failure of the hymnbook committee of 1971 to give historic continuity to . . . the traditional MB Kernlied"[116] and its emphasis on discipleship.

On the one hand, having a denominational hymnbook created a sense of musical uniqueness and its shared repertoire a sense of belonging to a body of like-minded believers. On the other hand, the apparent disregard of the MB musical tradition by hymnbook committees compiling *The Church Hymnal* and the *Worship Hymnal* demonstrated the dangers of an easy identification with Evangelicalism. In this transition Mennonite Brethren were beginning "to see themselves as part of a transdenominational [Protestant] fellowship,"[117] and moving "from an 'outsider' or an 'insider' to a 'participant' status."[118] Their musical choices were indicative of opting for being only one of many pluralistic options rather than a radical, counter-culture denomination. And so they moved with other evangelicals from congregational gatherings calling people to discipleship to "respectable" musicians inviting individuals to worship.

FROM PUMP ORGAN TO ELECTRONIC ORGAN

Changes in musical instrumentation paralleled these transitions in mid-century MB hymnody. Many Mennonite Brethren congregations entered the 1940s with upright pianos or pump organs in their sanctuaries. By 1960 many a pump organ had been retired to a Sunday school classroom, and upright pianos in urban church sanctuaries had been replaced by both a grand piano and a modest electronic organ. Renting organs for special occasions like weddings was often an intermediary step to acquiring them for regular church service use.[119] The perception that "only spiritually dead churches [had] organs"[120] and that using organs would "kill congregational singing,"[121] had given way to arguments that one can use discretion, yet enliven congregational song through musically sensitive organ accompaniment.[122] A church that in its infancy was criticized for its unruly musical practices, was now concerned about adding vitality to its music-making.[123]

Not only were churches graced by new instruments. The use of these musical instruments also changed. Choral anthems and oratorio selections generally required instrumental accompaniment, so pianists and organists were expected to do more than provide a starting pitch or replicate choral parts. Instead, they played accompaniments using and testing their skills and training.

Pianos and organs were, however, no longer solely instruments of accompaniment. With the advent of more formal musical training for young people, they became solo performance instruments as well. By the early 1940s, the practice of congregational singing during the offering,[124] for example, had given way to instrumental offertories, invariably hymns played by a pianist or organist.

Church members claimed it was awkward to pass on an offering plate while holding a songbook. They argued it was "more practical" to listen to the offertory than to juggle a songbook and offering plate, "and besides, no other church sang" during the offering.[125] In many churches the offering itself had been moved from its post sermon position to the middle of the service[126] because, as John Regehr observed, "the offering destroy[ed] the spirit . . . especially if you hear[d] the clinking."[127]

Visits by church choirs to other MB and various Protestant congregations had made lay musicians aware of alternative options for order and content of worship services. They now adopted these without questioning their philosophical basis. In fact, says church organist Walter Thiessen of Saskatoon, Mennonites often incorporated musical changes "without thinking twice" or asking, "Is this theologically right or not?"[128] Instead, as Mennonite Brethren, like other evangelicals, saw themselves more as an integral part of a pluralistic society, they often made an easy transition to middle class values.

The impetus, as John Stackhouse suggests, was post-war affluence which often applied to church ministries an interesting blend of "general cultural conservatism and consumerism."[129] By 1960, a finished recreation room and an organ in the church sanctuary were simply two varying expressions of mid-century MB identification with Canadian society and in particular, with evangelical churches. The change was one of modernization facilitated by Evangelicalism.

FROM HOME MISSIONS TO CHRISTIAN EDUCATION

The role of church music within the Canadian Conference of Mennonite Brethren Churches changed significantly during the period leading to mid-century. By the 1960s music-making at conference gatherings was no longer a significant part of the agenda. This centrality was already lost when the *Sängerfeste* of the 1920s and mass choirs of the 1930s gave way to business meetings and incidental congregational songs at annual conference gatherings.[130] The impact of this change was, however, expressed in 1955 and again in 1960 when churches were encouraged to elect more choir leaders as delegates to annual conferences.[131] Before that time, it was assumed they were present.

Second, musical directives at the conference level become less oriented toward outreach. Both the city mission work of Erdman Nickel in Winnipeg in the 1920s and radio outreach beginning in the 1940s were initiated by the conference and reached out to young people, then involved them in ministry. Music was thus an integral component of local youth work, with its dual emphasis on personal growth and outreach ministries. After 1944, the focus shifted to fostering national conference unity, emphasizing Mennonite theological distinctive and enlivening local church music-making, particularly in the realm of congregational song. By 1960 the geographical scope of conference music ministries had widened to include sending pianos to South America and hymnbooks to Germany but the emphasis on involving youth musically in outreach ministries appears to have been lost.

Some of the changes can be attributed to the formation of institutions to carry out these functions on behalf of the conference. For example, after MBBC's music department assumed educational responsibilities formerly accorded to the Dirigentenkurse, the conference decided in 1953 to discontinue these conducting workshops. Similarly, larger scale radio broadcasting under the conference rubric seems to have substituted for smaller scale local church radio broadcasts. In this centralization of radio broadcasting, Canadian Mennonite Brethren demonstrated acceptance not only of a societal, but also an evangelical, ethos of professionalization. They did so, however, without sufficient attention to how this strategy would affect the call of congregational members to discipleship in the area of musical outreach ministries.

CONCLUSION

Most striking among Canadian MB musical transitions of this era were the shift from gospel songs to worship hymns and the professionalization of music evangelism. Language change had facilitated the hymnodic transition but not determined its direction. Mennonite Brethren, who had been given the option by a convert from Lutheranism to embrace an Anabaptist musical orientation had opted instead to embrace an ethos of worship and evangelical respectability.

Similarly, the centralization and professionalization of music evangelism via the media had removed itself from local church emphases on "keeping the youth" through involvement in that area. Those of sectarian persuasion appreciated the coming of tent evangelism but those with churchish commitments often chose professionalism in musical ventures that valued both text and music, but were divorced from their musical roots by an aborted composition program at its denominational college.

Innovations like congregational singing from denominational hymnbooks and listening to electronic organ offertories had given to mid-century Canadian MB churches a reasonable degree of uniformity. While rural and urban churches frequently changed at varying paces, they were, nevertheless, moving in a similar direction. For many churches, this direction had been chosen more by concerns for replicating a modernizing pattern etched by the larger evangelical movement, than by commitment to a Mennonite past. Ironically, this merging occurred at the historic moment that descendants of colonially dominated peoples in Africa and America were seeking not only equality but a separate identity. Mennonite Brethren, by contrast, were singing hymns of worship and donning matching choir robes to lose their distinctiveness and merge their identity with that of the larger evangelical milieu of Canadian society.

Canadian Mennonite Brethren and Language Transition

Gerald C. Ediger

In 1907 a correspondent to the Russian Mennonite periodical *Friedenstimme* wrote, "If we are conscious of our peoplehood, the use and understanding of the German language is essential. Correct German thinking, correct German feeling, correct German speaking will always be a blessing and also promote correct Christian thinking and action."[1] A little over a decade later, J. W. Neufeld, a Mennonite Brethren minister in both Canada and the United States, complained in the Mennonite Brethren periodical *Zionsbote* that among first-generation Mennonite Brethren immigrants English had become so mixed with German that it was scarcely recognizable, and the second generation spoke only English. In his mind, there was no doubt that German would soon be lost, with serious results for Mennonite Brethren faith.[2] In the summer of 1945, B. B. Janz toured the young adult mission efforts of Alberta and shared his reflections with H. F. Klassen.[3] Sadly pessimistic, the only certainty Janz saw in the future was the "ruin of all that is good." Unless German could be retained long enough to facilitate a smooth transition to English, he feared inevitable "rupture and pain, misunderstanding and contempt."[4] The June 25, 1952 issue of *Mennonitische Rundschau,* a Canadian Mennonite Brethren paper published in Winnipeg, carried the third installment of an article entitled *"Der Preis der Zweischprachigkeit"* by Isaak Regehr of Coaldale, Alberta. The plight of the German language, he lamented, was like that of Ishmael in Genesis 21, sent into the desert with Hagar when he seemed to threaten Isaac. In the end, however, God rescued and blessed Ishmael because of Hagar's prayers; in the same way God also would rescue and bless the bilingualism of the Mennonites if they too earnestly pled with God.[5] Nine years later, in 1961, C. C. Peters, British Columbia Bible School teacher and leader of the Yarrow Mennonite Brethren Church, preached the last full-length defense of the German language to be heard at the Canadian Conference. Introducing and concluding his case with Philippians 2:5 and John 17:21 respectively,[6] he argued that the unity and integrity of the Mennonite Brethren Church depended on the retention of the German language. Within ten years, congregations that had worshipped together first in German and then in German and English, were splitting into separate English and German services.[7]

These vignettes point to a fundamental shift in the religious experience within the Mennonite Brethren Church. The process of Mennonite Brethren assimilation to North American society brought many changes, some of which were very subtle and beyond the awareness of most Mennonite Brethren believers. The threat posed to the alliance of German and Religion, however, was an immediate and tangible challenge Mennonite Brethren could only escape by leaving the church. A reading of Canadian Mennonite Brethren Conference proceedings, Mennonite Brethren-sponsored periodicals such as *Zionsbote*, *Mennonitische Rundschau*[8] and *Das Konferenz Jugendblatt*, and case studies of language transition in three Manitoba congregations—Winkler, North End/Elmwood and South End/Portage Avenue[9]—during the 1940s, 1950s and 1960s reveals that the assimilation of the English language into Mennonite Brethren faith and practice represented a fundamental issue in the church during the mid-twentieth century. The culture Mennonite Brethren brought with them from their former life in southern Russia adapted to Canadian ways in many respects, but they struggled to retain the central role played by the German language in their religious practice and expression. The issue of language continuity or shift became a question of deliberate public policy reaching from the foremost councils of the church to the membership meetings of local congregations. By the 1960s the fight to retain High German as the language of Mennonite Brethren piety and religious practice had ended and the process of Mennonite Brethren becoming *"verenglischced"*[10] was all but complete.

The period of language transition for conference institutions stretched from the 1940s to the mid-1960s. By 1965 English was the official working language of the Canadian Conference[11] and the language of the official organ of Canadian Mennonite Brethren.[12] The three congregations used as case studies lagged somewhat behind the Conference but by 1971 all three had converted their main Sunday morning worship services to English.[13] The year 1952 marks a high point of emotional crisis after which the English reality seeded in the youth of the 1930s and 1940s rapidly matured to bear the fruit of complete transition in the 1960s.

Several critical junctures punctuated the period before 1952. Language was a concern of Canadian leaders from the beginning of the conference in 1910.[14] A decade later, however, Canadian Mennonite Brethren who had immigrated to North America in the 1870s (*Kanadier*) appeared ready to begin the transition process along with their American co-religionists. The Canadian process, however, was interrupted in the 1920s as a new wave of German-speakers, the *Russländer*, overwhelmed the *Kanadier*. The newcomers took immediate steps to protect their heritage of *Deutsch und Religion*.[15] Nevertheless, the immigrant *Russländer* failed to convince their children that Mennonite Brethren religion and the German language were a necessary unity. By 1947 English was becoming a significant fact of religious life among younger Canadian Mennonite Brethren.[16] Their leaders had no choice but to acknowledge that language was becoming a serious problem for the church.

Mennonite Brethren were of different minds regarding German and English from the very beginning of the transitional period. Some saw bilingualism as regrettable but necessary. Believing that an eventual transition was inevitable, they were willing to take steps in that direction.[17] Conversely, others took parallel steps to preserve, strengthen and entrench the German language.[18] Thus, the disruptive and disuniting potential of the *Sprachfrage* (language question) was evident from the outset. The ready linguistic assimilation of first-generation Canadian *Russlander*, however, doomed the campaign of the German-retainers before it began. This set the stage for twenty years of linguistic tension and painful transition.

The 1950s and 1960s were a period of formal and institutional language change. This period began with the establishment in 1950 of the most obvious symbol of the futile German-retention effort: the Canadian Conference Committee for the Preservation of the German Language.[19] Created as a poor substitute for the failure of Mennonite Brethren schools to mount a coordinated effort at German retention,[20] the committee was most effective at providing systematic documentation of the advance of English. Pro-German rhetoric of the early 1950s revealed the extent to which some identified their Mennonite Brethren faith with their heritage of German language and ethnicity. The German language was the defensive perimeter guarding the integrity of Mennonite Brethren distinctives and identity.[21] Parents who failed to speak High German at home were derelict in their duty.[22] Children and youth who did not make every effort to learn German were one step away from apostasy. Mennonite Brethren leaders who neglected the urgent struggle to retain the German heritage for the church were failing in their God-appointed mandate. Biblical precept and example were exploited for the cause, and the retention of the German language was declared God's absolute will for the Mennonite people.[23]

Against this backdrop, the official record documents the relentless advance of English in those sectors of the church most concerned with children and youth. At the same time, progressive leaders prepared for transition. The *Youth Worker* and the*M.B.S.S. Instructor* were established within two years of the organization of the German Committee.[24] As early as 1945,[25] and increasingly into the 1950s, some Conference leaders saw a subculture of Mennonite Brethren youth assuming English as its language of piety and mission. In response, they produced a series of publications designed to retain the youth for the church and serve the needs of rising English-speaking lay leaders, while also bridging the language gap by incrementally altering the ratio of German to English in their content. Congregational German school activity peaked in 1951 after which it declined to virtual extinction fifteen years later.[26] By 1958 English was being used in more than 95 percent of Sunday schools and youth groups across the Conference.[27] Front-ranking Conference leaders had given up any pretense of protecting a premier status for German among Canadian Mennonite Brethren. During the late 1950s and early 1960s a proposal for an English family-oriented periodical slowly gained acceptance,[28] English and German became equally permissible on the Conference floor,[29] and the Committee for the German Language was disbanded.[30] All these events prepared the way for the final decision in 1965 to make English the official language of the Canadian Conference.[31] Tracing language transition at the Conference level offers a necessary but limited perspective on the language-related religious experience of Mennonite Brethren in the 1940s, 1950s and 1960s. Detailed analyses of three congregations and their process of language shift also reveal much about the significance language has had for Mennonite Brethren religion. The examination of an originally

Kanadier congregation in small-town Winkler and two urban *Russländer*-dominated congregations in Winnipeg—North End/ Elmwood and South End/Portage Avenue—shows a common period of transition that stretches from around 1950 to the late 1960s.

In 1949, as front-ranking Conference leaders were acknowledging the *Sprachfrage*, the Winkler congregation was already using English in Sunday school and youth programs while North End and South End reported themselves to be solidly German.[32] In the next three years all three recognized that their children were losing the ability to function in German. Two congregations, Winkler and South End, discussed the need for English in the Sunday morning worship service.[33] None, however, took any action—as might be expected at a time when most decision-makers still believed that the German language could and should be salvaged as a permanent feature of Mennonite Brethren experience. By 1955 all three congregations had installed full-time professional pastors[34] and by 1957 all three pastors had initiated Christian education committees in the congregations.[35] Meanwhile, the North and South End congregations had acknowledged English in the Sunday schools and youth programs.[36] All three congregations had introduced English Sunday evening services as well. In Winkler and North End the youth specifically initiated these, while at South End the admission of English content to the Sunday evening service was an explicit recognition of non-German-speaking youth.[37] Weekday youth programming had become almost totally English. These developments paralleled the transformation of the *Youth Worker* and the *Instructor* into English resources for Christian education. Allowing an English sermon in Sunday morning worship was a crucial next step. While this innovation cannot be documented for Winkler, in 1958 both Elmwood and South End substituted an English sermon for the traditional *Gebetstunde.* They did so after a two year process initiated by their respective Christian education committees.[38] Again, the larger Conference process and the congregational process were roughly in step as 1959 saw the publication of an English translation of the *Gesangbuch*, a resource deliberately designed for bilingual worship.

For almost a decade the three congregations practiced bilingual worship, and in each case the transition from bilingual to unilingual English worship proved the most difficult. In Winkler the Christian Education Committee led the process. The membership came to the very brink of splitting on the issue in 1967 before the bilingual majority capitulated for the sake of preserving the congregation intact.[39] That same year, after a four-year process, Elmwood members reversed a previous rejection of their council's recommendation, and agreed that their main Sunday morning service become totally English.[40] In 1961 South End had divided into the bilingual Portage Avenue and the unilingual German Central congregations.[41] Portage Avenue repeatedly reaffirmed its determination to remain bilingual until 1970 when its members also accepted separate German and English Sunday morning services.[42] In all three cases the final stage of transition occurred immediately after a pastoral resignation and before a new pastor had completely taken over leadership. While pastoral transition probably provided the occasion for the formal transition, it is also true that by 1965 the Canadian Conference had withdrawn nearly all support for German as the language of continuing Mennonite Brethren faith and practice. With the Conference now publishing both the *Mennonite Brethren Herald* and the *Mennonitische Rundschau* and giving members their choice of one or the other, the unity of *Deutsch und Religion* had been broken. The decline and eventual extinction of Mennonite Brethren bilingualism was in sight.

The main steps of transition in the three cases are coincident with one another, and with the process in the Conference at large. Nevertheless, even though all three congregations were located in Manitoba, and though the leaders and members of these congregations in frequent contact with each other, the internal transition of each seems self-contained. There is no explicit evidence of one depending upon or borrowing from another. In surveying the three case studies, however, the similarities are more striking than the differences. One might expect that Winkler, with its much longer history and *Kanadier* background would have had an easier and earlier transition than North End/Elmwood and South End/Portage Avenue. However, this was not true. Winkler did declare a higher amount of English usage in Sunday school and youth in 1949,[43] and in view of the German instruction available in public school neither had a congregational German school. It also is impossible to document the onset of bilingual preaching from the congregational records. These, however, are the most significant differences between the rural Winkler and the two urban congregations in Winnipeg.

The commonalities among the three congregations are more striking. Winkler adopted unilingual English worship the same year as Elmwood. Winkler's brush with bitter division was even more clearly language-related than the separation that racked South End/Portage Avenue. All three recognized the language challenge within a few years of each other and almost two decades later completed the process within a four-year span. The process of language confrontation and concrete change followed two significant and related innovations in each case: the introduction of the professional pastorate, and the institutionalization of the needs of children and youth in a Christian Education Committee. In all three instances the pastor specifically introduced the Christian Education Committee, and took a pro-English advocacy role on behalf of the younger segment of the congregation. Combining these similarities with the similar chronologies of change followed by each, shows that the *Kanadier-Russländer* and urban-rural distinctions did not result in significant differences in their language transition.

This conclusion is further supported by instances where two congregations shared a common feature in contrast to the third. In Elmwood and South End youth were engaged in English-language community outreach at the periphery of the congregation well ahead of any significant internal linguistic accommodation.[44] In both cases, members refused to integrate the recipients of these ministries into the mainstream of the congregation. Winkler and South End, the congregations that suffered the most tension, made extensive use of questionnaires to raise the awareness of members and try to forge a consensus among them. Elmwood, the congregation that suffered the least overt strife also had the pastor with the longest tenure, I. W. Redekopp (1954-1967). He also was the most skilled and capable pastor, although J. H. Quiring made an effective start in Winkler (1955-1962). Both came from the ranks of the Bible college faculty, and both tried to implement language transition as a positive program of incremental change. Jacob Neufeld of South End (1950-1961) was not as well trained, was less aggressive by nature, and led a congregation with a history of internal tension. As a result, he almost collapsed under the strain of trying to meet the needs of a growing English minority while shackled to an unresponsive German majority.[45] Part of the trauma faced by both Elmwood and South End was the difficult choice between an English sermon that would serve as a significant signal of inclusion for the younger segment of the congregation, and the Sunday morning *Gebetstunde* that served as an important participatory experience for older members. Giving up the *Gebetstunde* was a costly concession for the aging German establishment, and having made this sacrifice, it was not soon ready to be segregated from the emerging English majority and relegated to a shorter German service of obviously inferior status.

This synopsis has outlined the scope and sequence of Mennonite Brethren language transition in the 1940s, 1950s and 1960s. It remains to identify some key factors that contributed to the transitional process. This chapter highlights some factors at the expense of others because of the nature of its sources. It relies on internal documents that present the story of language transition from the perspective of two specific groups: denominational and congregational leaders, and Mennonite Brethren who contributed to periodicals. Thus, the voice of most members is heard only through their yea or nay in the voting process. A study including material from oral sources or sources exterior to the Mennonite Brethren community could conceivably reveal other important dynamics. Furthermore, this investigation does not touch the larger and more general factors inherent in the social assimilation of any immigrant group into a new and different host society. These limitations, however, do not prevent the disclosure of some internal dynamics that affected the exchange of English for German in the church.

The immigrant experience created the potential dynamic for change. Mennonite Brethren, who with other Mennonites had maintained the unity of religion and High German within a larger Russian-speaking context, now faced a new English-speaking social reality. As immigrants in Canadian society, they did not, in the long term, maintain the linguistic boundaries around their religious experience despite the determined efforts of many to do so. A primary factor in the process relates to education. In Russia Mennonites had largely controlled their own education, but in North America this was impossible.[46] Mennonite Brethren in the United States confronted the challenge around the turn of the century.[47] After 1910 *Kanadier* Mennonite Brethren in Canada founded the Herbert Bible School and sought to protect their privilege of extracurricular German religious instruction in the public schools. The fact remains, however, that Mennonite Brethren children were being educated in English, and the coming of the *Russländer* did nothing to change this. The Bible schools, the graded German Sunday school curriculum, the congregational German school, all of which received significant impetus with the coming of the *Russländer*, were intended in part to substitute for the German day-school of the Russian Mennonite colonies. They failed, however, to capture Canadian-born Mennonite Brethren children and youth for the German language. As the process advanced, education was also enlisted on the pro-English, pro-transition side of the issue. Whatever some in the constituency hoped, the Mennonite Brethren Bible College, founded in 1944, was bilingual from the start. Periodicals such as the *Jugendblatt*, the *Youth Worker* and the *Instructor* all focused on the Christian education of young people. The transition process in the three case-studies received significant impetus from Christian education committees. Thus, education ranks as a factor of first importance in Mennonite Brethren language transition.

A second factor promoting transition is related to the first. Mennonite Brethren had a relatively new history as a renewal movement among Mennonites, and a soteriology explicitly based on personal conversion. The religious dynamic of their 1860 schism from the *Kirchliche* Mennonites, the predominant Mennonite group in Russia, came from a conviction that authentic Christianity consisted of crisis conversion, occasioned by a profound sense of personal sinfulness, leading to a daily life of ethical purity and public witness, validated by the *Gemeinde* (congregation) in adult baptism and protected by rigorous congregational discipline.[48] This religious ideology had several implications for language and religion. When combined with the idealism of youth, it was a powerful motivation for outreach and mission. It also militated against a nominal faith satisfied with formal observance and passive religious allegiances.

Evidence of this religious activism can be found among the youth of both North End/Elmwood and South End. They mounted sizable English extension Sunday schools at arm's length from the congregation and organized other English language ministries, ranging from rescue mission work to tract distribution on the street. Thus, as Mennonite Brethren youth were educated in English, and attended Bible schools that drew inspiration from North American revivalism, they moved out into their English-speaking communities. In the process they thoroughly integrated their personal Mennonite Brethren faith with the English language.

This was the new reality that dawned on B. B. Janz, minister of the MB Church in Coaldale, Alberta, in 1945 after a first-hand examination of young-adult summer outreach ministries in Alberta. For Janz the unity of Mennonite Brethren religion and German was ruined. He already feared the possibility of schism and only hoped that a bilingual phase could be extended long enough to avoid it.[49]

This introduces the tertiary factor of language transition, the role of leadership. The failure of German-language educational efforts and the integration of English and practical religion by the youth apparently convinced many front-ranking leaders that bilingualism was, at best, a stress-relieving step on the way to full language transition. Seen in this light, the Canadian Mennonite Brethren purchase of the Christian Press, a printing establishment in Winnipeg, and the *Rundschau* in 1946[50] balanced the 1945 introduction of the bilingual *Jugendblatt*.[51] It was, in the words of B. B. Janz, an effort to "regulate the situation."[52] The Committee for the Preservation of the German Language served quite well as a safety vent for pro-German rhetoric but it had little effect on the pace of the transition process. H. F. Klassen of the Christian Press, which provided the *Rundschau* for Mennonite German enthusiasts, also launched the *Mennonite Observer* in 1955 at a strategic juncture.[53] The leader-driven buy-out of the Press also helped to introduce the *Mennonite Brethren Herald*.

At the local level, most of the pastors recruited from the ranks of the Mennonite Brethren Bible College faculty who served the three case-study-congregations took progressive steps to promote language transition. Of the case-study pastoral leaders, only D. K. Durksen of North End took a definite pro-German stance. Hermann Lenzmann of Winkler tried to maintain the bilingual status quo. The remaining pastors all took their own steps to move the process of transition along to a peaceful conclusion. Thus, while many leaders were not militantly pro-English, they viewed transition to English as inevitable. They were unwilling to sacrifice their youth or the unity of their congregations and conference on the altar of German retention. Simultaneously, they struggled to meet the needs of the older generation and preserve as much goodwill as possible on the road to complete transition. There is no doubt that language was one of the most intractable issues facing denominational and congregational leaders in the 1940s, 1950s and 1960s.

If education, mission and outreach, and leadership all tend to explain the advance of language transition, what are the factors that created the problem in the first place? Why did Mennonite Brethren not simply progress through a smooth and orderly incremental exchange of English for German? Immigration must be given chronological priority as a factor creating the problem of language. While this study has restricted itself to the Canadian scene, another investigation waits to be made for Mennonite Brethren in the United States, almost all of whom arrived in the 1870s. It is certain that by 1920 some pro-German supporters there had all but given up. They recognized that the second generation was almost completely English and that the cause of German-speaking Mennonite Brethren faith was virtually lost.[54] By 1929 English content had become a necessity in Sunday school material intended for American Mennonite Brethren.[55] In 1943 English became their official language, and ten years later they published an English hymnal.

The *Kanadier* Mennonite Brethren, on the threshold of commencing their transition in the 1920s, were then numerically overwhelmed by the staunchly German Russländer. This development delayed the Canadian transition for a generation. The smaller German Mennonite immigration after World War II did not materially slow the pace of transition in the Conference at large, but it probably had some local effect. Thus, it is possible that the segment of the South End congregation that became the German-speaking Central congregation consisted largely of these more recently arrived immigrants. Still, it was the *Russländer* that led the fight to retain the German language. They did so for two major reasons.

First, the German language represented a significant hedge protecting Mennonite Brethren identity and community from the encroaching dangers of English Canadian society. If personal religion and evangelism provided one important aspect of Mennonite Brethren self-understanding, the separate integrity of the congregation, the *Gemeinde*, was another. For Mennonite Brethren thrown into an alien social environment, the *Gemeinde* represented an ethos of separation from the world. It was the primary social institution providing identity, meaning and purpose in the midst of daily life. For ordinary members, it represented their strongest tie to an increasingly idealized past, and a refuge from the strangeness of their new world. The exclusive use of

German in the *Gemeinde* offered a powerful mark of differentiation and a hedge against dangerous assimilation to the ways of what older Mennonite Brethren considered the "barbarians" around them.[56]

The sentiments of *Rundschau* contributors such as J. J. Janzen and Gerhard Cornies in 1950,[57] both of whom appear not to have been leaders, provide two examples of this attitude. South End and Elmwood provide two more telling examples. In 1952, as the reaction against the creeping encroachment of English was at its peak, the South End congregation voted to end sponsorship of its decade-old English mission Sunday school. South End was unwilling to integrate young English-speaking converts from non-Mennonite backgrounds into its *Gemeinde*.[58] Even more specific is the example of Elmwood in 1965 when members rejected a proposal sponsored jointly by the Good Tidings Sunday school, the Christian Education Committee and the council, to end bilingual worship in favor of segregated worship so that community people could be integrated into an English worship service. The fact that English was already a part of the Elmwood service is very instructive. By 1965 the issue was not the introduction of English, but the retention of German. Mennonite Brethren members were willing to overrule their leaders to retain the German and keep *Engländer* out.[59]

The second factor that contributed to the volatility of the German question for Mennonite Brethren was that during the 1940s, 1950s and 1960s, at least some members believed that the German language deserved a sacred status. The German language was a natural extension of the strongly chauvinist attitudes many, if not most, *Russländer* immigrants harbored for their adopted German heritage. Thus, German was not only a hedge against worldly corruption but a positive gift from God to the Mennonite people. It is at this crucial point that the language issue points to the ethnocentricity of Mennonite Brethren religion in this period. While the evidence is muted in the official record, it is sufficient to validate this important conclusion. In 1949 F. C. Thiessen, a leading Mennonite Brethren educator from British Columbia declared it to be God's will that Mennonite Brethren children be born into German-speaking families. God did not intend Mennonite Brethren to adopt the English language.[60] At the 1951 convention David Neuman of the Ontario Youth Committee alluded to the concern of youth that their elders were ethnocentric and not bibliocentric in their faith.[61] Later at the same convention, the German Committee felt constrained to confront the confusion of language and salvation in the first sentence of its initial report to the Conference.[62] In the 1952 *Rundschau* typeface controversy, correspondents used biblical citations to charge editor H. F. Klassen with his responsibility to defend the German language.[63] Isaac Regehr, in his 1952 *"Der Preis der Zweisprachigkeit,"* implied that German was the divinely-ordained birthright of the Mennonite people. To reject it was to commit the sin of Esau in selling Isaac's blessing for a mess of pottage.[64] The tendency to make the German language itself central and essential to Mennonite Brethren religion was probably more prevalent among rank and file members than leaders, but the pain and turmoil of the language transition is at least partly explained by this factor.

The significance of language transition for Mennonite Brethren is implicit in six factors: education, mission, leadership, the realities of immigrant life, religious and ethnic separation, and a tendency to sacralize one's mother tongue. All these elements illustrate the complex and even contradictory nature of the cultural dynamics at work. The opposing forces set in motion by cultural assimilation and mission on the one hand, and an ideology of separation and cultural superiority on the other, proved so intractable that, in a sense, the fears of schism were finally proven true. A generation after the arrival of the *Russländer,* Mennonite Brethren were compromising their core value of a bonded congregational unit as congregation after congregation made the painful decision to split its worshipping community based on lingusitic preference. This conclusion alone is sufficient to show that language transition was a highly significant feature of Mennonite Brethren experience. It must be taken into account when seeking to understand Canadian Mennonite Brethren religion in the middle of the twentieth century.

Endnotes

INTRODUCTION

1. "A Statement to the Conference," presented by the Board of Reference and Counsel, *Report of the Forty-fifth General Conference of the Mennonite Brethren Church of North America, July 21 to 26, 1951, Winkler, Manitoba, Canada*, 126. (All General Conference reports hereafter cited as *General Conference Report*).

2. Ibid., 126-127.

3. Ibid., 126.

4. Ibid., 128.

5. Ibid., 130.

6. Ibid., 127.

7. "Summarized Report of the Mennonite Brethren Conference Seminary Commission," Ibid., 118-119.

8. Committee of Reference and Counsel report, *1948 General Conference Report*, 106-107.

9. See Leo Driedger, *Mennonite Identity in Conflict*, Studies in Religion and Society, vol. 19 (Lewiston, N.Y.: Edwin Mellen Press, 1988).

10. See Robert Wiebe, *The Search For Order: 1877-1920*, The Making of America Series, vol. 4. (New York: Hill and Wang, 1967). Wiebe makes this point in chapters 1 and 2 about small communities generally in the United States.

11. I have explored more of this theological pluralism in "Differing Historical Imaginations and the Changing Identity of the Mennonite Brethren," in *Anabaptism Revisited: Essays on Anabaptist/Mennonite studies in honor of C. J. Dyck*, Walter Klaassen, ed. (Scottdale, Pa.: Herald Press, 1992), 155-172.

12. John H. Lohrenz, *The Mennonite Brethren Church* (Hillsboro, Kans.: Board of Foreign Missions of the Conference of the Mennonite Brethren Church of North America, 1950), 64.

13. E. K. Francis, *In Search of Utopia: The Mennonites In Manitoba* (Altona, Man.: D. W. Friesen & Sons Ltd., 1955), 209.

14. John Peter Schmidt, "Pilgrims in Paradise: Sixty Years of Growth in the Mennonite Brethren Churches of British Columbia" (D. Min. dissertation, Fuller Theological Seminary, 1991), 77.

15. *75 Years of Fellowship: Pacific District Conference of the Mennonite Brethren Churches, 1912-1987*. Esther Jost, ed. (Fresno, Calif.: Pacific District Conference of the Mennonite Brethren Churches, 1987), 121.

16. see Peter M. Hamm, *Continuity and Change Among Canadian Mennonite Brethren*, Religion and Identity, vol. 3 (Waterloo, Ont.: Wilfrid Laurier University Press, 1987), 57.

17. See A. H. Unruh, *Die Geschichte der Mennoniten-Bruedergemeinde, 1860-1954* (Hillsboro, Kans.: General Conference of the Mennonite Brethren Church of North America, 1955); Peter M. Friesen, *The Mennonite Brotherhood in Russia (1789-1910)*, J. B. Toews, et al., trans. and ed. (Fresno, Calif.: Board of Christian Literature, General Conference of Mennonite Brethren Churches, 1978); John F. Harms, *Geschichte der Mennoniten Bruedergemeinde* (Hillsboro, Kans.: Mennonite Brethren Publishing House, 1925); John A. Toews, *A History of the Mennonite Brethren Church: Pilgrims and Pioneers* (Fresno, Calif.: Board of Christian Literature, General Conference of Mennonite Brethren Churches, 1975).

18. "Report of the Committee of Reference and Counsel," *1954 General Conference Report*, 20.

"WAR, PEACE AND NONRESISTANCE AT MIDCENTURY"
- *Abe Dueck*

1. Paul Toews, "The Long Weekend or the Short Week: Mennonite Peace Theology, 1925-1944," *Mennonite Quarterly Review* [Hereafter *MQR*] 60 (1986): 38-57; Paul Toews, "The Impact of Alternative Service on the American Mennonite World: A Critical Evaluation," *MQR* 66 (1992): 615-627.

2. Toews, "The Long Weekend," 57.

3. Toews, "The Impact of Alternative Service," 620.

4. Ibid., 627.

5. Toews, "The Long Weekend," 53.

6. Ted D. Regehr, "The Influence of World War II on Mennonites in Canada," *Journal of Mennonite Studies* 5 (1987): 73-89.

7. John Richard Burkholder and Barbara Nelson Gingerich, eds., *Mennonite Peace Theology: A Panorama of Types* (Akron, Pa.: Mennonite Central Committee Peace Office, 1991), 60. This booklet emerged from the 1989 MCC Peace Theology Colloquium and was used as a basis for discussions at the sixth Peace Theology Colloquium in Clearbrook, B.C. in June 1991. A further series of papers was given in response. See *Conrad Grebel Review* 10 (Fall 1992).

8. Leo Driedger and Donald B. Kraybill, *Mennonite Peacemaking: From Quietism to Activism* (Scottdale, Pa.: Herald Press, 1994).

9. Ibid.

10. Ibid.

11. Ibid. See also Leo Driedger, "The Peace Panorama: Struggle for the Mennonite Soul," *Conrad Grebel Review* 10 (1992): 289-308.

12. P. M. Friesen states that Abraham Schellenberg gave him two reasons for leaving Russia, the first of which was that he was convinced that religious freedom would be taken away from all alien church denominations. Peter M. Friesen, *The Mennonite Brotherhood in Russia (1789-1910) [Alt-Evangelische Mennonitsche Bruederschaft in Russland (1789-1910): im Rahmen der mennonitischen Gesamtgeschichte]*, trans. and ed. J. B. Toews, et al. (Fresno, Calif.: Board of Christian Literature, General Conference of Mennonite Brethren Churches, 1978), 496.

13. Theron F. Schlabach, *Peace, Faith, Nation: Mennonites and Amish in Nineteenth-Century America*, The Mennonite Experience in America, vol. 2 (Scottdale, Pa.: Herald Press, 1988), 252-253.

14. James C. Juhnke, *Vision, Doctrine, War: Mennonite Identity and Organization in America, 1890-1930*, The Mennonite Experience in America, vol. 3 (Scottdale, Pa.: Herald Press, 1989), 304.

15. The Canadian statistics were derived from tables of congregational memberships in Frank H. Epp, *Mennonites in Canada, 1920-1940: A People's Struggle for Survival* (Scottdale, Pa.: Herald Press, 1982), 269-289.

16. The role of Peter C. Hiebert, although significant, is not comparable to the role of Benjamin B. Janz. Janz was much more a spokesman for Canadian Mennonite Brethren and for the entire Russian Mennonite community than was Hiebert in the U.S. Furthermore, Janz was the chief proponent of a particular point of view with respect to alternative service. His major liability, of course, was his lack of fluency in English. On Hiebert, see the biography by Wesley J. Prieb, *Peter C. Hiebert: He Gave Them Bread* (Hillsboro, Kans: Center for Mennonite Brethren Studies, 1990). On Janz see John B. Toews, *With Courage to Spare: The Life of B.B. Janz (1877-1964)* (Winnipeg: The Board of Christian Literature of the General Conference of the Mennonite Brethren Churches of North America, 1978).

17. See William Janzen, "Relations Between Canadian Mennonites and their Government during World War II," *MQR* 66 (1992): 492ff.

18. Albert N. Keim, *The CPS Story: An Illustrated History of Civilian Public Service* (Intercourse, Pa.: Good Books, 1990), 80-81.

19. Guy Franklin Hershberger, *The Mennonite Church in the Second World War* (Scottdale, Pa.: Mennonite Publishing House, 1951), 39; Melvin Gingerich, *Service for Peace: A History of Mennonite Civilian Public Service* (Akron, Pa.: The Mennonite Central Committee, 1949), 90-92.

20. T. D. Regehr, "Lost Sons: The Canadian Mennonite Soldiers of World War II," *MQR* 66 (1992): 465.

21. *Beratungen und Bestimmungen der elften jährlichen Delegiertenversammlung der Ontario Konferenz der Mennoniten Brüdergemeinden, abgehalten in Virgil, Ontario am 24.*

und 25. Oktober 1942 (Hereafter *Ontario Conference Reports*), 30.

22. 1943 *Ontario Conference Report*, 25.

23. Ibid. These men still had to qualify as conscientious objectors. See David W. Fransen, "Canadian Mennonites and Conscientious Objection in World War II," (M.A. Thesis, University of Waterloo, 1977), 125 ff., and William Janzen, *The Limits of Liberty: The Experience of Mennonite, Hutterite, and Doukhobor Communities in Canada* (Toronto: University of Toronto Press, 1990), 163-244.

24. *Report of the Fiftieth Annual Conference of the Central District held in the Mennonite Brethren Church at Lustre, Montana, October 10-13, 1959*, 31.

25. *Minutes and Reports of the United States Area Conference of the Mennonite Brethren Church of North America* (1957), 35; (1959), 45; (1960), 57.

26. This table was compiled from tables in *The Mennonite Mosaic: Identity and Modernization*, eds. J. Howard Kauffman and Leo Driedger (Scottdale, Pa.: Herald Press, 1991), 174, and J. B. Toews, Abram G. Konrad and Al Dueck, "Mennonite Brethren Church Membership Profile: 1972-1982," *Direction* 14 (Fall 1985): 15.

27. The statements are provided in Appendix II of John E. Toews and Gordon Nickel, eds., *The Power of the Lamb* (Winnipeg: Kindred Press, 1986), 131-183. Statements by provincial conferences are not included in the appendix. This creates a somewhat misleading impression, because by 1940 Canada had approximately 50 percent of the MB membership in North America. Furthermore, the Ontario Conference of MB Churches was accepted as a district conference in 1939 and then became a member of the Canadian Conference in 1946. Its resolutions are not included.

In 1954 Canada and the United States became area conferences and subsequently the Canadian Conference continued to increase in size more rapidly than the U.S. Conference. Nevertheless, the district conference statements in the U.S. continue to be included whereas provinical statements are not included.

28. The Canadian figures are compiled from Bert Friesen, *Where We Stand: An Index of Peace and Social Concerns Statements by the Mennonites and Brethren in Christ in Canada, 1787-1982* (Winnipeg: Mennonite Central Committee Canada, 1986). Unfortunately, the equivelant U.S. publication, Urbane Peachy, ed., *Mennonite Statements on Peace and Social Concerns, 1900-1978* (Akron, Pa.: Mennonite Central Committee U.S. Peace Section, 1980), does not provide a similarly comprehensive index of statements. The U.S. figures and General Conference figures are compiled on the basis of statements in *The Power of the Lamb*.

It should be noted that Saskatchewan was divided into two districts until 1966, although there was also a provincial conference beginning in 1946. Also, the Canadian Conference (except Ontario) was a district of the General Conference until 1954 and the U.S. Conference met for the first time in 1957.

29. Burkholder, *Mennonite Peace Theology: A Panorama of Types*. The ten types identified by Burkholder are 1) Historic nonresistance; 2) Culturally engaged pacifism; 3) Social responsibility; 4) Apolitical nonresistance; 5) The pacifism of the Messianic community; 6) Radical pacifism; 7) Realist pacifism; 8) Canadian pacifism; 9) Liberation pacifism; and 10) Neo-sectarian pacifism.

30. *Report of the Forty-fourth General Conference of the Mennonite Brethren Church of North America, August 28 to September 2, 1948, Mountain Lake, Minnesota, 103-104*; A. H. Unruh, *Die Geschichte der Mennoniten-Bruedergemeinde: 1860-1954* (Hillsboro, Kans.: The General Conference of the Mennonite Brethren Church of North America, 1955), 792.

31. Ibid., 790-92.

32. Quoted in John B. Toews, *With Courage to Spare*, 110.

33. Ibid., 109.

34. As cited by Frank H. Epp, *Mennonites in Canada, 1920-1940*, 570.

35. Ibid., 571.

36. *The Power of the Lamb*, 159.

37. Ibid., 161.

38. See *Task Force Report on Mennonite Central Committee (Canada), July 1980,*

(Winnipeg: Board of Spiritual and Social Concerns, Canadian Conference of Mennonite Brethren Churches of North America, 1980).

39. J. A. Toews, *True Nonresistance Through Christ: A Study of Biblical Principles* (Winnipeg: The Board of General Welfare and Public Relations of the Mennonite Brethren Church of North America, 1955).

40. *Verhandlungen der achtundvierzigsten Kanadischen Konferenz der Mennoniten-Bruedergemeinde von Nord-Amerika, abgehalten in Nord-Kildonan, Manitoba, vom 5 bis 9 Juli, 1958*.

41. J. A. Toews, *Alternative Service in Canada during World War II* (Winnipeg: Publication Committee of the Canadian Conference of the Mennonite Brethren Church, 1959).

42. Culbert G. Rutenber, *The Dagger and the Cross: An Examination of Christian Pacifism* (Nyack, N.Y.: The Fellowship of Reconciliation, 1950).

43. *Peace Conference Lectures* (Hillsboro, Kans.: Tabor College, 1953).

44. John B. Toews, "The Origins and Activities of the Mennonite *Selbstschutz* in the Ukraine (1918-1919)," *MQR* 46 (1972): 36.

"DECADES OF TRANSITION: NORTH AMERICAN MENNONITE BRETHREN IN POLITICS" - *John Redekop*

1. James C. Juhnke, *A People of Two Kingdoms: The Political Acculturation of the Kansas Mennonites*, Mennonite Historical Series, no. 10 (Newton, Kans.: Faith and Life Press, 1975), esp. ch. 4 and 8.

2. John H. Redekop, "Mennonites and Politics in Canada and the United States," *Journal of Mennonite Studies* 1 (1983): 79-105.

3. Leland Harder, *Doors to Lock and Doors to Open: The Discerning People of God* (Scottdale, Pa.: Herald Press, 1993), ch 12.

4. John H. Redekop, *A People Apart: Ethnicity and the Mennonite Brethren* (Winnipeg: Kindred Press, 1987).

5. Leo Driedger, *Mennonite Identity in Conflict*, Studies in Religion and Society, no. 19 (Lewiston, N.Y.: The Edwin Mellen Press, 1988); Miriam E. Warner, "Mennonite Brethren: The Maintenance of Continuity in a Religious Ethnic Group." Ph.D. diss., University of California, Berkeley, 1985; Donald Kraybill, "Modernity and Identity: The Transformation of Mennonite Ethnicity," paper delivered at Conrad Grebel College, Waterloo, Ont., 30 May 1986; James Urry, *None But Saints: The Transformation of Mennonite Life in Russia, 1789-1889* (Winnipeg: Hyperion Press, 1989).

6. Howard John Loewen, *One Lord, One Church, One Hope, and One God: Mennonite Confessions of Faith in North America, An Introduction*, ed. Willard M. Swartley, Text-Reader Series, no. 2 (Elkhart, Ind.: Institute of Mennonite Studies, 1985), 80-81.

7. John A. Toews, *A History of the Mennonite Brethren Church: Pilgrims and Pioneers* (Fresno: Board of Christian Literature, General Conference of Mennonite Brethren Churches, 1975), 344.

8. *Bericht über die zehnte Bundeskonferenz der Mennoniten-Brüdergemeinde Abgehalten in Reno County, Kansas, Nordamerika am 12. u. 13 Oktober, 1888* (Hereafter GC Report), 12.

9. 1890 GC Report, 31.

10. War-Time Elections Act, T-I George V, 39 Statutes of Canada § 154 (f) (1917).

11. 1943 GC Report, 67.

12. 1966 GC Report, 24-25.

13. *The Canadian Parliamentary Guide* edited sequentially by Arnott Magurn, Ernest Chambers, A. L. Normandin, G. Pierre Normandin and, since 1990, Kathryn Flanagan and Katherine Miller. Until 1988 it was "Published with the Patronage of Parliament" privately in Ottawa. Since 1989 it has been published in Toronto by Info Globe.

14. Frank C. Peters, "The Scriptural Basis for Nonresistance," *The Christian Leader*, 20 Oct. 1959, 4-5; Clarence Bauman, "Focal Elements In the Anabaptist-Mennonite Peace Position," *The Christian Leader*, 3 Nov. 1959, 4-5, 24; and 17 Nov. 1959, 4-5.

15. Orlando Harms, "Our Government and We," *The Christian Leader*, 20 Sept. 1960, 2.

16. John H. Redekop, "Comments on the Anti-Communist Movement," *The Christian Leader*, 1 May 1962, 4-5; John H. Redekop, "Is the United States a Christian Country?" *The Christian Leader*, 15 Oct. 1963, 4-5; John H. Redekop, "Evangelical Christianity and Political Ideology," *The Christian Leader*, 10 Nov. 1964, 4-5.

17. *The Christian Leader*, 2 Feb. 1965, 19.

18. *Mennonite Encyclopedia* (Scottdale, Pa.: Mennonite Publishing House, 1955-1959).

19. James C. Juhnke, *A People of Two Kingdoms*, 248; Perry J. Bush, "Drawing the Line: American Mennonites, the State and Social Change, 1935-1973," *The Mennonite Quarterly Review* 65 (Apr. 1991): 202.

20. John H. Redekop, "The State and the Free Church," in *Kingdom Cross and Community: Essays on Mennonite Themes in Honor of Guy F. Hershberger*, eds. John Richard Burkholder and Calvin Redekop (Scottdale, Pa.: Herald Press, 1976), 179-195.

21. J. Howard Kauffmann and Leland Harder, *Anabaptists Four Centuries Later: A Profile of Five Mennonite and Brethren in Christ Denominations* (Scottdale, Pa.: Herald Press, 1975), 157.

22. Mark A. Noll, "The End of Canadian History," *First Things*, Apr. 1992, 31.

23. *Toronto Globe and Mail*, 12 Jan. 1993, A4.

"THE ECONOMIC TRANSFORMATION OF CANADIAN MENNONITE BRETHREN - *Ted Regher*

1. According to the Canadian census, 86.9 percent of Canada's 111,380 Mennonites lived on farms or in small rural towns and villages in 1941. (CANADA *Census of Canada*, 1942, Table 37, Population by principal religious denominations and sex, for counties and census division). The census statistics cited here, and membership figures cited later in this paper, should be used with caution. The census figures, of course, include all those who indicated on the census form that they were "Mennonite." Only about half of that number were actually members of any Mennonite church. The church membership figures, of course, do not include unbaptized young people or other adherents, but the census figures almost certainly also include some cultural or ethnic Mennonites who rarely or never attended a Mennonite church. The membership figures published in the yearbooks of the Northern District (later the Canadian Conference) of the Mennonite Brethren Church of North America sometimes carry exactly the same figures for particular churches or provinces for three or four years before they are updated, and membership figures for some congregations are sometimes left blank. In addition, many of the immigrants of the 1920s who had been members of a Mennonite church in the Soviet Union, accepted short-term farm or other employment or began farming in a district where there was no nearby Mennonite church. Such people did not become members of any Canadian Mennonite church until they had established themselves in a new community. As a result, the church membership statistics are less than completely reliable. What is quite clear, however, is that from 1940 through 1960 the membership increases came almost exclusively from ethnic Mennonite people—not from neighboring non-Mennonite people.

2. A more detailed explanation of the reasons for Amish concerns regarding aspects of modern technology is given in Donald B. Kraybill, *The Riddle of Amish Culture* (Baltimore: The Johns Hopkins University Press, 1989).

3. These statistics were provided by the staff at the Center for Mennonite Brethren Studies in Fresno, California, and are based on the membership figures given in the annual conference yearbooks for the years indicated. In most cases the numbers indicate membership on 31 December of the previous year. Since no conference yearbook was published in 1940, the

figures for 1941 are used.

4. *Verhandlungen der fünfzigsten Kanadischen Konferenz der Mennoniten-Brüdergemeinde von Nord-Amerika, abgehalten in Virgil, Ontario, vom 2. bis 6. Juli 1960*. Several speakers at the annual meeting of the Canadian Conference reviewed the history and development of the Canadian conference and commented on various aspects of the membership statistics. It is indicative of the minor inaccuracies in the statistics that the membership of the conference in 1960 is given as 14,075 on page 4, but as 14,185 on page 260 of the 1960 Conference Year Book.

5. It is true that a disproportionate number of the immigrants of the 1920s had been teachers, preachers or other professionals in Russia before the revolution or under the Soviet regime. Some, including my grandfather, my father, an uncle and an aunt, tried very hard to reestablish themselves in Canada in their former careers. Both the Canadian Mennonite Board of Colonization and the Canadian Pacific Railway's Canada Colonization Association believed that the immigrants should establish farming communities, but that those so inclined might find teaching positions in rural, agricultural Mennonite communities. Many of the former teachers and preachers nevertheless had to find their livilihood in agriculture.

6. The most detailed information on some of these land sales, and the subsequent problems faced by the Mennonite farmers, is available in the Canadian Pacific Railway Papers, 1886-1958, in the Glenbow-Alberta Archives. See for example Box 173, File 1719, which documents the sale of the Whitman Farm near Hussar, Alberta, to a group of Mennonites from Saskatchewan. The *Western Weekly Law Reports* document a number of cases in which Mennonite purchasers were unable or unwilling in the 1930s to meet financial obligations they had undertaken in the late 1920s.

7. The Railway Agreement of 1925 gave the Canadian Pacific and the Canadian National Railways effective control over the recruitment of European agriculturalists. Both national railways were eager to attract Mennonites from the Soviet Union and other immigrants who could be settled on vacant or underdeveloped railway lands. Together the two railways organized the Canada Colonization Association, but competitive tactics also led to the creation by both railways of their own special operating departments designed to serve new settlers—the Department of Colonization and Development of the Canadian Pacific Railway and the Department of Colonization and Agriculture of Canadian National Railways. This led to a reduced use and an unwillingness to provide funds for the oepration of the Canada Colonization Association by Canadian National Railways, leaving that association as one of the operating departments of the Canadian Pacific Railway. Other Canadian Pacific Railway departments active in the promotion of Mennonite immigration and colonization were the Colonization Finance Corporation and the Department of Natural Resources.

8. A. A. Toews, "Sind wir als Siedler wirtschaftlich vorwaerts gekommen?" presented at *Die 9. Vertreterversammlung der mennonitischen Siedler Albertas im Bethause der Mennonitengemeinde zu Tofield am 14. und 15. Juli 1939*, in *Der Bote*, 14 Feb. 1940, 8. The translation is mine.

9. Ibid.

10. G. E. Britnell and V. C. Fowke, *Canadian Agriculture in War and Peace, 1935-1950* (Stanford: Stanford University Press, 1962).

11. The demand for cereal grains increased once war-devastated areas occupied by enemy forces were liberated, and by 1945 the demand for wheat and bread in liberated Europe absorbed all available grain covered either by government export credits or United Nations Relief and Rehabilitation contracts. Canadian grain prices were carefully controlled by the government during the war, and those controls were only removed gradually after the war to prevent windfall profiteering. This meant that operating margins for heavily indebted farmers remained problematic.

12. A. H. Unruh, "Zur Siedlungsfrage," *Mennonitische Rundschau*, 16 Sept. 1942, 4.

13. These figures, like the ones from Table 1, were provided by the Center for Mennonite Brethren Studies in Fresno, California.

14. K. J. Rea, *The Prosperous Years: The Economic History of Ontario, 1939-75* (Toronto: University of Toronto Press, 1985); John T. Saywell, *"Just call me Mitch:" The Life of Mitchell F.*

Hepburn (Toronto: University of Toronto Press, 1991); Britnell and Fowke, *Canadian Agriculture in War and Peace.*

15. V. C. Fowke, *The National Policy and the Wheat Economy* (Toronto: University of Toronto Press, 1957). In British Columbia both the dairy farmers and the poultrymen had established effective supply management schemes in the 1930s. Mennonite farmers participated in those schemes, and were consequently much less vulnerable to international market fluctuations than was the case for berry producers in the province.

16. *Stabilization Controls and What They Do,* a handbook prepared by an interdepartmental committee composed of representatives of the Departments of Finance, Labour, Agriculture, the Wartime Prices and Trade Board, and the War Information Board, December 1943, National Archives of Canada, Record Group 64, Vol. 1555.

17. The willingness of Mennonite Brethren to accept integrated economic institutions stands in sharp contrast to the continuing emphasis groups such as the Hutterites and Old Order Mennonites and Old Order Amish placed on the maintenance of their own separatist economic institutions. The (Old) Mennonite Church in Ontario, and the Northwest Conference of the Mennonite Church in western Canada participated in some of the new institutions but worked hard to maintain some of their traditional organizations as well. Even the General Conference Mennonites devoted a good deal of time and attention to ways whereby they could maintain a significant degree of economic control. Such matters, as far as I can discover, were not debated at Mennonite Brethren conferences, nor were they the subject of scholarly or public discussion in the journals and newspapers published by Mennonite Brethren.

18. J. Winfield Fretz, *The Waterloo Mennonites: A Community in Paradox* (Waterloo: Wilfrid Laurier University Press, 1989).

19. Donald Kraybill, in *The Riddle of Amish Culture,* suggests that Amish insistence on the use of the horse in field operations set practical limits to the size and complexity of Amish farms. The Church of God in Christ, Mennonite, accepts modern technology, but carefully watches the businesses of its members and orders those who grow too large to reduce their operations or sell branches of their businesses.

20. The term capitalist, as used here, is meant simply as a description of individuals who were able to accumulate and use capital. The most obvious uses of capital are to hire and pay for the labor of others, and to purchase technology, supplies and raw materials.

21. Executive Committee Minutes, 18 September 1943, which includes Dr. J. W. Fretz, "Report on my Trip to Canada to Study Mennonite Colonization." Mennonite Central Committee Papers, IX-5-1, Archives of the Mennonite Church Goshen, Ind. (Hereafter referred to as Fretz 1943 Report.)

22. J. Winfield Fretz, *Christian Mutual Aid: A Handbook of Brotherhood Economics* (Akron, Pa.: The Mennonite Central Committee, 1947), 8-9.

23. Ibid., 6.

24. Ibid, 3.

25. Ibid., 87.

26. William Janzen, *Limits on Liberty: The Experience of Mennonite, Hutterite, and Doukhobor Communities in Canada* (Toronto: University of Toronto Press, 1990), 245-286; Bert Friesen, *Where We Stand: An Index of Peace and Social Concerns Statements by Mennonites and Brethren in Christ in Canada, 1787-1982* (Winnipeg: Mennonite Central Committee Canada, 1986), 190.

27. It is interesting to contrast the experience of the Mennonite Church with those of General Conference and Mennonite Brethren. The latter two accepted direct government support. The Mennonite Board of Missions and Charities refused such direct support, but established policies, particularly for the institutions in the United States, which seemed to make them even more dependent on government social policies. Clients, patients or guests in the charitable institutions of the Mennonite Church were expected to pay for the services received, according to their ability. That ability, however, quickly came to be defined as the precise amount of their old age pension, disability or welfare checks. Fees at the facilities moved, in

locked step, with State welfare policies. Individuals who did not receive government support and did not have the necessary money themselves were refused admission unless they could find family or congregational sponsors who would pay the appropriate fees. Congregations were expected to cover any deficit between the financial ability of their members and the established fees. In effect, these charitable institutions depended on government policies, but obtained the money indirectly. The government, nevertheless, insisted that minimum standards be met by the institution if it accepted individuals who were receiving some sort of social assistance, and almost every major renovation in the homes was only made after government saftey, health or fire inspectors complained that the existing facilities were unsatisfactory. None of this quite fit the old separatist model of mutual aid.

28. The only Mennonite economic institutions which specifically restricted membership to Mennonites were the Mennonite credit unions, but the membership restrictions in most of those cases were due to federal banking legislation. Canadian Credit Unions enjoyed significant federal tax advantages and were not subject to the infamous "double liability" provisions of Canadian banking legislation. The established chartered banks, not the credit unions, insisted on the membership and other restrictions under which the credit unions were allowed to operate.

29. Fretz 1943 Report, 37.

30. The best general history of the Mennonite community at Yarrow is Agatha E. Klassen, ed., *Yarrow: A Portrait in Mosaic* (Yarrow, B.C.: A. E. Klassen, 1976).

31. A good example of the newer and more cautious Growers' Co-operative is the Abbotsford Growers Co-operative Union, founded late in 1947, and working closely with a federation of all berry growers in the Fraser Valley. One of the most controversial decisions made by this cooperataive was to order all members to reduce their plantings of Newburgh raspberries by 50 percent. (Protokoll, 25 January 1949).

32. Fretz 1943 Report, 22.

33. P. H. Regehr, *Er fuehret . . .: Geschichte der Coaldale Mennonitischen Kaeserei, 1928-1958* (Coaldale, Alta.: Kaeserei, 1959). The date in the title should apparently be 1938, but there had been limited cheese-making facilities at Coaldale earlier.

34. The Annual Reports of the Alberta Department of Agriculture list all the cheese factories in Alberta. At various times about half of these were in predominantly Mennonite communities, most in southern Alberta since the large and well established Northern Alberta Co-operative Dairy Producers dominated the market in the northern half of the province. The primary market for Alberta produced cheese was, of course, local, but British Columbia had only two small cheese factories in the 1940s and drew most of its cheese requirements from outside markets—initially from the Ottawa Valley but increasingly during the war from Alberta.

35. Fretz mentions this contract in his report. A considerable diversification of irrigation farming to include a variety of vegetables and other row crops was also greatly aided by the food requirements of the Prisoner of War camps. David Ewert stated in his personal recollections at the conference on the Mennonite Brethren Church at Mid-Century (February 1993) that members of the Mennonite Brethren Church at Coaldale who were carpenters were not permitted to accept employment in the building of the prisoner of war camps. Yet the Mennonite-controlled local cheese factory sold cheese and milk to the camps, and hundreds of the prisoners worked on farms owned by Mennonite Brethren. The prisoners working on Mennonite farms were invited to attend worship services at the Mennonite Brethren Church in Coaldale, and occupied the last two or three rows of seats in that church.

36. Both the egg grading station and the cold storage plant were only made possible because the provincial government provided substantial marketing or start-up assistance.

"ECONOMIC DEVELOPMENTS AMONG THE UNITED STATES MENNONITE BRETHREN - *Calvin Redekop*

1. The figures cited in this section are taken from the *Information Please Almanac,* 43rd ed. (Boston: Houghton Mifflin Company, 1990), unless otherwise indicated.

2. There is a vast amount of American economic history; one source providing background for this paper is Thomas C. Cochran and William Miller, *The Age of Enterprise: A Social History of Industrial America* (New York: Harper and Row, 1961). These authors suggest that after 1830, the West was being settled more by speculators than by families concerned about a way of life(37ff). If this is true, it indicates how different were the motives of the immigrant Mennonites who came fifty years later.

3. My own family illustrates the process. My grandfather, Benjamin Redekop, and his family left Naumenkov, Ukraine in 1913, settled first at Main Centre, Saskatchewan, and then homesteaded in Montana in 1916. He helped establish the MB congregation at Lustre, Montana

4. A. H. Unruh, *Die Geschichte der Mennoniten-Bruedergemeinde: 1860-1954,* (Hillsboro, Kans.: The General Conference of the Mennonite Brethren Church of North America, 1955), 480. I have relied heavily on this book for information on the description of many MB congregations. He does not, however, include all the congregations. The table, though lengthy, is very helpful in gaining a picture of the growth, spread, and movement of the Mennonite Brethren Conference.

5. This description is derived from data compiled by the staff of the Center for Mennonite Brethren Studies in Fresno, Calif. Only those congregations that survived to 1960 are listed. Congregations homesteading or settling in new areas, but that disbanded due to drought, westward movement, or schism and moved elsewhere are listed in Table 2.

6. Based on best available estimates; information may not always be entirely accurate.

7. Based on data compiled by staff of Center for MB Studies, Fresno, and Unruh, *Geschichte der Mennoniten-Bruedergemeinde.*

8. Unruh, *Geschichte der Mennoniten-Bruedergemeinde.*

9. Membership data derived from conference yearbooks of the various conferences.

10. The U.S. yearly average population increase was 1.3 percent between 1930 and 1980.

11. Reports of the annual conference provide the best direct source for the ethos, basic concerns and activities of the conference. From these reports, however, one would have no idea whether the membership was rural or urban. An occasional comment about the lack of finances is made, while the major concerns are congregational discipline, theological orthodoxy, missions and evangelism.

12. Periodicals such as *Mennonite Life* and *Mennonite Community* do provide a number of community studies, including several MB congregations/communities, but they generally are weak on specific information on the economic life of the community.

13. *Mountain Lake, Minnesota: 1886-1986, Written by the Centennial Committee on the Occasion of our Community's 100th Anniversary*, ed. Gary Richter (Mountain Lake, Minn.: Centennial Book Committee, 1986), 72; Will Klassen, letter to author; Raymond F. Wiebe, *Hillsboro: The City on the Prairie* (Hillsboro, Kans.: Multi Business Press, Inc., 1985), 172; Mennonite Brethren reports of annual conferences.

14. There is considerable unclarity regarding the supposed three groups. *Mountain Lake, 1889-1986* suggests only two groups settled near Mountain Lake and one near Carson, while Unruh indicates three groups settled near Mt. Lake.

15. Based on *Mountain Lake: 1886-1986* and data provided by Will Klassen of Mt. Lake.

16. Totals include non-Mennonites, hence the numbers for GC and MB will not always add up.

17. Comparing the total number of GC and MB population with their relative involvements in city business activity would be very interesting, but these figures were not available to me when writing this chapter.

18. J. Winfield Fretz, has variously cited Mountain Lake as a model of cooperative spirit. Indications that the cooperative spirit was giving in to individualistic competition is indicated by the fact that there were five service and oil stations owned by Mennonites in 1936. See Fretz, *Christian Mutual Aid: A Handbook of Brotherhood Economics* (Akron, Pa.: The Mennonite Central Committee, 1947).

19. Ibid.

20. The membership of the Hillsboro MB congregation was about half that of the population of Hillsboro itself, according to table 6. A number of the congregation members were undoubtedly farmers so the figures can only suggest the profile.

21. This information was supplied and/or checked by Ray F. Wiebe, local Hillsboro historian. I express my thanks to him for this fine service. Unfortunately, I was not able to make similar categories for Mountain Lake and Hillsboro.

22. Based on data in Wiebe, *Hillsboro: The City on the Prairie*; and *The Blue Jay*, the student yearbook of Tabor College.

23. Totals again include non-Mennonites, hence figures do not add up.

24. Marion W. Kliewer states there were 140 businesses in Hillsboro in 1954. This compares closely to my figures. Kliewer, "Hillsboro—Mennonite Community Center," *Mennonite Life* 9 (Jan. 1954): 12-15.

25. Meaningful comparisons of the business profiles of the Mennonite groups in Mountain Lake, Hillsboro and Reedley within the MB context would require accurate membership figures of all the congregations plus their occupational classifications.

26. This was also true of many Canadian Mennonite communities such as Altona. See Esther Epp-Tiessen, *Altona: the Story of a Prairie Town* (Altona: D.W. Friesen & Sons Ltd., 1982).

27. Data drawn from *Polk's Directory of Fresno, California*, 1940, 1956.

28. Even though Hillsboro had no flour mills, there were many in other neighboring towns, including several in the Buhler area and numerous ones in the Newton area. Mountain Lake had one, which however was no longer operating by 1940.

29. A tabulation of the occupational pursuits of A. Warkentin and Melvin Gingerich, eds., *Who's Who Among Mennonites* (North Newton, Kans.: A. Warkentin, 1943), reveals that only six Mennonite Brethren are listed as being in business or professions: four of these were bankers, all born between 1871 and 1889, while another was an undertaker, born in 1903, and the other an owner of a hatchery, born in 1894.

30. Ibid.

31. I assume that Mennonites were going into the commercial world as well, but the evidence is relatively sparse and defection of Mennonites from the fold may be the reason.

32. The number of professors, medical doctors and ministers included indicates the unreliability of the book as a representative sample. J. J. Hostetler, ed., *Mennonite Business and Professional People's Directory, 1978* (Scottdale, Pa.: Mennonite Industry and Business Associates, 1978). The only other tabulation of Mennonites in business, provides some insight for 1940-1960. Regarding educational levels, the Mennonite Brethren did not differ at all from the other groups. J. Howard Kauffman and Leland Harder, *Anabaptists Four Centuries Later: A Profile of Five Mennonite and Brethren in Christ Denominations* (Scottdale, Pa.: Herald Press, 1975), 59.

33. Miriam Warner's study focused on a congregation in California during the early 1980s. Warner, "Mennonite Brethren: The Maintenance of Continuity in a Religious Ethnic Group," (Ph.D. diss.: University of California, 1985).

34. Kauffman and Harder, *Anabaptists Four Centuries Later*.

35. I am grateful for J. Howard Kauffman who provided this information from the CMP computer files of the 1973 research.

36. J. Howard Kauffman and Leo Driedger, *The Mennonite Mosaic: Identity and Modernization* (Scottdale, Pa.: Herald Press, 1991).

37. Both columns for Reedley are derived from *Polk's Directory of Fresno, California*, 1945 and 1956. The accuracy of the percentages are not very useful, since the directory itself is not fully accurate.

38. The Warkentin and Gingerich data provides an overwhelming impression that the MB membership is overly represented in the professional occupations, especially medicine, dentistry, chiropractors, education, university positions, institutional and governmental administration, as compared to the other Mennonite groups. Astounding is the number of Ph.D and M.D. degrees awarded to persons (both GC and MB) born between 1875 and 1900. This phenomenon needs careful analysis.

39. John D. Unruh, *In the Name of Christ: a History of the Mennonite Central Committee and Its Service, 1920-1951.* (Scottdale, Pa.: Herald Press, 1950), 377-380.

40. Though Unruh does not specify, these figures apparently include both U.S. and Canadian membership. The population for the General Conference is an estimate.

41. These terms are defined below.

42. That is to say, the mix of personal abilities, availability of resources and economic need. For example in Mountain Lake the need for building contractors provided such an opportunity.

43. This does not deny the continuing exodus of young people from every Mennonite community, but this also reflects the national scene.

44. This is equally true of Canadian communites such as Altona. See Epp-Tiessen, *Altona* and Fretz, *Christian Mutual Aid*. I propose that the loss of cooperatives can be seen as a "transition process" to the individualistic society for Mennonites.

45. This process has not been extensively studied or documented. Harold S. Bender outlines these influences in an important article entitled "Outside Influences on Mennonite Thought," in *Proceedings of the Ninth Conference on Mennonite Educational and Cultural Problems,* (North Newton, Kans.: Bethel College Press, 1953), 33-41. He mentions the especially great infiltrating power of the radio for fundamentalism.

46. Robert K. Merton, *Social Theory and Social Structure* (Glencoe, Ill.: The Free Press, 1957). These terms can also be defined as alternatives to the famous "Gemeinschaft" versus "Gesellschaft" types of social structure introduced by Toennies.

47. Ibid.

48. This thesis is developed more fully in Calvin Redekop, Stephen Ainlay and Robert Siemens, *Mennonite Entrepreneurs* (Baltimore: John Hopkins University Press, 1995).

49. This perception was strongly reinforced during interviews with Mennonite entrepreneurs of the major Mennonite groups in my entrepreneurial research in 1985-1986. This tendency, however, is decreasing due to the greater interaction between the various Mennonite groups. See George Homans, *The Human Group* (New York: Harcourt Brace, 1950) for the classic major discussion of this idea.

50. I have maintained that the Mennonites do not fully fit Weber's thesis, but the Pietist influence does seem to offer some plausibility that the Mennonite Brethren are more "cosmopolitan" and hence "Capitalist" than other groups. For an analysis of Anabaptist/ Mennonite economics thesis, and the Mennonite Brethren differences see Redekop, Ainlay and Siemens, *Mennonite Entrpreneurs.*

"SHE HATH DONE WHAT SHE COULD: - *Valerie Rempel*

1. J. C. Penner and Adolf I. Frantz, *Through the Years: A History of the Mennonite Brethren Church of Shafter, California, Its Organization and Its Development, 1918-1968* (Shafter, Calif.: Mennonite Brethren Church, 1968), 37.

2. *Protokoll der Konferenz der M. B. Gemeinde von N. Amerika, abgehalten in der Gemeinde York und Hamilton Co., Nebraska, am 10, Oktober, 1881.* (Hereafter *GC Report*).

3. In 1894 the first missionaries sent out by the North American Mennonite Brethren, Henry and Elizabeth Unruh Kohfeld, went to work among the Comanche Indians in Oklahoma. They were joined in 1896 by the first single woman sent out by the conference—Maria B. Regier. Mrs. H. T. Esau, *First Sixty Years of M.B. Missions* (Hillsboro, Kans.: The Mennonite Brethren Publishing House, 1954), 28-39. In 1899 the first foreign missionary contingent was sent to

India. John A. Toews quotes A. E. Janzen as follows: "The initial group of four M.B. missionaries to India was made up of a preacher and his wife, a teacher and a nurse. By way of preparation and divine calling this group had embodied within its number the potential of the Lord's method—preach, teach, heal; a preacher, a teacher, a nurse were in the staff." This group was composed of one man, the preacher, and three women. The four were N. N. and Susie (Wiebe) Hiebert, Elizabeth Neufeld, and Anna Suderman. John A. Toews, *A History of the Mennonite Brethren Church: Pilgrims and Pioneers* (Fresno: Board of Christian Literature, General Conference of Mennonite Brethren Churches, 1975), 401.

4. *60th Anniversary: 1893-1953, Mennonite Brethren Church, Corn, Oklahoma* (Corn: Mennonite Brethren Church, 1953).

5. In an account prepared for their seventy-fifth anniversary (1980), Esther Jost wrote, "During the early years of the Reedley Church, several women were sensitive to the need of supplementing the missionary efforts of the church. In November 1913, the women met in the home of Mrs. H.R. Janzen, organized a Nahverein (sewing society), and elected Mrs. Janzen as their chairman. Eager to begin their services, the women donated money and materials for their first missionary project. This work was called to the attention of the church by Pastor John Berg, and as a result, the Women's Missionary Society was accepted as an organization of the Reedley Mennonite Brethren Church. At the end of the year, the society sent $50.00 each to missionaries H. C. Bartel and F. J. Wiens in China and $125.00 to the missionary field in India. The highlight of the group was their mission sale in 1919, which netted $1,545.00. This money was used for missionary and relief purposes in India and Russia." Esther Jost, *The Church Alive in its 75th Year: 1905-1980* (Reedley, Calif.: Mennonite Brethren Church, 1980), 105.

6. Herman J. Neufeld and Mrs. Neufeld, "The History of the Mennonite Brethren Church of Buhler, Kansas" (Diss., Tabor College, 1949), 74.

7. Ibid.

8. "History of the Sewing Circles of the M.B. Church of Shafter," Shafter Mennonite Brethren Church Records, Center for Mennonite Brethren Studies, Fresno, Calif., (Hereafter Shafter Church Records), Microfilm roll 77, frames 1405-1406. Mrs. P. P. Rempel served as the group's Bible teacher until March of 1942, and was apparently held in very high regard by the membership. Among the listing of projects is payment for a caretaker for Mrs. Rempel's yard, the installation of a cooler, and the secret remodeling of her house to install a bathroom while Mrs. Rempel and her daughter were taken to the beach for a short vacation. The unnamed historian wrote, "we don't know who was happier, Mrs. Rempel and Ann [her daughter], or those of us that had a share in it."

9. *60th Anniversary*.

10. Ibid.

11. Jost, *The Church Alive*, 107.

12. *1943 GC Report*, 64.

13. *Report of the Thirty-sixth Pacific District Conference of the Mennonite Brethren Church of North America, held at Reedley, California, November 18 to 21, 1945.* (Hereafter *PDC Report*), 40. The cost of furnishing a room was $250.00.

14. *Report of the Thirty-ninth Conference of the Mennonite Brethren Churches of the Southern District, held in the M.B. Church of Hillsboro, Kansas, October 16-19, 1948.* (Hereafter *SDC Report*), 35. A contribution of $50.00 from the Hillsboro Sewing Circle is noted in the financial report.

15. J. J. Seibel and Mrs. Seibel, eds., *Fiftieth Anniversary: Mennonite Brethren Church, Harvey, North Dakota, 1898-1948* (Harvey: Mennonite Brethren Church, 1948), 14.

16. Seibel and Seibel, 11. Total income for this time period is recorded as $4,281.98. $2,704.01 went for local projects, while $1,587.05 was channeled into mission-related projects: ($800.00 for care packages, $376.25 for "missions, widows and needy," and $410.80 for "mission schools, children's homes and radio work.")

17. Though the Krimmer Mennonite Brethren congregations were not a part of the Mennonite Brethren Church in the 1940s, they are included in this discussion because of the merger of the two groups in 1960.

18. Joseph A. Kleinsasser, *A History of Bethel Mennonite Brethren Church, Yale, South Dakota* (Sioux Falls, S. Dak.: J. A. Kleinsasser, 1979), 81.

19. Ibid., 80.

20. *60th Anniversary.*

21. *50th Anniversary: Zion Mennonite Brethren Church, Dinuba, California* (Dinuba: Zion Mennonite Brethren Church, 1961), 16.

22. Lydia Martens, "Fifth Anniversary," file "Scrapbook, Volume I, 1948-1958," Pacific District Conference of Mennonite Brethren Churches Women's Missionary Service Records, Center for Mennonite Brethren Studies, Fresno, Calif. (Hereafter PDC WMS).

23. She was also able to provide the following data: "Ten of the societies have used the method of the mission sale for income. Eight groups sew only for missionaries and relief, while some of the ten that have the sales sew for relief also. Estimated cash income is approximately $20,000, plus materials for relief estimated about again as much, amounting to a total of about $40,000. Projects that have received support are foreign missions, with the largest amount going into the general treasury, helping outgoing missionaries. Other projects are: Relief, MCC, as well as some home relief; home missions, such as: our local churches working among migrants, child evangelism, Home for the Aged in Reedley, Tabor College, P.B.I., and Immanuel Bible School. Then there are such additional projects as Red Cross, Release Hour, North Carolina Mission, Christian Radio Programs, Los Angeles Children's Home, Grace Children's Home, American Bible Society." Given subsequent reports in the district year books, these estimates were probably high. Martens, "Fifth Anniversary" PDC WMS.

24. Ibid.

25. Ibid.

26. In her fifth anniversary piece, Martens recalled that "with only a half day of conference left, numerous people voiced their opinion that we do something about organizing before the conference ended. Since I had been asked to make the survey report, I was asked to take the initiative and call for a meeting the next day, but the time was so short and everyone was anxious to leave for their homes, so we set a date to meet two or three weeks later in Reedley to organize." Martens, "Fifth Anniversary," PDC WMS.

27. Ibid.

28. Waldo Wiebe to J.B. Toews, 12 November 1948, Shafter Church Records, Microfilm Roll 77, frame 1387.

29. Ibid.

30. Meeting of the Shafter Relief Workers, 3 November 1948, Shafter Church Records, Microfilm Roll 77, frame 1560. A history of the sewing circle records the event thus: "On November 4, 1948, we planned to go to Reedley where the different sewing circles met to plan and to organize a Women's Missionary Service, but Rev. Waldo Wiebe didn't want us to go so we didn't, but as most of the other circles were present, a Women's Missionary Service was organized on November 14, 1948." "History of the Sewing Circle of the M.B. Church of Shafter, 1923-1966," Microfilm Roll 77, frame 1410, Shafter Chuch Records.

31. "We'll admit that we felt a bit discouraged," wrote Lydia Martens. "Then, on November 14, Sunday afternoon, making last minute preparations for the meeting, we met our pastor outside, he greeted us in his usual friendly way, encouraged us just to be calm, go ahead and wished us God's blessing. I cannot tell you what a comfort his words meant to me at that hour. It was a balm to our souls, and we found new courage to go ahead." Martens, "Fifth Anniversary," PDC WMS.

32. The main text of the letter reads, "After consulting with the brethren H.R. Wiens and B.J. Braun, we felt it would not be a proper procedure to read your letter to the group for as much as the Conference had passed a resolution recommending that this organization be effected. We personally honor the expression of your position, but felt that we were not authorized to express a public opposition towards the matter which had been ordered by the Conference body. It would be the proper procedure to register such an opinion to the Conference instead of to the sisters who have preceded on the strength of our Conference recommendation. I trust that you will understand us in our judgement." J.B. Toews to Waldo Wiebe, 18 November 1948,

Microfilm Roll 77, frame 1388, Shafter Church Records.

33. Mrs. Martens later wrote, "We also thank the Lord for those who were opposed, for it caused us to pray much, and search our hearts to see whether we were really seeking only the glory of God. We praise His name that prayer changes things, for some of those who were most opposed, after they fully understood what we were seeking to accomplish, are in full accord with us, and help in the work that we are trying to promote." Martens, "Fifth Anniversary," PDC WMS.

34. Chairman, Mrs. David Letkeman of Dinuba; Vice-Chairman, Lydia Martens of Reedley; Secretary/Treasurer, Mrs. Abe Gerbrandt of San Jose; and a committee to work with them (Susie Issac of Shafter, Emma Bartel of Rosedale, Calif., Mrs. J. J. Heinrichs of Dallas, Oregon, Mrs. H. G. Wiens of Fresno, Calif., and Mrs. Art Loewen of Winton, Calif. Organizational Meeting of the M.B. Missionary Service, 14 November 1948, PDC WMS.

35. Ibid.

36. The financial report for the annual meeting held in 1950 indicates receipt of $39.20 during 1949, and $0.0 up to that date in 1950. Women's Missionary Service Meeting, 31 October 1950, PDC WMS.

37. Women's Missionary Service meeting, 31 October 1950, PDC WMS. Although the name *M.B. Missionary Service* was chosen, the organization has invariably been called the Women's Missionary Service, or WMS, beginning with the November 13, 1951, annual meeting minutes. Article I of the first constitution accepted (1954), notes the name as the "M.B. Women's Missionary Service of the Pacific District Conference."

38. *1950 PDC Report*, 21-22.

39. Ibid, 20.

40. Constitution, M.B. Women's Missionary Service, PDC WMS.

41. The eight-member committee included the president, vice president, secretary-treasurer, corresponding secretary, and the chairs of the Missionary Sewing Committee, the M.C.C. Committee, the Home for the Aged Committee, and the Missionary Program Committee. Note the change in nomenclature from Chairman to President.

42. M.B. Women's Missionary Service Meeting, 15 November 1954, PDC WMS.

43. Ibid.

44. Missionary Rally, 17 March 1955, file "Executive Meetings," PDC WMS.

45. This is the first record of membership assessment for a WMS project. M.B. Missionary Service Executive Committee meeting, 12 April 1955, PDC WMS.

46. M.B. Missionary Society Executive Committee Report for the Year 1955, file "Annual Meetings," PDC WMS.

47. Women's Missionary Society Meeting, 31 October 1950, PDC WMS.

48. For example, circles were informed of Beatrice Warkentin's needs (she was a missionary widowed in India) and were encouraged to send cash donations directly to her. M.B. Women's Missionary Service Executive Committee meeting, 17 April 1953, PDC WMS.

49. Ibid.

50. M.B. Missionary Service Executive Board meeting, November 10, 1956, PDC WMS; M.B. Missionary Service meeting, 12 November 1956, PDC WMS.

51. M.B. Missionary Service Executive Meeting, 21 November 1957, PDC WMS.

52. "To the loyal thinking conference women the fact that there was no unity, no conference budget on the women's level, and very little understanding of conference needs presented an ever increasing concern. Not nearly all of the money collected in the circles was being given to conference mission work. More and more independent organizations finding the Mennonite Brethren women easy prey were presenting their causes in glowing language oft with heartrending sincerity, and these organizations were cashing in on ever increasing sums of money. The result was that loyalty to conference causes was suffering and lack of funds was hampering conference work." Waldo D. Hiebert, "History of the Women's Missionary Service of the Southern District of the Mennonite Brethren Church of North America," (photocopy, 1956), 5. Copy available in Center for Mennonite Brethren Studies, Fresno, Calif.

53. Hiebert attributes their failure to meet at the next conference to a lack of vision on the

part of the hosting congregation's women. He writes that the Hillsboro women would have been happy to organize the previous year, but "felt that taking the initiative would not be well received since they were the host church." Hiebert, 6.

54. This may have been due to the presence of Marie Gerbrandt. Hiebert notes that she served as chairperson of the Senior Women's Group at the Hillsboro M.B. church and "had lived in California for many years and was, therefore, familiar with the Pacific District Women's Organization." Hiebert, 7.

55. Ibid.

56. Ibid.

57. Other officers included Helen Franz, Vice-Chairman; and Rachel Hiebert, Secretary-Treasurer. Ibid.

58. Women's Missionary Service: 1954-1955, folder 11, Southern District Conference of Mennonite Brethren Churches Women's Missionary Service Records, Center for Mennonite Brethren Studies, Hillsboro, Kans. (Hereafter SDC WMS).

59. Hiebert, 8.

60. *1954 SDC Report*, 54.

61. Ibid.

62. Mrs. Waldo Hiebert to members of the Women's Missionary Service, 18 January 1955, folder 11, SDC WMS.

63. Ibid.

64. Ibid. The circles responded positively. The treasurer's report for November 1, 1954 to October 31, 1955, the first year of formal organization, listed the collection of $1,842.00 for the mission projects ($1,045 for the maternity hospital and $765 for the Denver congregation). Treasurer's Report, 1 November 1954-31 October 1955, folder 11, SDC WMS.

65. Women's Missionary Service Executive Committee meeting, 22 September 1955, folder 11, SDC WMS.

66. Women's Missionary Service meeting, 24 October 1955, folder 11, SDC WMS.

67. Ibid.

68. Partial Report and Decisions of the Business Meeting of the Women's Missionary Service of the Southern District Conference, 24 October 1955, folder 11, SDC WMS.

69. Partial Report and Decisions of the Business Meeting of the Women's Missionary Service of the Southern District Conference, 24 October 1955, folder 11, SDC WMS.

70. Annual Report, Southern District Prayer Chairman, 22 October 1956, folder 11, SDC WMS.

71. "Southern District Women Sponsor Mission Rallies," *The Christian Leader*, 22 April 1958, 21.

72. 1956 SDC Report, 100.

73. In March of 1956 the Executive Committee members discussed "the question as to what we should do about requests for finances which come to us on the sidelines . . . such as requests from Texas and Arkansas." Women's Missionary Service Executive Committee meeting, 15 March 1956, folder 11, SDC WMS.

74. Ibid.

75. Helen Franz to Ferne Hiebert, 14 January 1958, folder 13, SDC WMS.

76. This may be due to the timing of organizational starts. The Missionary Service in the Pacific District organized in the wake of World War II and the massive relief efforts mounted by both the Mennonite Brethren Board of General Welfare and Mennonite Central Committee. Relief work may not have had the same urgency in the mid-1950s.

77. "The Works Various Circles Do, Presented at Conference Meeting, 1957," folder 13, SDC WMS.

78. Women's Missionary Service meeting, 20 October 1958, folder 13, SDC WMS.

79. Women's Missionary Service Financial Report, 20 October 1958-19 October 1959, folder 15, SDC WMS.

80. Folder 15, SDC WMS.

81. Women's Missionary Service meeting, 19 October 1959, folder 15, SDC WMS.

82. Toews, 192.

83. Elfreda Fast to Esther [Ebel], 14 February 1959, folder 15, SDC WMS.

84. Mrs. Marion [Esther] Kliewer to Mrs. Pete E. Heinrichs, 27 February 1959; and to Mrs. Menno Prieb, 27 February 1959, folder 15, SDC WMS.

85. Women's Missionary Service Officers Meeting, 11 September 1959, folder 15, SDC WMS.

86. Mrs. Kliewer wrote, "I am not sure if you were the lady who called at the Board of Foreign Missions Office this past week, but I think you might be. For your interest and information I am sending you a few pieces of literature concerning our Southern District Women's Missionary Service. Enclosed are the recommendations which must have been adopted in 1955 and which I believe have been sort of a guide since then." Mrs. Marion Kliewer to Mrs. Wayne Faul, 28 March 1959, folder 15, SDC WMS.

87. *Report of the Fifty-first Conference of the Central District, held in the Mennonite Brethren Church at Mountain Lake, Minnesota, October 8-11, 1960*. (Hereafter CDC Report), 49.

88. 1957 CDC Report, 11-12.

89. 1959 CDC Report, 50.

90. Ibid., 50.

91. Ibid., 50-51.

92. Ibid., 51.

93. Officers elected to serve were Mrs. Waldo Dick of Mountain Lake, Minnesota, Chairman for a three-year term; Mrs. Rueben Dirks of Huron, South Dakota Vice-Chairman for a two-year term; Mrs. Clifford Reimche, Martin, North Dakota, Secretary-Treasurer for a two-year term; and Mrs. Henry Regier of Madrid, Nebraska, Devotional leader for a one-year term. 1960 CDC Report, 49.

94. Ibid.

95. 1961 CDC Report, 52.

96. Ibid., 52-53. Records note $500 to Rosella Toews, $400 to Martha Kroeker, $750 to John and Viola Wiebe, and $20 to the Kenneth Mungers.

97. For example, the Rosehill M.B. Circle of Munich, North Dakota, submitted the following report of their work to *The Challenger*: "We support a Korean orphan. Each member pledges $10.00 a month. We also send out Christmas bundles to the M.C.C. Each member donates. We have had a yearly mission sale. Items were donated and also sewed at our Circle. Our money then is distributed to various places, as: Back to the Bible Broadcast, other radio broadcasts, and some of our missionaries are remembered with a special gift. One missionary whom we try to remember in a very special way is Miss Mathilda Wall who grew up in Munich and was a member of the Rosehill church. Some of our projects consisted of gathering money for our new church parsonage, to buy drapes, paint, refrigerator, etc. The parsonage was built two years ago. We served lunches at auction sales, funerals, wedding receptions and baby showers. We have helped outfit several missionary couples as the Lord laid it upon our hearts. Also at our meetings we do embroidery work, quilt and tie quilts, letters from various missionaries are read and missionaries are remembered in prayer. There are also many other projects in which we have tried to help support the work of the Lord, such as the American Sunday School Mission, the American Bible Society, etc." Mrs. Ed Fadenrecht, "Societies Report," *The Challenger*, November 1962.

98. "Central District Women's Missionary Services Meet at Henderson, Nebraska," *The Challenger*, November 1962, 1.

99. Ibid.

100. Mrs. Waldo Dick, "W.M.S. President Writes," *The Challenger*, November 1962, 3.

101. Their stated purpose was as follows: "A. To promote spiritual growth and to become inspired for service through our fellowship of women in our conference. B. To promote the program of Missions, Relief, and Education of the District Area, and General Conference by: (1) giving our prayer and moral support; (2) fostering of interest in this program; (3) giving our financial support." The officers included president, vice-president, secretary, treasurer and

devotional chairman. Constitution of the Mennonite Brethren Women's Missionary Service of the Central District Conference, folder 22, SDC WMS.

102. For example, notes on a sermon by G. W. Peters at a missionary rally in 1956 report that "After reading Acts Chapter 9 verses 36 and to the end he showed us the importance of the work of the Missionary Service. Comparing the work of the Missionary Service and the life and work of Dorcas. Also that God is keeping a record and will give the reward." Missionary Rally, 15 March 1956, file "Executive Meetings," PDC WMS. J.B. Toews was a frequent speaker at WMS rallies and conferences, first as a pastor, then as Mission Board staff member, and later as president of the Mennonite Brethren Biblical Seminary. Minutes report the following sermon summary: "J. B. Toews of the Mission Office brought the challenge of the afternoon and based his message on Matt. 15:21-28. He spoke on the many women of faith listed in the Bible. When a crucial hour came in the history of man there was always a woman of faith to stand in the gap. . . . The work of women should not be minimized. Womanhood of our generation is awakening to the responsibility they have. Women are not to feel secondary but to lead the Cause of Christ to victory." Women's Missionary Service of the Southern District Meeting, n.d., folder 19, SDC WMS. On another occasion, Dr. Jacob A. Loewen informed WMS members that "Home is built around mother. In mother the children find a pattern of sacrifice." Women's Missionary Service of the Southern District, Annual Meeting, 20 October 1958, folder 13, SDC WMS.

"CANADIAN MENNONTE WOMEN'S SOCIETIES: MORE THAN MEETS THE EYE" - *Gloria Neufeld Redekop*

1. *Vereine* is the German word for "societies." The singular form, used elsewhere in this paper is *Verein*.

2. Jacob P. Bekker, *Origin of the Mennonite Brethren Church*, trans. D. E. Pauls and A. E. Janzen (Hillsboro, Kans.: The Mennonite Brethren Historical Society of the Midwest, 1973), 25-26.

3. *Frauen Missions Verein* means "Women's Mission Society."

4. *Männer Missions Verein* means "Men's Mission Society."

5. Samuel Floyd Pannabecker, *Open Doors: The History of the General Conference Mennonite Church*, Mennonite Historical Series, no. 11 (Newton, Kans.: Faith and Life Press, 1975), 288.

6. Maria Derksen, "Report—1944," in *Fifty Years: Ebenezer Verein (1936-1986)*, eds. Nettie Neufeld and Jessie Peters (Steinbach, Man.: Ebenezer *Verein*, 1987), 14.

7. Translation from the original German poem by Heinz Janzen, composed in the late 1940s.

8. Arelee MB Women's Missionary Fellowship, letter to author, January 1989.

9. Gloria Neufeld Redekop, "Mennonite Women in Canada: State of the Research," (a paper in partial requirement for a Ph.D. program in Religious Studies., University of Ottawa, 1989).

10. Pauline Bradbrook, "A Brief Account of The Church of England Women's Association in Newfoundland," *Journal of the Canadian Church Historical Society* 28 (Oct. 1986): 93.

11. Ruth Compton Brouwer, "Transcending the 'Unacknowledged Quarantine': Putting Religion into English-Canadian Women's History," paper presented to the joint session of the Canadian Society of Church History and Canadian Historical Association Annual Meeting, Kingston, Ont., 5 June 1991, 2-3.

12. Ibid.

13. Alison Prentice, et al. *Canadian Women: A History* (Toronto: Harcourt Bruce Jovanovich, 1988), 334.

14. Between 1947 and 1959, 112 new Mennonite women's societies were organized, whereas between 1960 and 1987, only sixty-six additional societies were formed. Margaret Gossen Toews, *South Western Ontario Women in Mission (1925-1987)* (n.p., 1987); Anita Froese, *Manitoba Mennonite Women in Mission (1942-1977)* (Winnipeg: Manitoba Mennonite Women in Mission, 1977); Mary Bartel, *Saskatchewan Women in Mission* (n.p.: Saskatchewan Women in Mission, 1977); Anne Neufeld, ed., *History of Alberta Mennonite Women in Mission (1947-1977)* (Coaldale: Alberta Mennonite Women in Mission, 1977); Martha Rempel, *History of B.C. Mennonite Women in Mission (1939-1976)* (Chilliwack: British Columbia Mennonite Women in Mission, 1976); all published histories of CMC and MB local congregations; and Gloria Neufeld Redekop, "Survey on Women's Fellowships of the Conference of Mennonites in Canada and the Canadian Mennonite Brethren," November 1988.

15. Prentice, et al. *Canadian Women: A History*, 311; Anne Bargen, "Too Gifted to Become a Mere Housewife?" *The Canadian Mennonite*, 7 Sept. 1956, 2; B. Charles Hostetter, "The Husband's Part in Happy Home Building," *The Canadian Mennonite*, 27 Aug. 1954, 6; B. Charles Hostetter, "The Wife's Part in Happy Home Building," *The Canadian Mennonite*, 3 Sept. 1954, 6.

16. *Yearbook of the Forty-Seventh General Conference of the Mennonite Brethren Church of North America, Held at the Mennonite Brethren Church, Yarrow, B.C., October 20-23, 1957*, 106.

17. John Webster Grant, *The Church in the Canadian Era* (Burlington: Welch Publishing Company, 1988), 57.

18. Earl Merrick, *These Impossible Women: 100 Years, The Story of the United Baptist Woman's Missionary Union of the Maritime Provinces* (Fredericton: Brunswick Press, 1970), 33.

19. Class lecture for the course, "The Mennonite Brethren Church," Mennonite Brethren Biblical Seminary, Fresno, Calif., 1982.

20. Mrs. W. Wiebe, "Women and the Church," in *A Century of Grace and Witness: 1860-1960*, ed. Walter Wiebe (Hillsboro, Kans.: Mennonite Brethren Publishing House, 1960), 72.

21. Louise Enns, "Ladies Fellowship Groups, Clearbrook MB Church," in *History of the Clearbrook MB Church: 1936-1986* (n.p., 1986), 97.

22. National Council of Women of Canada, *Women of Canada: Their Life and Work* (n.p.: National Council of Women of Canada, 1900; reprint ed., 1956), 298.

23. Bartel, *Saskatchewan Women in Mission*, 29.

24. My research of CMC and Canadian MB women's societies covers only societies organized within churches which were established between the first year of Russian Mennonite immigration to Canada (1874) and the last year of immigration (1952). I have traced the growth and development of these societies from their years of establishment until 1988.

25. Information on naming was obtained from Toews, *South Western Ontario Women in Mission*; Froese, *Manitoba Mennonite Women in Mission*; Bartel, *Saskatchewan Women in Mission*; Neufeld, *History of Alberta Mennonite Women in Mission*; Rempel, *History of B.C. Mennonite Women in Mission*; and all published histories of CMC and MB local congregations.

26. Translation of German names are as follows: *Nähverein*—"Sewing Circle"; *Wohltätigkeitsverein*—"Charity Society"; *Verein Helfende Hände*—"Helping Hands Society"; *Tabea Verein*—"Tabea Society"; *Maria Martha Verein*—"Mary Martha Society"; *Abendglocken Verein*—"Evening Bells Society"; *Schnetke Conference*—"a meeting with a variety of components"; and *Sonnenstrahl Verein*—"Sunbeam Society."

27. The percentage of the "Other" category is high because thirteen women's societies called their groups simply *Verein*.

28. Information was obtained from reports of MB women's societies within local congregation histories. Since we do not have access to as much source material about MB women's societies, the number of names of societies is fewer than in CMC women's societies.

29. Translation of names not mentioned in note 26 are: *Missionskränzchen*—"Mission Sewing Group" and *Schwesternbund*—"Sister's Union."

30. Biblical references are from the King James Version, since that version was most commonly used in Mennonite churches in this time period. This particular translation of the Bible did not use inclusive language. Thus, the words "men" and "brethren" appear in biblical references cited in this paper.

31. Maria Derksen, "Report—1944," 14.

32. Toews, *South Western Ontario Women in Mission*, 5.

33. Neufeld and Peters, *Fifty Years: Ebenezer Verein*, 13.

34. Froese, *History of Manitoba Mennonite Women in Mission*, 15.

35. *Leamington Mennonite Brethren Church* (n.p.: n.d.), 38.

36. Katherine Harder, ed. *The Greendale Mennonite Brethren Church (1931-1981)* (Cloverdale, B.C.: Greendale Mennonite Brethren Church, 1981), 166-167.

37. Frank H. Epp and Marlene G. Epp, "The Diverse Roles of Ontario Mennonite Women," in *Looking Into My Sister's Eyes*, ed. Jean Burnet (Toronto: Multicultural History Society of Ontario, 1986), 233.

38. Katie Funk Wiebe, "Women in the Mennonite Brethren Church," in *Your Daughters Shall Prophesy: Women in Ministry in the Church*, ed. John E. Toews, et al.(Winnipeg: Kindred Press, 1992), 183.

"ECCLESIOLOGICAL DEVELOPMENTS, 1940-1960"
- *Richard Kyle*

1. Richard Kyle, "The Concept and Practice of Separation from the World in Mennonite Brethren History," *Direction* 13, no. 1/2 (1984): 33.

2. "The Christian Life," Our Confession of Faith: Section 5, *The Christian Leader*, 16 Aug. 1977, 12-13.

3. James C. Juhnke, *A People of Two Kingdoms: The Political Acculturation of the Kansas Mennonites* (Newton, Kans.: Faith and Life Press, 1975), 21, 54, 67, 106, 108, 110; Cornelius C. Janzen, "A Social Study of the Mennonite Settlement in the Counties of Marion, McPherson, Harvey, Reno, and Butler, Kansas" (Ph.D. diss., University of Chicago, 1926), 165-166; Kyle, "The Concept and Practice of Separation," 38.

4. Clarence Hiebert, "The Development of Mennonite Brethren Churches in North America-Some Reflections, Interpretations and Viewpoints," in *Pilgrims and Strangers: Essays in Mennonite Brethren History*, ed. Paul Toews (Fresno: Center for Mennonite Brethren Studies, 1977), 129-130; Hans Kasdorf, "Reflections on the Church Concept of the Mennonite Brethren," *Direction* 4, no. 3 (1975): 342; Richard Kyle, "The Mennonite Brethren and the Denominational Model of the Church: An Adjustment to the Pressures of North American Society," *Mennonite Life* 42, no. 3 (1987): 33; Peter M. Hamm, *Continuity and Change Among Canadian Mennonite Brethren*, ed. Hans Mol, Religion and Identity: Social-Scientific Studies in Religion, no. 3 (Waterloo: Wilfrid Laurier University Press, 1987).

5. Paul Toews, "Faith in Culture and Culture in Faith: The Mennonite Brethren in North America," *Journal of Mennonite Studies* 6 (1988): 43-44.

6. Orlando Harms, *A Conference in Pilgrimage: The Story of the Southern District Mennonite Brethren Conference and Its Churches* (Hillsboro, Kans.: Center for Mennonite Brethren Studies, 1992), 120.

7. J. B. Toews, "Mennonite Brethren Identity and Theological Adversity," in *Pilgrims and Strangers*, 133-154.

8. Hiebert, "The Development of Mennonite Brethren Churches," 117-124.

9. J. B. Toews, "The Influence of Fundamentalism on Mennonite Brethren Theology," *Direction* 10, no. 3 (1981): 21-22.

10. John A. Toews, *A History of the Mennonite Brethren Church: Pilgrims and Pioneers* (Fresno: Board of Christian Literature, 1975), 377.

11. Charles Caldwell Ryrie, *Dispensationalism Today* (Chicago: Moody Press, 1965), 22, 29; Toews, *A History of the Mennonite Brethren Church*, 377. For a critical view of dispensationalism see Clarence B. Bass, *Backgrounds to Dispensationalism: Its Historical Genesis and Ecclesiastical Implications* (1960, reprint, Grand Rapids: Baker Book House, 1977).

12. George M. Marsden, "Fundamentalism," in *Eerdmans' Handbook to Christianity in America*, eds. Mark A. Noll et al., (Grand Rapids: William B. Eerdmans Publishing Company, 1983), 384. For general information on fundamentalism see George M. Marsden, *Fundamentalism and American Culture: The Shaping of Twentieth-Century Evangelicalism: 1870-1925* (New York: Oxford University Press, 1980); Ernest R. Sandeen, *The Roots of Fundamentalism: British and American Millenarianism: 1800-1930* (Chicago: The University of Chicago Press, 1970); Norman F. Furniss, *The Fundamentalist Controversy, 1918-1931*, ed. Lewis C. Curtis, Yale Historical Publications (New Haven: Yale University Press, 1954); Louis Gasper, *The Fundamentalist Movement* (The Hague: Mouton & Company, 1963); Stewart G. Cole, *The History of Fundamentalism* (1931; reprint, Westport, Conn.: Greenwood Press Publishers, 1971).

13. Toews, *A History of the Mennonite Brethren Church*, 378.

14. Toews, "Mennonite Brethren Identity," 144; Toews, *A History of the Mennonite Brethren Church*, 255.

15. Toews, "Mennonite Brethren Identity, " 144.

16. Ibid., 144-145.

17. Ibid., 145.

18. Ibid.

19. Richard Kyle, *From Sect to Denomination: A Study of Mennonite Brethren Church Types* (Hillsboro, Kans.: Center for Mennonite Brethren Studies, 1985), 116.

20. Wesley Prieb, interview with author, 15 Dec. 1992; Vernon Wiebe, interview with author, 19 Dec. 1992.

21. Toews, *A History of the Mennonite Brethren Church*, 378.

22. Kyle, *From Sect to Denomination*, 116-117.

23. Ibid., 119.

24. A. E. Janzen and Herbert Giesbrecht, comps. *We Recommend . . . Recommendations and Resolutions of the General Conference of the Mennonite Brethren Churches* (Fresno: Board of Christian Literature of the General Conference of Mennonite Brethren Churches, 1978), 167; Toews, *A History of the Mennonite Brethren Church*, 387.

25. Janzen, *We Recommend*, 167; Toews, *A History of the Mennonite Brethren Church*, 387.

26. Elmo Warkentin, "The Federal Council of Churches and the Association of Evangelicals Compared," *The Christian Leader*, 15 Jan. 1947, 5-6.

27. Some examples include the following: Orlando Harms, "Communist Clergymen at Evanston?" *The Christian Leader*, 1 May 1954, 2; Helen Sigrist, "What can we do about Communism?" *The Christian Leader*, 1 May 1954, 5, 15; Orlando Harms, "The World Council of Churches," *The Christian Leader*, 15 Aug. 1954, 2.

28. Wesley J. Prieb and Don Ratzlaff, *To a Higher Plane of Vision: Tabor College—The First 75 Years* (Hillsboro, Kans.: Tabor College, 1983), 17-18; Wesley Prieb, interview with author, 22 Dec. 1992.

29. Wesley Prieb, interview with author, 22 Dec. 1992; Toews, "The Influence of Fundamentalism," 23.

30. Arthur Willems, "How to Detect the First Signs of Modernism," *The Christian Leader*, 1 March 1947, 6.

31. Oswald J. Smith, "What is Modernism and How Can It Be Detected?" *The Christian Leader*, June 1945, 9-10; Walfried Dirks, "Mennonitism and Modernism," *The Christian Leader*, 15 Jan. 1947, 9; Krist Gudnason, "The Marks of a Modernist," *The Christian Leader*, May 1944, 3-4; H. Giesbrecht, "Some Recent Literature on the Recent 'Fundamentalism Controversy'," *The Voice* 8, no. 1 (1959): 20-23.

32. Dirks, "Mennonitism and Modernism," 9.

33. Reprint of a series of articles by Oswald T. Allis entitled, "Evangelism and 'The New Version'." They ran in the following issues of *The Christian Leader*: 15 Nov. 1952; 1 Dec. 1952; 15 Dec. 1952; 1 Jan. 1953; 15 Jan. 1953; 1 Feb. 1953; and 15 Feb. 1953.

34. R. M. Baerg, "The Blessed Hope of the Church," *The Christian Leader*, 1 May 1952, 12-14.

35. Wesley Prieb, interview with author, 22 Dec. 1992.

36. Harold S. Bender, "The Anabaptist Vision," *Church History* 8, no. 1 (1944): 3-24.

37. Wesley Prieb, interview with author, 15 Dec. 1992; Prieb, *To a Higher Plane of Vision*, 20; Wesley J. Prieb, "The Biblical Context Within Which Some Men Decided to Become COs in World War II," *The Mennonite Quarterly Review* 66 (1992): 455.

38. Wesley Prieb, interview with author, 15 Dec. 1992; Abraham E. Janzen, *Glimpses of South America* (Hillsboro, Kans.: Mennonite Brethren Publishing House, 1944); A. E. Janzen, *His Second Coming* (Hillsboro, Kans.: Forward Printing Company, 1934); A. E. Janzen, *The Two Kingdoms and Closely Related Events* (Hillsboro, Kans.: Mennonite Brethren Publishing House, 1927).

39. Vernon Wiebe, interview with author, 19 Dec. 1992.

40. Paul Toews, "Differing Historical Imaginations and the Changing Identity of the Mennonite Brethren," in *Anabaptism Revisited: Essays on Anabaptist/Mennonite Studies in Honor of C. J. Dyck*, ed. Walter Klaassen (Scottdale, Pa.: Herald Press, 1992), 163-164; John A. Toews, "In Search of Identity," *The Mennonite Brethren Herald*, 10 March 1972, 2-4, 25. See also Elfrieda Toews Nafziger, *A Man of His Word: A Biography of John A. Toews* (Winnipeg: Kindred Press, 1992).

41. Some examples include J. A. Toews, "Eschatological Views of the Early Mennonites (Anabaptists)," *The Voice* 3, no. 2 (1954): 23-24; J. A. Toews, "Ideological Roots of Anabaptism: A Study of Early Mennonite History," *The Voice* 5, no. 2, (1956): 12-15.

42. Frank C. Peters, "The Scriptural Basis for Nonresistance," *The Christian Leader*, 20 Oct. 1959, 4-5, 8; C. Wall, "My Concept of Biblical Nonresistance," *The Voice* 9, no. 2 (1960): 4-7; Clarence Bauman, "Focal Elements in the Anabaptist-Mennonite Peace Position," *The Christian Leader*, 3 Nov. 1959, 4-5, 24; and 17 Nov. 1959, 4-5; Orlando Harms, "Nonresistance and the Christian," *The Christian Leader*, 1 Nov. 1956, 4-5.

43. Henry H. Dick, "The Uneasy Conscience of the Mennonite Brethren," *The Christian Leader*, 12 Jan. 1960, 4-5, 19; and 26 Jan. 1960, 4-5, 18.

44. G. W. Peters, "Motivations in Founding the Mennonite Brethren Church," *The Christian Leader*, 15 Nov. 1960, 4-5, 13; and 29 Nov. 1960, 4-5, 19.

45. Toews, "Differing Historical Imaginations," 165; Kyle, *From Sect to Denomination*, 118-119.

46. Kyle, "The Mennonite Brethren and the Denominational Model of the Church," 31.

47. Rodney J. Sawatsky, "Domesticated Sectarianism: Mennonites in the United States and Canada in Comparative Perspective," *Canadian Journal of Sociology* 3 (1978): 234-241; John E. Toews, "Theological Reflections," *Direction* 14, no. 2 (1985): 66-67; Frank H. Epp, *Mennonites in Canada, 1920-1940: A People's Struggle for Survival* (Scottdale, Pa.: Herald Press, 1982), 242, 334-335.

48. Toews, "Differing Historical Imaginations," 165. For more on the opening of these institutions see Paul Toews, "'A Shelter in a Time of Storm': The Establishment of Schools in the Pacific District," in *75 Years of Fellowship: Pacific District Conference of the Mennonite Brethren Churches, 1912-1987*, ed. Esther Jost (Fresno: Pacific District Conference of the Mennonite Brethren Churches, 1987), 57-70; Wesley Prieb, interview with author, 21 Jan. 1993.

49. Toews, "Differing Historical Imaginations," 165-166.

50. Janzen, *We Recommend*, 32-42.

51. Toews, *A History of the Mennonite Brethren Church*, 306.

52. Orlando Harms, interview with author, Aug. 1992.

53. J. A. Toews, "The Church As a Brotherhood: A Study in Early Mennonite Theology," *The Voice* 4, no. 5 (1955): 14; Abe Dueck, "Church Leadership: A Historical Perspective," *Direction* 19, no. 2 (1990): 19-20.

54. Kyle, *From Sect to Denomination*, 45; Toews, *A History of the Mennonite Brethren Church*, 302-304; Dueck, "Church Leadership," 22-23.

55. Toews, "Faith in Culture and Culture in Faith," 42, Dueck, "Church Leadership," 23-24; George Shillington, "Authority in Church Leadership," *Direction* 12, no. 1 (1983): 23-26.

56. Vernon Wiebe, interview with author, 19 Dec. 1992. Wesley Prieb, interview with author, 15 Dec. 1992.

57. Toews, *A History of the Mennonite Brethren Church*, 306; Orlando Harms, *The Journey of a Church: A Walk Through One Hundred Years of the Life and Times of the Hillsboro Mennonite Brethren Church, 1881-1981* (Hillsboro, Kans.: Center for Mennonite Brethren Studies, 1987), 173.

58. Toews, *A History of the Mennonite Brethren Church*, 306.

59. Frank H. Epp, *Mennonites in Canada, 1786-1920: The History of a Separate People* (Toronto: Macmillan of Canada, 1974), 37-39.

60. Juhnke, *A People of Two Kingdoms*, 117.

61. Vernon Wiebe, interview with author, 19 Dec. 1992; Kyle, *From Sect to Denomination*, 125.

62. Vernon Wiebe, interview with author, 19 Dec. 1992; Shillington, "Authority in Church Membership," 24; Kyle, *From Sect to Denomination*, 125; Toews, *A History of the Mennonite Brethren Church*, 307.

63. Laurence Davis, "The Work of the Ministry," *The Christian Leader*, 1 June 1954, 5; "Paul's Hitherto Unpublished Letter," *The Christian Leader*, 15 June 1948, 15-16; Charles S. Walton, Jr., "A Layman Speaks," *The Christian Leader*, 15 Dec. 1947, 14.

64. "The Preacher's Vacation," *The Christian Leader*, July 1943, 16.

65. Arthur Jost, "Vacations for Ministers," *The Christian Leader*, 15 Aug. 1953, 5.

66. David D. Allen, "How a Church Can Help the Pastor," *The Christian Leader*, 15 Oct. 1947, 3-5; Lawrence Davis, "The Work of the Ministry," *The Christian Leader*, 15 May 1954, 4-5; and 1 June 1954, 4-5, 11.

67. K. F., "The Ideal Minister," *The Christian Leader*, July 1943, 8-9; Carl M. Lehman, "What Do We Expect of Our Pastor," *The Christian Leader*, 15 Oct. 1947, 7; Lawrence Davis, "The Work of the Ministry," 15 May 1954, 4-5; and 1 June 1954, 4-5, 11.

68. Harold Jantz, "An Immigrant People Have Settled Down in Canada: Two Decades of Change," *Mennonite Brethren Herald*, 15 Jan. 1982, 2-5; Toews, *A History of the Mennonite Brethren Church*, 308-309; Dueck, "Church Leadership," 24-25.

69. Kyle, *From Sect to Denomination*, 124-125; Toews, *A History of the Mennonite Brethren Church*, 309.

70. Dueck, "Church Leadership," 25; Toews, *A History of the Mennonite Brethren Church*, 309; Shillington, "Authority in Church Leadership," 24-25; Hamm, *Continuity and Change*, 110-111.

71. Toews, *A History of the Mennonite Brethren Church*, 309; Hamm, *Continuity and Change*, 110-111.

72. Victor Adrian, "The Ministry of the Deacon," *The Voice* 14, no. 6 (1965): 4; Toews, *A History of the Mennonite Brethren Church*, 312-313.

73. Toews, *A History of the Mennonite Brethren Church*, 313-314.

74. Wesley Prieb, interview with author, 15 Dec. 1992.

75. J. Howard Kauffman and Leland Harder, *Anabaptists Four Centuries Later: A Profile of Five Mennonite and Brethren in Christ Denominations* (Scottdale, Pa.: Herald Press, 1975), 306, 309; Kyle, *From Sect to Denomination*, 125-126.

76. Wesley Prieb, interview with author, 15 Dec. 1992; Kyle, *From Sect to Denomination*, 126.

77. Peter M. Friesen, *The Mennonite Brotherhood in Russia (1789-1910) [Alt-Evangelische Mennonitische Bruederschaft in Russland (1789-1910): im Rahmen der mennonitischen Gesamtgeschichte]*, trans. and ed. J. B. Toews, et al. (Fresno: Board of Christian Literature, General Conference of Mennonite Brethren Churches, 1978), 475-476; Toews, *A History of the Mennonite Brethren Church*, 76-77.

78. Toews, *A History of the Mennonite Brethren Church*, 195-205; Kyle, *From Sect to Denomination*, 121; Janzen, *We Recommend*, 94; Hamm, *Continuity and Change*, 131.

79. Toews, *A History of the Mennonite Brethren Church*, 205-206.

80. Ibid., 205-206; Kyle, *From Sect to Denomination*, 121.

81. Toews, *A History of the Mennonite Brethren Church*, 205-206.

82. Ibid., 207-210.

83. Hamm, *Continuity and Change*, 131-132; Toews, *A History of the Mennonite Brethren Church*, 207-208.

84. Toews, *A History of the Mennonite Brethren Church*, 210; "A Preview of the General Conference," *The Christian Leader*, 15 Oct. 1954, 5.

85. C. F. Plett, *The Story of the Krimmer Mennonite Brethren Church* (Winnipeg: Kindred Press, 1985), 33-40; Toews, *A History of the Mennonite Brethren Church*, 176-184.

86. Plett, *The Story of the Krimmer Mennonite Brethren Church*, 311-321; Toews, *A History of the Mennonite Brethren Church*, 190-192.

87. Plett, *The Story of the Krimmer Mennonite Brethren Church*, 318-326; Toews, *A History of the Mennonite Brethren Church*, 191-192.

88. Janzen, *We Recommend*, 97-99; Plett, *The Story of the Krimmer Mennonite Brethren Church*, 325-327; Toews, *A History of the Mennonite Brethren Church*, 191-193.

"URBANIZATION OF CALIFORNIA MENNONITES"
- *Kevin Enns-Rempel*

1. *Bericht über unsere Conferenz, abgehalten in Nebraska, Hamilton Co., am 12. November 1883*, 15.

2. In this paper, the definition of "urban area" will be any city of 50,000 or more residents. This is a much higher number than has been used in other studies of Mennonite urbanization, which generally utilize the 1790 United States census definition of any town with a population of over 2,500 as "urban." Using this definition means that Hillsboro, Kansas falls into the same category as Los Angeles, California—hardly a useful comparison. For examples of studies utilizing the lower definition, see J. Howard Kauffman and Leland Harder, *Anabaptists Four Centuries Later: A Profile of Five Mennonite and Brethren in Christ Denominations* (Scottdale, Pa.: Herald Press, 1975), 54; and J. Howard Kauffman and Leo Driedger, *The Mennonite Mosaic: Identity and Modernization* (Scottdale, Pa.: Herald Press, 1991), 36.

3. All statistics on MB Church membership in this chapter are drawn from annual district conference reports. These figures have been compiled into a statistical database maintained by the Center for Mennonite Brethren Studies, Fresno, Calif.

4. Johann Ratzlaff, correspondence from Glendora, 23 June 1895, *Zionsbote*, 3 July 1895, 4. See also Justina Ratzlaff, correspondence from Glendora, *Zionsbote*, 26 August 1896, 3.

5. Peter and Maria Wall, "Aus California," *Zionsbote*, 26 November 1902, 2-3.

6. Maria Wall, correspondence from Los Angeles, 1 July 1903, *Zionsbote*, 15 July 1903, 4.

7. Ibid.

8. Peter and Maria Wall, correspondence from Los Angeles, 14 September 1903, *Zionsbote*, 23 September 1903, 3-4.

9. Peter Wall, correspondence from Los Angeles, 12 April 1904, *Zionsbote*, 20 April 1904, 8; Peter and Maria Wall, correspondence from Los Angeles, 9 May 1904, *Zionsbote*, 25 May 1904, 7.

10. Peter and Maria Wall, correspondence from Los Angeles, 15 August 1904, *Zionsbote*, 24 August 1904, 3.

11. Cornelius and Katharina Nickel, correspondence from Long Beach, *Zionsbote*, 7 September 1904, 7.

12. Johann Harms, "Ein Tauffest in Long Beach, Californien," *Zionsbote*, 26 April 1905, 3.

13. Franz C. Penner, correspondence from Escondido, 19 February 1907, *Zionsbote*, 27 February 1907, 3; "Thrifty People Here," *Escondido Times*, 15 February 1907, 3.

14. The 1906 list describes the congregation as "Anaheim" rather than "Los Angeles"; both designations refer to the same group.

15. J. F. Harms, *Geschichte der Mennoniten Brüdergemeinde* (Hillsboro, Kans.: Mennonite Brethren Publishing House, [1924]), 168-170; *Verhandlungen der fünfzehnten Westlichen Distrikt-Konferenz, abgehalten zu Reedley, California, vom 29. Oktober bis 2. November, 1924*, 12-13. [All cited hereafter as PDC Report.]

16. John A. Toews, *A History of the Mennonite Brethren Church: Pilgrims and Pioneers* (Fresno: Board of Christian Literature, General Conference of Mennonite Brethren Churches, 1975), 199.

17. "*Bericht vom Felde,*" 1913 PDC Report, 29.

18. Ibid., 34.

19. B. H. Nikkel, correspondence from Bakersfield, *Zionsbote*, 11 March 114, 2; 1914 PDC Report, 51-52.

20. H. and L. Kohfeld, correspondence from Bakersfield, 7 August 1913, *Zionsbote* 13 August 1913, 2.

21. 1924 PDC Report, 12-13; J. D. Hofer, correspondence from Los Angeles, 17 November 1925, *Zionsbote*, 25 November 1925, 7.

22. A. W. and Margaret Friesen, correspondence from Los Angeles, 24 June 1927, *Zionsbote*, 6 July 1927, 7-8; 1929 PDC Report, 41.

23. 1945 PDC Report, 22.

24. 1946 PDC Report, 16-17.

25. 1947 PDC Report, 25.

26. 1954 PDC Report, 19.

27. B. D. Schultz, correspondence from San Jose, 24 November 1925, *Zionsbote* 9 December 1925, 4.

28. J. J. Unruh, correspondence from San Jose, 26 January 1927, *Zionsbote*, 2 February 1927, 10-11.

29. J. J. Unruh, correspondence from San Jose, 7 October 1927, *Zionsbote*, 19 October 1927, 8.

30. P. F. Wiebe, correspondence from Sunnyvale, 11 March 1940, *Zionsbote*, 20 March 1940, 7; Richard Gerbrandt, "A History of Lincoln Glen Church, San Jose, California," photocopy [available in Center for MB Studies, Fresno], 1988; 1940 PDC Report, 10.

31. Bethany Mennonite Brethren Church Records, Center for Mennonite Brethren Studies, Fresno, Calif.

32. Richard B. Rice, William A. Burrough and Richard J. Orsi, *The Elusive Eden: a New History of California* (New York: Alfred A. Knopf, 1988), 443-446.

33. Board of Home Missions meetings, 2 July 1951 and 21 May 1952, PDC Home Missions Records, Center for MB Studies.

34. Board of Home Missions Executive Committee meeting, 15 September 1952, PDC Home Missions Records, CMBS; 1952 PDC Report, 30.

35. Board of Home Missions meetings, 14 February 1953, 10 March 1953, 9 April 1953, 25 May 1953, PDC Home Missions Records, CMBS.

36. 1953 PDC Report, 14.

37. Board of Home Missions meetings, 30 March 1954 and 29 June 1954, PDC Home Missions Records, CMBS.

38. "San Jose trip of some of the members of the Board for Home Missions and one member of the Board of Trustees of the M.B. Pacific District Conference," 3 May 1956, PDC Home Missions Records, CMBS.

39. Board of Home Missions and Board of Trustees meeting, 7 May 1956, PDC Home Missions Records, CMBS.

40. 1955 PDC Report, 18.

41. "Report from Arthur Wiebe on the visit to the Valley Mennonite Brethren Church, Pacoima, California, on June 17, 1956," PDC Home Missions Records, CMBS.

42. Board of Home Missions minutes, 24 October 1957; "Report of a trip to the Los Angeles area by some of the members of the Executive Committee and the Executive Secretary of the Board for Home Missions of the M.B. Pacific Conference," 3-4 March 1958; Board of Home Missions Executive Committee minutes, 18 March 1958, PDC Home Missions Records, CMBS.

"MUSICAL TRANSITIONS AMONG CANADIAN MENNONITE BRETHREN" - *Doreen Klassen*

I wish to thank Jack Heppner, Jacob Klassen, and Evelyn Labun, who commented on earlier versions of this chapter.

1. Wesley Berg, "From Piety to Sophistication: Developments in Canadian-Mennonite Music After World War II," *Journal of Mennonite Studies* 6 (1988): 89-92.

2. John G. Stackhouse, Jr. *Canadian Evangelicalism in the Twentieth Century* (Toronto: University of Toronto, 1993), characterizes Evangelicalism as centered around "three concerns—doctrinal orthodoxy, personal piety, and evangelism" (181).

3. John A. Toews, *A History of the Mennonite Brethren Church: Pilgrims and Pioneers* (Fresno: Board of Christian Literature, General Conference of Mennonite Brethren Churches, 1975), 377-379.

4. Ibid., 376.

5. Ibid., 376-377.

6. Ibid., 375.

7. Stackhouse, *Canadian Evangelicalism*, 203.

8. Ibid., 184, 196. Stackhouse notes the identification of Mennonites with the "sectish" or more conservative strains of Evangelicalism. He also observes that cooperation among evangelicals did not necessarily constitute ecumenism or formal union (p. 180).

9. Ibid., 190.

10. Walter Thiessen, interview with the author, Saskatoon, Saskatchewan. 3 September 1984, "Mennonite Music-making in Canada, 1920-1970," Centre for Mennonite Brethren Studies, Winnipeg, Manitoba, MM-69-1/5. Thiessen concludes, "I'm afraid nowadays the chickens have come home to roost, because our choirs are not as youth oriented as they used to be."

Primary source materials for this paper are taken from "Mennonite Music-making in Canada, 1920-1970," a study I undertook for the Centre for Mennonite Brethren Studies (CMBS) in Winnipeg in the summer of 1984 with funding by Canada's Secretary of State Multiculturalism Branch. Tape recordings and transcriptions of the interviews are deposited at CMBS Winnipeg. All subsequent references to interview transcriptions from this project indicate the project name (MM), interviewee number (e.g., 69), tape number (e.g., 1) and page number of the transcription (e.g., 5).

11. *Evangeliums-Lieder* is the popular designation for *Evangeliums-Lieder 1 und 2 (Gospel Hymns) mit deutschen Kernliedern*, comp. and ed. Walter Rauschenbusch and Ira D. Sankey (Chicago: Biglow and Main, 1897); *Neue Zions-Lieder*, comp. and ed. J. J. Franz and D. B. Towner (Hillsboro, Kans.: Mennonite Brethren Publishing House, 1919); *Liederperlen* (St. Louis: Concordia Publishing House, 1905); *Ausgewaehlte Lieder des Evangeliums/Selected Gospel Songs*, ed. A. P. Mihm, H. von Berge and G. H. Schneck (Cleveland: Religious Book Repository, 1927).

12. David D. Duerksen, Winnipeg, Manitoba, 2 August 1984, MM-8-1/5. Duerksen recalled his father's (D. K. Duerksen) and my grandfather's (John M. Hiebert) choir work at the Melba School, near Horndean, Manitoba, as being "part of [their] Christian commitment," characterized by "a real concern for young people." See also H. P. Neufeldt, MM-54-1/9; Mrs. Nicholai Fehderau, MM-12-1/30.

13. John Regehr, Winnipeg, Manitoba, 29 May 1984, MM-2-1/4, recalls, "When I came back [from Coaldale], before I gave all my earnings to my parents, I asked whether I could buy a violin. So I wrote to Eaton's mail order and got a $10 violin . . . So I learned to play violin with a lesson book and this finger board that you paste on."

14. J. B. Janz, "Gemeindechorarbeit," *Konferenz-Jugendblatt der Mennoniten Bruedergemeinden in Canada* [hereafter *Konferenz-Jugendblatt*] August 1946, 9.

15. J. Benjamin Janz, Vauxhall, Alberta, 26 August 1984, MM-51-1/24.

16. In 1938 there were a total of fifty-one choirs, thirty-eight of them mixed choirs with 1148 singers. *Verhandlungen der 30. Nördlichen Distrikt-Konferenz der Mennoniten-Brüdergemeinden von Nord-Amerika, abgehalten vom 8. bis zum 12. Juli 1939, zu Coaldale, Alberta*, 38. By 1950 Canadian MB churches had sixty-three church choirs—fourteen youth, six male and four women's—with a total membership of 2500. *Verhandlungen der vierzigsten Kanadischen Konferenz der Mennonite Brüdergemeinden von Nord-Amerika, abgehalten zu Abbotsford, B.C. vom 29. Juli bis 3. August, 1950*, 102. All subsequent citations from Northern/Canadian Conference proceedings will refer to "*Canadian Conference Report*," with the year and page number.

17. At its 2 May 1954 meeting, the Scott Street MB Church Music Committee decided the following: the age for church choir membership would be 18 for females and 19 for males; reception of members would be held twice a year, in April and October; their church members would be given preference but others of unblemished Christian character could also join. Scott Street MB Church Records, Centre for Mennonite Brethren Studies, Winnipeg, Man., microfilm reel 26, frame 271.

18. 1942 *Canadian Conference Report*, 15. Articles in *Konferenz-Jugendblatt* during the 1940s reiterate the assumption that youth work is equivalent to choir work with the youth.

19. Frank Brown, Winkler, Manitoba, 3 June 1984, MM-5-1/14.

20. Friedrich Schweiger, "Ein Besuch unter den Saengern in Russland, *Zionsbote*, 26 September 1894, 2, as quoted and translated in Peter Letkemann, "The Hymnody and Choral Music of Mennonites in Russia, 1789-1915," (Ph.D. diss., University of Toronto, 1985), 416. This quotation reiterates the focus on "*Aussprache der Vokale, richtige Phrasierung und gute Betonung*" (pronunciation of vowels, correct phrasing and good accentuation) in Russian Mennonite choral singing of the late nineteenth and early twentieth centuries, p. 410. See also pp. 410-429.

21. Janz, MM-51-1, says he emphasized rhythm, while Fehderau, MM-12-1, states he used contrastive dynamics to draw attention to the text.

22. Cipher or number notation was introduced to Mennonites in the Ukraine by Heinrich Franz in 1860. He introduced it "[in order] to improve the quality of singing among students in the school and through their influence to improve the congregational singing in Gnadenfeld." (Letkeman, "The Hymnody," 152). Considered to be more accessible to the untrained musician, this system uses the numbers 1-7 placed on, above or below a given line to indicate pitch, and short lines above or punctuation marks to the right of these numbers to indicate duration.

23. Margaret Janz, Vauxhall, Alberta, 26 August 1984, MM-51-1/6.

24. Nicholai Fehderau, Kitchener, Ontario, 6 August 1984, MM-12-1/18.

25. 1947 *Canadian Conference Report*, 177.

26. Fehderau, MM-12-1/60.

27. Justina Wiebe, Winkler, Manitoba, 3 June 1984, MM-4-2/22.

28. Susie Warkentin, "Vancouver, B.C.," *Konferenz-Jugendblatt*, February-April 1950, 37.

29. Helen Enns, "Sängerfest in Springstein!" *Konferenz-Jugendblatt*, May-August 1951, 26. In a program which featured nine German and one English musical selections, the reader is told, "While Sister Anne Kroeker, Elm Creek, quietly played: "Fairest Lord Jesus," the collection was gathered."

30. A song festival in Winkler, Manitoba featured a trumpet duet of "Onward Christian Soldiers" by John Voth and Henry Dyck. "Song Festival at Winkler, Man.," *Konferenz-Jugendblatt*, February-April 1950, 44.

31. Stackhouse, *Canadian Evangelicalism*, 202.

32. Stackhouse notes that evangelical fervor frequently ignored its male dominated ethos in an attempt "to get the job done." Ibid.

33. Regehr, MM-2-1.

34. Justina Wiebe, MM-4-1/12, mentions "that time when basketball became very important, and then they started switching the Friday night [choir practice] to Saturday night." John Boldt's article, "Friday Night is Choir Practice," *Konferenz-Jugendblatt*, May-June 1952, 28, indicates this was already an issue in 1952.

35. Scott Street MB Church Records, frames 230-250.

36. Ibid., frames 271, 279, 282, 294, 407, 493, 2223.

37. Ibid., frames 2119, 2128.

38. Helmut Janzen, Clearbrook, British Columbia, 29 August 1984, MM-55-1/1.

39. See Wesley Berg, *From Russia with Music: A Study of the Mennonite Choral Singing Tradition in Canada* (Winnipeg: Hyperion Press, 1985), particularly Chapter VI, "Flourishing and Decline 1944-1960." This chapter focuses on Conference of Mennonites in Canada choral singing, but touches on MB activity as well.

40. Peter Letkemann, "Singing the New Song Together: MB-GC Relations in Music," paper presented at the symposium "Inter-Mennonite Relations: MB's and GC's in Canada," Winnipeg, Manitoba, 4-5 November 1982, 10.

41. Wesley Berg, "Choral Festivals and Choral Workshops Among the Mennonites of Manitoba and Saskatchewan, 1900-1960, with an Account of Early Developments in Russia," (Ph.D. diss., University of Washington, 1979), 155.

42. Ben Horch, "The Mennonite Brethren Church: History of Its Musical Development, 1860-1984," 29 June 29 1984, 14, MM 1984-125, CMBS Winnipeg.

43. *Kernlieder* is the term generally used for German translations of nineteenth-century American gospel songs which became part of Mennonite experience in Russia. The term denotes the perception that the songs contain the kernel or essence of the gospel. In my conversations with him, Ben Horch often referred to *Kernlieder* as "songs of hurt and hope" or "Mennonite blues" songs. This focus on hope in meeting the challenges of everyday life distinguished *Kernlieder* from other American gospel songs with their emphasis on deliverance "in the sweet bye and bye."

44. Regehr, MM-2-1/21.

45. Regehr, MM-2-1/22.

46. Benjamin and Esther Horch, Winnipeg, Manitoba, 26 May 1984, MM-1-1/31.

47. Horch, "The Mennonite Brethren Church," 9. See also Bertha Klassen, *Da Capo: "Start Once From the Front": A History of the Mennonite Community Orchestra* (Winnipeg: Centre for Mennonite Brethren Studies, 1993).

48. Horch, "The Mennonite Brethren Church," 24.

49. Ibid., 24.

50. Based on forty-five respondents to a conference-wide survey reported in 1947 *Canadian Conference Report*, 177. Since many churches were singing annual Christmas and Easter cantatas, the total of 60 books may have included cantatas as well.

51. Janz, MM-51-1/28.

52. See e.g., 1944 *Canadian Conference Report*, 51; 1947 *Canadian Conference Report*, 176-178; 1950 *Canadian Conference Report*, 100-102; 1955 *Canadian Conference Report*, 99-101.

53. 1947 *Canadian Conference Report*, 177.

54. Fehderau, MM-12-1/17.

55. 1947 *Canadian Conference Report*, 176.

56. Victor Martens, Kitchener, Ontario, 6 August 1984, MM-11-1/9, 1/7.

57. Henry P. Neufeldt, Clearbrook, British Columbia, 28 August 1984, MM-54-1/11.

58. Janz, MM-51-1/14.

59. Peter J. Dick, St. Catherines, Ontario, 10 August 1984, MM-23-2/3.

60. Duerksen, MM-8-1/14.

61. The publication of Benjamin Spock's *Child and Baby Care* in 1946 is only one example of a growing awareness within mid-century Canadian society of developmental stages of childhood and the need for educational methods and materials appropriate to these stages. In this light, *Neues Singvoegelein* and Rodeheaver's *Songs for Little Singers No. 1* were recommended for use in Canadian MB Sunday Schools in the early 1950s. 1952 *Canadian Conference Report*, 87; 1953 *Canadian Conference Report*, 75, 77.

62. Ben and Esther Horch, interview with Hilda Dueck, 1981, author's transcription, MM-1984-125, CMBS, Winnipeg.

63. The *Carillon News* of 31 May 1957 reported on Brunk's campaign in Steinbach.

64. Frank W. Peers, *The Politics of Canadian Radio Broadcasting 1920-1951* (Toronto: University of Toronto Press, 1969), 367.

65. See John G. Stackhouse, Jr., "The Protestant Experience in Canada since 1945," in *The Canadian Protestant Experience: 1760-1990*, ed. G. A. Rawlyk (Burlington: Welch Publishing Company, 1990), 200. Stackhouse considers the post-war increase in church attendance and support of church programs as a "get back to normal" response. He notes, however, that the inadequacy of "Sunday School faith" to deal with war-induced anxieties also led other individuals to "the abandonment of traditional Christianity."

66. John Regehr, MM-2-1/19, says, "We got a radio in 1939 when it looked like war was going to break out."

67. Toews, *A History of the Mennonite Brethren Church*, 320.

68. John W. Lane, Jr., "What is the Radio Doing to You?," *Konferenz-Jugendblatt*, October-December 1948, 55-56.

69. Herman Voth, "'The Gospel Hour' von CHWK, Chilliwack, B.C." *Konferenz-Jugendblatt*, February-April 1950, 36.

70. 1941 *Canadian Conference Report*, 30.

71. 1942 *Canadian Conference Report*, 15.

72. "'Lighthouse of Hope' Radio Broadcast," *Konferenz-Jugendblatt*, January-April 1953, 44-45;

73. The name of this quartet was used for the radio program conducted by the Coaldale MB young people on CHAT, Medicine Hat, Alta., every Sunday morning. See: Erna Penner, "Gospel Bells Radio Program," May-June 1954, 3-4. *Konferenz-Jugendblatt* 1954 10(54):3-4.

74. "Moments of Blessing," *Konferenz-Jugendblatt*, March-April 1955, 20.

75. Horch, MM-1-1/46. Mennonite interest in quartet singing occurred in an era in which there was widespread interest in quartet singing, as exemplified by the founding of the Society for the Preservation of Barber Shop Quartet Singing in America, Inc. (1938), and its female counterpart, Sweet Adelines, Inc. (1947).

76. John Regehr, MM-2-1/1, recalls how youth imitated "what the older fellows did in the Bible School" at local *Jugendverein* meetings.

77. "'Lighthouse of Hope' Radio Broadcast," *Konferenz-Jugendblatt*, January-April 1953, 44-45.

78. Toews, *A History of the Mennonite Brethren Church*, 320.

79. Interview with Rudy Sawatzky, now of Steinbach, Manitoba, 9 June 1994. Sawatzky recalls driving to Saskatoon for the 7:30 a.m. live broadcast, which, he says, "really got people into the church." Unlike many other MB churches of the time, he says, "Our church was English-speaking because most of our members had moved there from Mountain Lake, Minnesota."

80. Peter J. Dick, "Gospel Tidings—the First MB Radio Program in Canada." *Konferenz-Jugendblatt*, April 1950-April 1951, 16.

81. Toews, *A History of the Mennonite Brethren Church*, 320.

82. Peter J. Dick, "Gospel Tidings," 6.

83. Because of the danger of American dominance of the Canadian air waves in the 1920s, the formulation of Canadian broadcast policy at that time could have been directed primarily at the issue of developing Canadian media content. Instead, the 1928 review and resulting Aird Report were occasioned by a religious controversy: Jehovah Witness radio programs who used "hate language" to criticize mainline churches. After 1932, Broadcast policy was regulated by the Canadian Radio Broadcasting Commission, but 1940s religious radio broadcasts were susceptible to the memory of this controversy. Other policies specified the percentage of live versus recorded programming, yet these underlay the need for a distinctive Canadian media identity. See John Herd Thompson and Allen Seager, *Canada, 1922-1939: Decades of Discord* (Toronto: McClelland and Stewart, 1985), 180-183, 256.

84. Albert A. Shea, *Broadcasting the Canadian Way* (Montreal: Harvest House, 1963), notes that "with the advent of television local radio became more dependent on local advertisers" (p. 36). Consequently, local ratings were a deciding factor in the retention or deletion of local radio programs.

85. Frank Foster, *Broadcasting Policy Development* (Ottawa: Franfost Communications, 1982), 101.

86. Fehderau, MM-12-1/28.

87. Foster, *Broadcasting Policy*, 142. Peers, *The Politics*, also identifies 1944-47 as an era "when radio stations were established in smaller communities," (p. 367). This made radio broadcasting a viable option for many smaller MB churches across the prairies.

88. In a discussion of Anabaptist music-making, Harold S. Bender quotes Christian Neff as saying, "They sang themselves into the hearts of many, clothed in popular tunes." "Music, Church," in *The Mennonite Encyclopedia*, ed. Harold S. Bender and C. Henry Smith, vol. 3 (Scottdale, Pa.: Mennonite Publishing House, 1957), 791.

89. The late Nicholai Fehderau, MM-12-1, recounted for me how he as a youth in the Ukraine had moved from the Kirchliche to the MB church because of the music. Similarly, Frank Brown, MM-3-1, shared how he left the Sommerfelder church in southern Manitoba to join the Winkler MB Church because the musical vitality attracted him.

90. *Glaubensstimme für die Gemeinde des Herrn*, ed. Julius Kobner (Hamburg: Baptistische Verlags Bundhandlung, 1890).

91. 1914 *Canadian Conference Report*, 35.

92. 1944 *Canadian Conference Report*, 51.

93. Foreword to *Gesangbuch der Mennoniten Bruedergemeinde* (Winnipeg: The Christian Press, 1952), iii.

94. Ibid.

95. Ben Horch, "On the Subject of Mennonite Musical Traditions," Cassette tape to Peter Letkeman, March 1983. Author's transcription, MM-1984-125, CMBS Winnipeg.

96. Horch, MM-1-1/53.

97. Ben Horch, interview with Linda Mazurat for CBC Radio, 12 December 1983. Author's transcription, MM-1984-125, CMBS Winnipeg.

98. Ben Horch to Frank A. DeFehr, 17 August 1984, MM-1984-125, CMBS Winnipeg.

99. 1951 *Canadian Conference Report*, 93-94.

100. 1952 *Canadian Conference Report*, 87.

101. 1950 *Canadian Conference Report*, 62.

102. Peter Klassen, "Concerning Mennonites and Music—A Brief Appraisal," *Konferenz-Jugendblatt*, July-August 1955, 13.

103. Martens, MM-11-1/2.

104. In the Preface to *The Hymn Book* ([Winnipeg]: Canadian Conference of the Mennonite Brethren Church of North America, 1960), iv, the editors state that "the Mennonite Brethren fellowship felt as a whole that the matter of creating an English language parallel should not be left until spiritual, sociological and ethnic considerations create a situation of urgency." They identify the dominant factor necessitating this move as the "recognized bilingual 'status quo' already manifested in most of our churches throughout Canada."

105. Ibid.

106. Horch, "The Mennonite Brethren Church," 26.

107. Scott Street MB Church Records, frame 103.

108. Ibid., frame 250.

109. Like several other Canadian MB Churches, Scott Street MB began English language services in 1957. See the chapter by Gerald C. Ediger in this volume.

110. In an article entitled, "Reverence in the Hymn Singing of Our Church Created in the Sunday School," *Konferenz-Jugendblatt* November-December 1951, 29-30, Mrs. Ben [Esther] Horch encourages church educators to teach children hymns rather than choruses with no doctrinal, literary or musical value.

111. The fundamentalist Sunday School movement of the 1930s and 1940s had created an awareness of the need for a musical repertoire focussed on the needs of children. J. Wedel, "Unsere Gesangsaeche," *Konferenz-Jugendblatt* September 1944, 5-6, demonstrates MB acceptance of this assumption.

112. Duerksen, MM-8-1/2.

113. Orlando Schmidt, *Church Music and Worship Among the Mennonites* (Newton, Kans.: Faith and Life Press, 1981), 35. Schmidt notes that the "impact of revivalism" and emphasis on worship occur somewhat later among Mennonites than within "the church at large in North America."

114. James F. White, *Christian Worship in Transition* (Nashville: Abingdon, 1976), 78-85.

115. Ben Horch, written communication to Mr. Frank A. Defehr, President, Palliser Furniture, Ltd., 17 August 1984. Author's transcription, MM-1984-125, CMBS Winnipeg.

116. Ibid.

117. Stackhouse, "Canadian Evangelicals," 204.

118. Ibid., 203.

119. Dick, MM-23-1; Janz, MM-51-1/26.

120. Dick, MM-23-1/4.

121. Fehderau, MM-12-1-35, quoting John Boldt.

122. Fehderau, MM-12-1/35.

123. Toews, *A History of the Mennonite Brethren Church*, 57-58.

124. 1932 *Canadian Conference Report*, 3 refers to an offering during a congregational song, while 1931 *Canadian Conference Report*, 7 records that A. A. Smith, bass soloist from Minneapolis, Minn., provided the music for the offering.

125. Fehderau, MM-12-1/39.

126. 1935 *Canadian Conference Report*, 3 records a collection being held at the end of a service, during a choir song.

127. Regehr, MM-2-1/27.

128. Thiessen, MM-69-2/3.

129. Stackhouse, "The Protestant Experience," 206.

130. 1922-1950 *Canadian Conference Report*s.

131. 1955 *Canadian Conference Report*, 101; 1960 Canadian Conference Report, 200.

CANADIAN MB AND LANGUAGE TRANSITION
- *Gerald C. Ediger*

1. Quoted in John B. Toews, *Czars, Soviets and Mennonites* (Newton, Kans.: Faith and Life Press, 1982), 41.

2. J. W. Neufeld, "Etwas zum Nachdenken," *Zionsbote*, 15 Sept. 1920, 13-14.

3. B. B. Janz, "Aus andern Provinzen," *Das Konferenz-Jugendblatt der Mennoniten Bruedergemeinde von Manitoba*, March 1945, 13.

4. This English phrase hardly captures the power of the German "*Bruch und Schmerz, Verkennung und Verachtung.*"

5. Isaak Regehr, "Der Preis der Zweisprachigkeit," *Mennonitische Rundschau*, 25 June 1952, 3. Regehr's interpretation of bilingualism seems to have been a unilingual German Mennonite Brethren Church whose members were also fully competent to function in an English-speaking society.

6. Philippians 2:5 and John 17:21 read as follows: "Your attitude should be the same as that of Christ Jesus"; "That all of them may be, one, Father, just as you are in me and I am in you. May they also be in us so that the world may believe that you have sent me." (NIV).

7. The Winkler, Manitoba and Elmwood (Winnipeg, Manitoba) congregations ratified separate English and German services in 1967 and the Portage Avenue congregation in Winnipeg did the same in 1970.

8. The *Rundschau* was founded in 1880 as an inter-Mennonite newspaper and published in Elkhart, Ind. and later Scottdale, Pa. until 1923. In 1924 it was moved to Winnipeg and in 1945 a group of Mennonite Brethren bought the paper. Since that time it has functioned as a Mennonite Brethren periodical.

9. This discussion assumes the radical identification of Mennonite religion and the German language and culture in southern Russia, and the necessary background to the Mennonite migrations of the 1870s and the 1920s. See relevant materials by authorities such as Frank H. Epp, *Mennonites in Canada, 1786-1920: A History of a Separate People* (Toronto: Macmillan of Canada, 1974); Frank H. Epp, *Mennonites in Canada, 1920-1940: A People's Struggle for Survival* (Scottdale, Pa.: Herald Press, 1982); John A. Toews, *A History of the Mennonite Brethren Church: Pilgrims and Pioneers* (Fresno: Board of Christian Literature of the General Conference of Mennonite Brethren Churches, 1975); John B. Toews, *Czars, Soviets and Mennonites* (Newton, Kans.: Faith and Life Press, 1982); John B. Toews, *Perilous Journey: The Mennonite Brethren in Russia, 1860-1910*, Perspectives on Mennonite Life and Thought, no. 5 (Winnipeg: Kindred Press, 1988); James Urry, *None But Saints: The Transformation of Mennonite Life in Russia, 1789-1889* (Winnipeg: Hyperion Press, 1989). The interest of this study has been the actual process of Mennonite Brethren language shift and the experience of Mennonite Brethren at the congregational level. Benjamin Wall Redekop has written a thesis discussing Germanism and the German language as a factor of socio-religious integration and boundary maintenance for Canadian *Russländer* Mennonite Brethren between 1930 and 1960. Redekop, "The German Identity of Mennonite Brethren Immigrants in Canada, 1930-1960" (M.A. thesis, University of British Columbia, 1990).

10. This was a derisive term applied by the German-retainers to their co-religionists who were too easily abandoning their German heritage of language and culture for English.

11. "Election of Conference Secretary," *Minutes of the fifty-fourth Canadian Conference of the Mennonite Brethren Church of North America convened at Winkler, Manitoba July 4 to July 8, 1964*, 120. (Hereafter *Canadian Conference Report.*)

12. "Publications Committee," 1963 *Canadian Conference Report*, 103.

13. Winkler Mennonite Brethren Church Membership Minutes, 29 November 1967, Centre for Mennonite Brethren Studies, Winnipeg, Manitoba (hereafter CMBS), reel 90. Elmwood Mennonite Brethren Church Membership Minutes, CMBS, 6 December 1967, reel 92. Portage Avenue Mennonite Brethren Church Membership Minutes, CMBS, 16 February 1970, reel 82. Hereafter congregational records will be identified by congregational name and microfilm reel number.

14. "Schule," *Verhandlungen der zweiten Nördlichen Distrikt-Konferenz der Mennoniten Brüdergemeinde von Nord Amerika, abgehalten in der Gemeinde Bruderfeld am 10. und 11. Juli, 1911*, 14. (Hereafter *Northern District Report*.)

15. This is illustrated by a confrontation of Canadian and American Mennonite Brethren over the inclusion of English-language Bible passages in the Conference *Lektionshefte*. *Verhandlungen der 38. Generalkonferenz der Mennoniten-Brüdergemeinden von Nord-Amerika, angehalten vom 30. Mai bis zum 4. Juni 1930 in der Gemeinde zu Hepburn, Saskatchewan*, 45-46.

16. Bethany Bible School faced a challenge from its graduating students over language in 1935. Margaret Epp, *Proclaim Jubilee!: A History of Bethany Bible Institute* (n.p., [1976]), 44. The Northern District formed a special Bible school commission in 1939, in part occasioned by the language problem. "Schulbestrebungen in unseren Kreisen," 1939 *Northern District Report*, 24-27. Winkler Bible School had a detailed language policy in 1942. "Der Lehrplan der Bibelschule," *Auskunft ueber die Winkler Bibelschule "Pniel" 1941-42*, 5.

17. This is demonstrated by the changing attitude of *Mennonitische Rundschau* editor and Canadian Conference Youth Committee chairperson H. F. Klassen. In 1944 Klassen wrote that converting Mennonite Brethren youth programs totally to English would be a "sin." H. F. Klassen, "Fragen und Antworten," *Das Konferenz-Jugendblatt der Mennoniten Bruedergemeinde von Manitoba*, September 1944, 3. By 1951 he was warning older Mennonite Brethren that their identification of German and true Mennonite Brethren faith was alienating their youth and that the price was too high. "Jugendversammlung am 14. Juli, nachmittags," 1951 *Canadian Conference Report*, 12.

18. This is well-illustrated by the struggle over language in the early years of the Mennonite Brethren Bible College. Both A. H. Unruh and J. B. Toews as the College's first two presidents endorsed a clear parity of English and German in the College program. This elicited vociferous opposition from others determined to exploit the new College in the cause of German retention. "Schulesache: Das M.B. Bibel-College in Winnipeg," 1946 *Canadian Conference Report*, 98-105.

19. "Geschaftssitzung—Mittwoch nachmittags," 1950 *Canadian Conference Report*, 90-91.

20. "Eingereichte Fragen," 1948 *Canadian Conference Report*, 118; "Fortsetzung—Schulsache: Bibelschulen und Hochschulen," 1949 *Canadian Conference Report*, 54-58.

21. J. J. Janzen, "Mennonitische Tugenden," *Mennonitische Rundschau*, 12 April 1950, 4.

22. "Fortsetzung—Schulsache."

23. Isaak Regehr, "Der Preis der Zweisprachigkeit," *Mennonitische Rundschau*, 11 June 1952, 4; 18 June 1952, 2-3; 25 June 1952, 3.

24. "Jugendsache," 1952 *Canadian Conference Report*, 81-84; "Sonntagschul-Sache," 1952 *Canadian Conference Report*, 93.

25. This was the adoption of Manitoba's *Jugendblatt* as a youth paper for the entire Northern District. "Empfehlungen des Jugendkomitees der N. D. Konf. abgehalten in Yarrow, B.C. vom 16-17ten Juni," 1945 *Northern District Report*, 105-106.

26. This is based on a compilation of the number of congregations reporting a German school in the 1948-1966 *Canadian Conference Reports*.

27. "Komitee fur deutsche Sprache," 1959 *Canadian Conference Report*, 130.

28. The process of approving and financing a Conference-sponsored English family periodical took from 1957 to 1961. The *Mennonite Brethren Herald* began in 1962.

29. "M. B. Bible college," 1962 *Canadian Conference Report*, 162.

30. "Committee of Reference and Counsel," 1963 *Canadian Conference Report*, 117.

31. "Election of Conference Secretary," 1964 *Canadian Conference Report*, 120.

32. Canadian Conference Statistical Records, 1946-1966, CMBS, Winnipeg, Manitoba, boxes 19-21.

33. South End Council Minutes, 28 March 1949, reel 83; Winkler Council Minutes, 18 November 1951, reel 91; North End Annual Reports, 1951, reel 92.

34. South End Membership Minutes, 18 February 1950, reel 82; North End Membership Minutes, 24 September 1951, reel 92; Winkler Membership Minutes, 7 February 1955, reel 90.

35. Elmwood Council Minutes, 13 September 1954, reel 93; South End Membership Minutes, 18 May 1955, reel 82; Winkler Membership Minutes, 25 November 1957, reel 90.

36. Canadian Conference Statistical Records, 1946-1966, boxes 19-21.

37. South End Council Minutes, 28 March 1949, reel 83; Winkler Council Minutes, 2 January 1954, reel 91; Elmwood Membership Minutes, 23 August 1954, reel 92.

38. South End Mennonite Brethren Church Sunday Morning Bulletin, 14 September 1958; Elmwood Membership Minutes, 8 December 1958, reel 92.

39. Winkler Membership Minutes, 7 June 1967, reel 90.

40. Elmwood Membership Minutes, 6 December 1967, reel 92.

41. South End Membership Minutes, 3 May 1960, reel 82.

42. Portage Avenue Membership Minutes, 16 February 1970, reel 82.

43. Canadian Conference Statistical Records, 1946-1966, boxes 19-21.

44. In 1944 South End had a mission Sunday school with 150 registered students and an attendance of about seventy. South End Membership Minutes, 9 December 1944, reel 82. In 1951 The Elmwood *Jugendabend* program served more than two hundred young people who distributed tracts and Christian literature on the street and spoke to individuals about their spiritual welfare, distributed Christmas cheer, conducted street meetings, and ran an English summer Bible school for sixty children. North End Annual Reports, 1951, reel 92.

45. South End Council Minutes, 5 January and 19 January 1957, reel 83.

46. The role of education in the cultural retention of Canadian Mennonites has been presented in a paper by Frank H. Epp, "Educational Institutions and Cultural Retention in Canada: The Mennonite Experience," paper presented at the Canadian Historical Society, London, Ontario, 1 June 1978.

47. The earliest and most deliberate attempt by American Mennonite Brethren to mount an education-based resistance to English assimilation was their short-lived sponsorship of the German department at McPherson (Kans.) College in the late 1890s. P. F. Durksen, "Deutsches Department in McPherson College, McPherson Kansas," *Zionsbote*, 8 June 1898, 2.

48. Calvin Redekop has summarized the importance of the congregation in understanding the Mennonite ethos. Redekop, *Mennonite Society* (Baltimore: The Johns Hopkins University Press, 1989), 62-65.

49. Janz, "Aus andern Provinzen."

50. "Bericht von der Christian Press oder 'Die Rundschau' wie viele nicht nur die Zeitschrift, sondern auch das Geschaft nennen," 1946 *Canadian Conference Report*, 74.

51. "Emphfehlungen des Jugendkomitees der N. D. Konf. abgehalten in Yarrow, B.C. vom 16-27ten Juni," 1945 *Northern District Report*, 105-106.

52. "Die Konferenzbotschaft," 1954 *Canadian Conference Report*, 14.

53. "Bericht über Christian Press," 1956 *Canadian Conference Report*, 10.

54. Neufeld, "Etwas zum Nachdenken." Neufeld was a Russian-born ordained minister who emigrated to Canada in 1906, founded the Bethania, Saskatchewan congregation in 1913 and moved to the United States in 1920 where he ministered in the Los Angeles congregation for twenty-two years. John H. Lohrenz, *The Mennonite Brethren Church* (Hillsboro, Kans.: The Board of Foreign Missions of the Conference of the Mennonite Brethren Church of North America, 1950), 312.

55. "Eingereichte Fragen," 1929 *Northern District Report*, 72-74.

56. A general overview of the importance of the Mennonite Brethren *Gemeinde* and the German language in the context of cultural assimilation between 1930 and 1960 is supplied by Benjamin Redekop in a chapter entitled "Germanism and Brethren Congregational Life: The Struggle for Socio-Religious Integrity." Redekop, "The German Identity," 115-161.

57. Janzen, "Mennonitische Tugenden;" Gerhard Cornies, "Rettet die Muttersprache," *Mennonitische Rundschau*, 21 June 1950, 7 and 27 June 1950, 2.

58. Specifically, South End members decided "to transfer the English Sunday school to the Logan Street Mission so that the children will receive care as they grow older and when they want to become baptized." South End Membership Minutes, 24 January 1952, reel 82.

59. The Good Tidings Sunday School had 150 members with an average attendance of ninety including a class for mothers from the community. Elmwood Membership Minutes, 23 September 1965, reel 92.

60. "Fortsetzung—Schulsache," 54-58.

61. "Jugendversammlung am 14. Juli nachmittags," 12.

62. "Wir sind als Komitee wohl bewusst dass eine Sprache nicht selig macht." "Bericht vom Komitee fuer deutsche Sprache," 1951 *Canadian Conference Report*, 58.

63. K. K., *Mennonitische Rundschau*, 9 April 1952, 11.

64. Isaak Regehr, "Der Preis der Zweisprachigkeit," *Mennonitische Rundschau*, 25 June 1952, 3.

List of Contributors

Abe Dueck
> Director, Centre for Mennonite Brethren Studies
> Winnipeg, Manitoba

Gerald C. Ediger
> Professor of Historical Theology
> Concord College, Winnipeg, Manitoba

Kevin Enns-Rempel
> Archivist, Center for Mennonite Brethren Studies
> Fresno, California

David Ewert
> President and Professor of New Testament Emeritus
> Mennonite Brethren Bible College, Winnipeg, Manitoba

Waldo Hiebert
> Professor of Practical Theology Emeritus
> Mennonite Brethren Biblical Seminary, Fresno, California

Doreen Klassen
> Professor of Music and Drama
> Steinbach Bible College, Steinbach, Manitoba

Richard Kyle
> Professor of History and Religion
> Tabor College, Hillsboro, Kansas

Calvin Redekop
> Professor of Sociology, Emeritus,
> Conrad Grebel College, Waterloo, Ontario

Gloria Neufeld Redekop
> Independent Researcher
> University of Ottawa, Ottawa, Ontario

John H. Redekop
> Professor of Political Science (on leave),
> Wilfrid Laurier University, Waterloo, Ontario;
> Visiting Scholar,
> Trinity Western University, Langley, British Columbia

T. D. Regehr
      Professor of History,
      University of Saskatchewan, Saskatoon, Saskatchewan

Valerie Rempel
      Doctoral student, Department of Religion
      Vanderbilt University, Nashville, Tennessee

John B. Toews
      President and Professor of Missions and Theology Emeritus
      Mennonite Brethren Biblical Seminary, Fresno, California

Paul Toews
      Professor of History,
      Fresno Pacific College, Fresno, California;
      Executive Secretary of the Historical Commission,
      General Conference of Mennonite Brethren Churches,
      Fresno, California

Katie Funk Wiebe
      Professor of English Emeritus
      Tabor College, Hillsboro, Kansas